ONE ROUND RIVER

HENRY HOLT AND COMPANY
NEW YORK

ONE
ROUND
RIVER

The Curse of Gold

and the Fight for the

Big Blackfoot

RICHARD MANNING

Henry Holt and Company, Inc.
Publishers since 1866
115 West 18th Street
New York, New York 10011

Henry Holt® is a registered
trademark of Henry Holt and Company, Inc.

Published in Canada by Fitzhenry & Whiteside Ltd.,
195 Allstate Parkway, Markham, Ontario L3R 4T8.

Library of Congress Cataloging-in-Publication Data
Manning, Richard, 1951–
One round river : the curse of gold and the fight for the Big Blackfoot /
Richard Manning.—1st ed.
      p.   cm.
Includes bibliographical references (p.   ) and index.
ISBN 0-8050-4792-1 (hb)
1. Blackfoot River (Mont.)—Description and travel.   2. Blackfoot
River (Mont.)—Environmental conditions.   3. Manning, Richard, 1951–.
4. Logging—Montana—Blackfoot River.   5. Gold mines and mining—
Montana—Blackfoot River.   I. Title.
F737.B62M36   1998
978.6'85—dc21   97-27537

Henry Holt books are available for special promotions and premiums.
For details contact: Director, Special Markets.

First Edition 1998

Designed by Kate Nichols

Printed in the United States of America
All first editions are printed on acid-free paper. ∞

10   9   8   7   6   5   4   3   2   1

For the Blackfoot
and for all the people
who have fought and are fighting
for its life.

How innocent, how blessed, how luxurious life
would even be if we did not crave anything deeper
than the surface of the earth—in brief, if we were
satisfied by what is around us. . . . Gold is grabbed
up. . . . Man has learned to challenge nature. . . .
Would that it could be wholly banished from
our lives.

—PLINY

CONTENTS

ONE ROUND RIVER

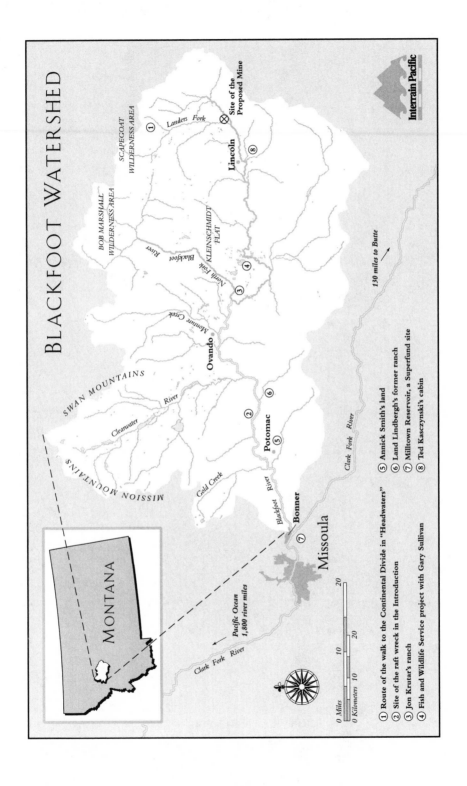

BLACKFOOT WATERSHED

SCAPEGOAT
WILDERNESS AREA

Landers Fork

⊗ Site of the
Proposed Mine

① Lincoln

⑧

BOB MARSHALL
WILDERNESS AREA

North Fork   Blackfoot   River

KLEINSCHMIDT
FLAT

④

③

SWAN MOUNTAINS

Monture Creek

River

Ovando

Clearwater

River

⑥

② Potomac

⑤

MISSION MOUNTAINS

Gold Creek

Blackfoot   River

Bonner

⑦ Missoula

Clark Fork River

130 miles to Butte

MONTANA

Pacific Ocean
1,800 river miles

Clark Fork River

0 Miles   10   20
0 Kilometers   10   20

① Route of the walk to the Continental Divide in "Headwaters"
② Site of the raft wreck in the Introduction
③ Jon Krutar's ranch
④ Fish and Wildlife Service project with Gary Sullivan
⑤ Annick Smith's land
⑥ Land Lindbergh's former ranch
⑦ Milltown Reservoir, a Superfund site
⑧ Ted Kasczynski's cabin

Interrain Pacific

INTRODUCTION

THIS IS WATER'S STORY, in particular the story of water shaped as a river. All that follows hinges on the simple fact that water flows down. It erodes, slices, cuts and carries the stuff of the earth to make and remake the earth. Water, the sun's energy that lifts it and the countervailing pull of gravity that returns it always to the sea, these together are the creator, the heart that pumps our planet's life. From the instant water strikes in the chaos of rain, gravity begins setting it in order. Gravity gathers drops to make rivulets that vein to streams that vein to rivers.

This is the universal and timeless force of the planet, yet I cannot picture or grasp the universal. It is beyond the scope of a single life to account for all rivers, or perhaps even for a single river. Knowing a river, however, provokes the effort. One eventually learns that one has been pulled in with raindrops. Just as rivers organize rain, they organize us. My life has known many rivers, but I know the Big Blackfoot best.

Perhaps you know it, at least its name. It is famous, the stream of Norman Maclean's novella *A River Runs Through It*. Maybe you believe you have even seen it in a film by the same name. You haven't. Robert Redford shot the film elsewhere, because the real river is a working river and required a stand-in, abused as it is by the recent forces of history—especially logging—that have so abused all of our waters. Hollywood retails images, not real rivers.

In the course of this book, I will argue that images lie at the root of the problem. A principal disease of our time is our extermination of reality to vivify imagery. I fight the temptation of imagination by trying to grasp the reality of a river. A river is an accretion of facts.

These are the facts particular to the Big Blackfoot: It winds together in western Montana where I live, assembled from three main forks. The main stem perks from groundwater and snowmelt in west-central Montana near Rogers Pass through the Continental Divide. Two other branches, Landers Fork and the North Fork, wind down from the Bob Marshall and Scapegoat Wilderness areas also along the Continental Divide. Grizzly bears live there, a fact I have verified firsthand. The Landers Fork joins the main stem just upstream of the dinky mountain town of Lincoln, a place recently made famous as the longtime hideout of Ted Kaczynski, the accused Unabomber.

By the time it clears Lincoln, the Blackfoot has gathered enough water to graduate from stream to river. From here downstream it will float a canoe year round and a raft in high water, and that's the best definition of the line between "river" and "stream" that science can devise. It passes through a vast and stunning valley—Ovando—pocked everywhere with evidence of glaciation and rimmed on its north with the peaks of the Bob Marshall. Frost can be expected here eleven months of the year. The river collects first its South Fork at Kleinschmidt Flat then Monture Creek. Downstream, downhill and west, after a lazy loll through a box canyon favored by bald eagles, the Clearwater joins. From here it caroms off Johnson Mountain to Johnsrud then to the town of Bonner, where the Blackfoot ends by joining the Clark Fork near the small city of Missoula—all in all, a run of 130 miles. The Clark Fork, Montana's biggest river in terms of volume, flows on west to Lake Pend

Oreille in northern Idaho, then to the Pend Oreille River, then to the Columbia River and to the tepid salt of the sea until the sun's heat lifts it into the clouds, and it returns as rain and snow.

These bare facts, however, tell almost nothing about the river. I tell you now it's mostly beautiful, and still I've told you almost nothing. Mostly clean and wild, still nothing. That it is underlain through most of its clear course with a diadem of red, green and yellow rocks that it and the glaciers have smoothed and rounded, that great speckled trout sulk in its pools, that ponderosa pine and Douglas fir larger than ships' masts tower from clean-cut cliffs in its private bends, still nothing.

A river cannot be described, or rebuilt from its elemental facts, just as it cannot be imagined alive into images. It must be lived, and that is our problem. Every time I consider the terrible threat that looms, I keep coming back to specific events in my own life, memories, the details that tell a life what it values. Seminal events that made me who I am are strung all up and down this river. The elemental fact is these events are mostly why I value this river, but it is not enough that I do. The threat is such that we must all learn to know rivers.

WHEN I WAS A NEWSPAPER REPORTER working in Missoula, I picked my way in a Jeep through the logging roads webbed in the Big Black-foot's basin. I was investigating corporate logging practices. I did what a newspaperman is supposed to do, which is fight, and it led to the best work in my fifteen years of responsibility for a small-town byline. My work got printed. The resulting machinations by the timber industry got me fired, and it was worth it.

ONE NIGHT a friend offered a late afternoon float on his raft for some fishing through the box canyon where the eagles live. My son and his mother, my wife then, came along, but the friend underestimated the distance. In pitch black, we were forced to stop floating, and we pulled the raft to the rocks along the canyon's sheer cliff walls to huddle in T-shirts through the long, implacable night.

ONCE A NEW LOVE and I took a test here, but we didn't know it was a test. We took her canoe through rapids, seeing whether we could pull and push together with sufficient harmony to overcome the troubles.

We failed. But mainly I remember that day by how beautifully her fury and drive presented themselves against the backdrop of that river.

ONCE I WALKED FIFTEEN MILES up Monture Creek into the wilderness, made camp by a brook then walked another four miles to a gunsight pass between two drainages. The pass was capped by a broad valley furred in lodgepole pine, heather and mountain ash, the ash then starting to redden at the touch of the first few frosts of September. I found a fat deadfall tree and sat in the sun it offered for hours, trying to measure the full depth of the quiet in an alpine valley that felt as if it had never seen another human. A sonic boom split the afternoon like the voice of a god, and the roar of it ricocheting off rock face and canyon pinned me flat to the earth. Hours later I shot an enormous mule deer buck, gutted it and hung it in a tree, its ham muscles still twitching in tissue's recall of flight. I walked the four miles back to camp for a packframe, made it by dark and slept a sleep of crucial and unrecallable dreams. When I returned to the pass the next morning, a grizzly had beat me to my deer, eating most of it in a night, stripping all the fat from the ribs, leaving only the hind legs but burying those and pissing on them to mark his claim.

He'd crunched the skull like a potato chip, and I found one of the molars he'd spit out into the mud. That's what I packed out that day, down Monture Creek until it wove back to the Big Blackfoot.

THE DAY I LOST my newspaper job I did what newspapermen have always done through all those years in a craft where a savings account is still called "fuck-you money": I gathered a few friends in a bar and we got roaring drunk. Late in the night a woman hauled me away, sobered me a bit and drove me in my pickup up the moonlit highway that threads along the Blackfoot. From what I remember, she had some serious things to say, but mostly she wanted to hide me from the mess for a bit in a place she knew upstream. She's my wife now.

ONCE I WAS FISHING the Blackfoot just below the box canyon, a fine summer's afternoon in August, but not seeing much of it, lost as I was in a fly fisher's concentration, focused like a Fresnel on the bugs and the fish taking the bugs. I snapped my rod tip back to the salute of backcast, and I lifted my head to honor it. Just at rod's apogee, a bald eagle flew overhead, inches above the flyrod's tip.

THE SPRING OF 1996 was the wettest we can remember here, and the snow clung to the mountains well into June, then the late but fiery summer sun set the snow loose all of a sudden, and it roared to record floods. Two teenagers tested the invincibility of their age against the river's and drowned within a couple of days of each other. A few weeks later a party of rafters on the nearby Clark Fork included a two-year-old child outfitted in an adult life vest. By late summer, searchers still had not recovered the child's body, despite an almost constant effort and considerable reward offered by the child's grandfather. This in a town where cocktail party chatter routinely covers the flow of the main stem (quoted in cubic feet per second) and pinpoints the location of new holes and sweepers.

On Father's Day of that year, my wife, Tracy, and my son, Josh, and I pumped up my thirteen-and-a-half-foot self-bailing raft, launched it at the Roundup Bridge and began the float to Johnsrud. It was the first time that year Josh had floated with me, and it was a matter of some significance, as it always is when Josh floats with me. He was twenty-two that spring, and every year he attains seems a gift because when he was eight, I nearly killed him in a raft.

Honesty will not allow me to recast that last clause into the less damning passive voice, or even substitute a new subject like "the river." The fact was, it was my fault and doing. It was another time when I knew less about rivers. I flipped a boat that had a child in it who had no business being on a flooded river. It was Mother's Day. His mother and I were trying to land the raft and had both stepped ashore when it happened—a heartbeat—then the boat was free, upside down and headed downstream on a swollen Idaho river, coffee-colored from the snowmelt water driving it. Near one edge of the raft a small head bobbed, barely visible then not visible as the rage of the river carried the raft away faster than I could run through the tangle of shoreline brush. Still I ran, tripping, then tangling in a barbed wire fence, but running until I found two kids on a motorcycle. They went to the small town nearby and within a half hour the town had emptied, everyone turning out to comb the banks of that river.

Two miles downstream of the accident, I stood on a bridge watching the river and trying to get used to the idea that my only child was dead. Maybe an hour after the flip, a searcher found the boat tangled in a sweeper—a fallen tree that arches just above the river's surface. Josh was with it, his life jacket still on, his arms wrapped in the safety line, which is a rope strung around the raft's circumference. He was unconscious and hypothermic with a body temperature of about 80 degrees. He was fine the next day.

Maybe that day is one of the things that keeps me coming back to rivers. I've rafted whitewater ever since, and am better at it now. Josh is old enough to be with me. That day on the Blackfoot we rode the rollers into the holes, whooping and hollering. I had decided early in the trip that no hole and no standing wave was too large to defy. The oars were in my hands, as was everything else.

The essence of a raft ride is a synergy between the person at the oars and the river. An oarsman on a river raft doesn't really row; the river does the work of moving the load from point A to B. The oarsman steers, mostly as an opportunist, pushing and prying the raft across the current to avoid rocks and other obstacles, and to position the raft so it takes standing waves and holes at the proper angle to avoid capsizing. He can avoid the worst the river offers by steering a conservative course, but that day I avoided nothing, setting up to plunge the raft through all the biggest holes and waves.

Holes are created by car-sized rocks that are barely submerged. The water flows over the rock, which lifts and channels it into a tongue that clears the rock then curls downward to form a hole, sometimes down a drop of six or eight feet. The downsweep then echoes back to an upward curve a few feet downstream at the opposite side of the hole, nadir followed by zenith in the amplitude of a standing wave form. Sometimes the upswing curls back on itself, a full curl like the loop-the-loop of a roller coaster. The raft bit into each of these holes like a toboggan through a ditch, dropping with the water over the face of each rock, dropping as the pit of our stomachs rose, then rising back upslope to teeter over the crest of each standing wave.

Tracy saw me setting up on that last big hole, the one with the particularly pronounced standing wave where the tongue of current lashed and roiled around the angry river god's face. For the record, she did say the hole was too big, but I had long before decided on my omnipotence, and I set up on it anyway, dead center and square, all as good as it could be. We dropped over the edge cleanly, seeming to linger in the relative peace of the fall, to hover for a second, then the raft tobogganed up the standing wave and angled ever back with the curl of the wave that was rolling back on itself. Our angle grew steeper and steeper in the climb, then we pointed straight up, perfectly vertical and suspended in the aching moment of balance just before the teeter back down and forward. I waited to feel the shift of our mass past the balance point from up to down. I felt it, but it went backward, not forward. Backward and down. Then came the second when the raft was standing completely vertically, its bow a clean and perfect thirteen and a half feet above its stern, but too brief a second to record and realize. By then our minds were not on the raft, but on our bodies and the vague recognition that they had achieved the apogee of a reverse roll, when all one's weight presses to the head. Then it was black, as I thought to myself: "Idiot."

We crossed then from daylight and noise to the silence of submersion and a cold that suddenly claims every molecule of breath. For a second, one simply surrenders to the baptism of the void, willingly crossing to the netherworld beneath the black surface of a spring-cold river. Then just as quickly my head broke the surface, as I fought to force at least some air back into my cold-flattened lungs. First I saw the red tube of the overturned raft a foot away, then next to it Tracy's head fighting for air and next to her, Josh's doing the same. We were fine, laughing even, when our lungs recovered enough air to permit it.

ALL OF THE ABOVE are insignificant stories when laid on the grand scheme of a river. I tell them only because they are a way of entering a river and that is the purpose of what is to come. All of us who know and love the Blackfoot know it with stories that are our own; none is the same. A river is not the straight line of a single story, but rather the round roils and eddies that bend and weave together into an infinite array of stories, together and back against each other through as much time as a good river has to give, which is all of time. None of us knows the same river, just as surely as it is never the same river twice to any one of us. It is, nonetheless, the common thread of the lives that live now and have lived in this quiet corner of the world.

At leisure of unburdened thought, I like to think of these cycles of stories as forming the "Round River" that Aldo Leopold spoke of in an essay by the same title. In the worst of times, we have thought of a river as that straight line that took things away, that washed away our worst sins like a high mountain sewer pipe. Leopold created the notion of the round river to urge conservation. If rivers' mouths dump back into their sources, then the garbage and abuse we heap on them would come back around to haunt us. It is only with the closing of our world, with the expansion of the human endeavor and human pollution to every edge of the world, that we finally begin to figure out that the joke here is on us. We see rivers as straight lines leading away only because of our warped perception. All rivers are really round. We don't dump our garbage on someone else, because there is only us. The river rolls back again and again in a never-ending loop of cycles as integral to our lives as the cycle of seasons.

These, however, are not times that afford the leisure of unburdened thought. In the best of times, we are measured and philosophical enough to think of the river as enclosing all of us, but every once in a while something comes along to jolt us back to clear battle lines. Events force this book to consider the Blackfoot not as a series of cycles of personal stories, but rather as a line as straight and hard as cash. As I write this, we who organize our lives according to this river must focus now away from the various eddies of our own lives. Instead, our attention is riveted straight upstream along the same line to a particular broad valley and a particular knob of a mountain near the junction of the main stem and the Landers Fork, a few miles below the Continental Divide and ten miles upstream from the town of Lincoln.

Phelps Dodge Corporation of Arizona has formed a partnership with a second mining corporation, Canyon Resources of Colorado, called the Seven Up Pete Joint Venture. The goal of the McDonald Project near Lincoln is to mine, to dig a hole a mile across and a half-mile wide, 1,300 feet deep, a hole that would be visible from outer space. The rock and dirt from the hole would be crushed and piled into a new mountain, but in layers, each layer woven with a network of sprinkler pipes that would irrigate the dirt and rock with a solution of sodium cyanide. It would trickle to the bottom and carry with it the minuscule amounts of gold in each square foot of dirt. This book is mostly about the fight to save the Blackfoot from this mine.

This book is about gold, so it must be about rivers. The two, as we shall see, have forever been inextricably intertwined. There is a new plague of gold mining throughout the West, one that has generally gone unnoticed in the nation as a whole. I think this is because the nation as a whole does not know rivers. My goal in this book is simple and straightforward: that it might be persuasive enough and vivid enough in its attachment to a river that it will stand as a case against buying gold in any form. To accomplish that, however, I cannot be satisfied with only addressing gold directly or even rivers directly. It must be the story of a river, a story that includes not just gold and rafters, but the range of human enterprise that this river brings to life. Only then might the reader know the real cost of a Rolex watch.

I have already mentioned logging, and that this river has seen some abuse. To stand on any stretch of it and stare to the hills that make it a river is to understand this. The hills are tiled with clear-cuts, which is probably why Redford found it unworthy of his film's backdrop. Likewise, there are open stretches along the valley floors where there ought to be bands of willows and shrubs winding with the meanders of tributary streams, but there are none. In some places, the stream picks its way through fields as hard used and barren as a parking lot. Cattle have caused this damage.

The Blackfoot is a working river, so the Blackfoot is a river of fights. The same people who are fighting the mine have fought logging and grazing. They have learned something in these fights, both sides. Accommodations have been made. By examining these battles—parallel to what the nation as a whole has experienced and is experiencing in its struggle to come to terms with nature's limits—this book will develop an idea: There is something fundamentally different between logging and grazing on the one hand and mining on the other. They create different battles. That difference says much about where we must go to cut a deal with all of our rivers that might ensure their future as well as a human future.

The Blackfoot is round because its small story wraps around the larger story of the Earth and the Earth's people.

HEADWATERS

THE HUMAN MEMORY of water runs deep in Montana. The Missoula Valley is famous for this, at least among geologists, who specialize in reconstructing the earth's deep memories. This place was the epicenter of one of the planet's most important and most recent catastrophes.

The record of this event is all indirect, drawn from the tracks and marks on these hills. One can read this history on any walk up any mountain trail that rims the Blackfoot and the rest of the streams in the web of the Clark Fork River, virtually all of Montana west of the Continental Divide. It is not subtle. Once a friend's father flew into Missoula on a clear crisp afternoon, got off the plane and announced, without any specific knowledge of the area's history, "This place was once all a great big lake." He is a geologist and could spot the water's tracks from a mile away, literally, even after the lake was more than 10,000 years gone. The rest of us can see it best in spring when a sprinkling of snow hits the hills—suddenly, perfectly flat tiers of terraces stand out, as if cut by bulldozers. They were cut by the water and ice of a lake's flat surface. One can spot it digging a posthole on the valley floor where gravels have been packed together nearly as hard as concrete by the great weight of the ancient lake.

It is named glacial Lake Missoula and once was as large as Lake Ontario. More than once, actually. The lake formed toward the end of the last glaciation, the end of the Ice Age, by an ice dam in what is now northern Idaho. Miles thick, the dam pooled an enormous body of water throughout what are now the river valleys of the region. The glaciers melted slowly in fits and starts, and periodically the dam would melt enough to float, draining this massive inland sea in a matter of a day. The lake flushed as many as forty times during the course of about 3,000 years, the first time as early as 16,000 years ago. The spectacular geology of the Columbia Basin, everything between the Blackfoot and the Pacific, is largely evidence of Lake Missoula, so much so that the existence of the lake was deduced from observances in Washington state. A highschool biology teacher, J. Harlen Bretz, spent his spare time wandering the Columbia Plateau scablands, until he finally figured out that the landscape had to have been the result of a great flood. He formally offered that controversial hypothesis in 1923. He was right, and it was quite a flood. It roared toward Washington at speeds up to fifty-eight miles an hour, its front lip a wall of water and ice 1,000 feet high. At one point, it gouged a pothole 164 feet deep.

Anthropocentric as it may be, what makes this event stand out in my mind against the great backdrop of catastrophe that shaped the planet is that all human reckoning of it may not be indirect. At the end of glaciation, there were already people in the region, people we call Clovis, whose progress from the Bering Land Bridge south through the continent is marked by fire pits and distinct stone points that reveal their hunting habits. They ate the camels, sloths, bison and woolly mammoths here at the time. They are the best candidates for direct ancestors of most American Indians.

Forty floods. Somebody could have seen these immense deluges, or more likely, wandered into the region while the enormous wounds were still evident. How many centuries' worth of water stories would these floods have created?

TO SEEK THE SOURCE one simply walks upstream, but walking upstream only finds the stream splitting to its forks again and again to teach that there are many sources. Pick one. Naming a river or deciding where it begins and ends is arbitrary. On the day in question, I was headed first up the Blackfoot, then up the Landers Fork a few miles until I could drive no more, because to really seek a source one must go walking. The road peters out low (in river-ese, low means downstream, close to its mouth) on the Landers Fork, but the stream goes on and up into formal, legal, congressionally sanctioned wilderness. This is the south edge of the Scapegoat Wilderness, which is a part of the sprawling Bob Marshall Wilderness complex, the first in the nation's wilderness system. From this edge one may walk for a day up to a divide then cross from the Blackfoot drainage to the Flathead, another tributary of the Columbia, or one may veer east over the Continental Divide onto the Dearborn drainage, which is headwaters to the Missouri, meaning from here the waters run all the way to the Gulf of Mexico. From either side of the divide one may walk straight north for ninety-five miles, in unroaded wilderness all the way, then for a minute out of wilderness to cross U.S. Highway 2 and a set of train tracks then into Glacier National Park, the Hudson Bay River drainage and on into Canada. The Bob Marshall is the source of pure waters.

It's July, hot and clear as Montana tends to be in July. I'm carrying a fanny pack, a plastic bottle of water, light binoculars and a map. I did have a plastic bottle of trail mix, but cached it early on the trail, since today would be about walking. I want to travel as lightly as possible so as to travel as far as possible. I am headed for the Continental Divide, to the source of the Blackfoot and back, a round trip of about twenty-four miles, and I will need all the daylight to make it. I am not the first to walk this trail.

There is no direct tie we know of from the Clovis people, who we suspect have walked this place, to the Salish, who we know were here. Lewis and Clark found the Salish here; they remain today. The Salish called this trail, the very bit of path my boots are now pounding, Cokahlarishkit, the going-to-the-buffalo trail. It was old by the time Meriwether Lewis used it in 1806, but one can still find the very stretch of it he used, using the same ancient marker that guided him, as I will later this trip. This trip is about finding our way.

Unlike many tribes hereabouts, the Salish admit to being newcomers, interlopers in the river valleys of western Montana. Their stories suggest they were from the region that is now northern California and southern Oregon. One story says an argument developed in this tribe when a duck flew by, with one person maintaining the quack came from the bill and the other partisans believing it was from the wings. The disagreement split the tribe. The bill side eventually decided to leave the country, traveling into the Snake River Plateau of southern Idaho then through Lolo Pass into the Bitterroot Valley of western Montana.

The valley was already occupied by the Pend Oreilles, another group of Salishin people with a language that differed from the newcomers' as much as British differs from American English. The two groups simply coexisted, peacefully, for centuries before whites came along.

Commonly, the Salish are called Flatheads, a term they object to, but descriptive of a practice common throughout the Pacific Northwest. Many of the tribes in the language group used a particular sort of cradle board that deliberately flattened the foreheads of infants, a deformation that was regarded as handsome and a sign of nobility. In some tribes, slaves were forbidden to flatten the heads of their infants. There is no record of the Salish of Montana ever doing this, although the Pend Oreilles report the Salish did when they first arrived in Montana, but quit. The Salish deny they ever did.

Both groups, however, agree that they were not the first to occupy the region, and that when they arrived they found a thriving population of giants, dwarfs and a less fantastic race labeled the Foolish Folk. The last was said to be a tribe of squat, bowlegged, nearly naked, bad-mannered and above all stupid people eking out a primitive sort of existence. The Salish highly regarded both manners and intelligence, so surviving stories have very little good to say about the Foolish Folk. It is understood that they buried their dead sitting upright, and some of them wore copper jewelry, which the Salish did not—an indication that these aboriginals may not have been nearly as primitive as the Salish would have it. There is copper in western Montana. As we shall see, the metal was the curse that preceded gold in recent times, responsible for environmental degradation on a monumental scale. This copper, however, is embedded in ores, and barring smelters, jewelry would require copper in its metallic form. The source of pure metallic copper was much farther east, meaning these Foolish Folk were plugged into a transcontinental trading network centuries before whites arrived, and the existence of such trading networks is well documented.

The Salish stories may be wrong, but in 1934, Edward Lozeau, a placer miner and a Pend Oreille, happened to find a corpse buried upright in the Foolish Folk fashion near the Clark Fork River downstream of Missoula. The necklace it wore held three beads of sheet copper.

According to Salish legend, the Foolish Folk were a river people, traveling everywhere in canoes. One day, a chief paddled his canoe over the Spokane Falls and died. His whole tribe followed him, and they died too, explaining the extinction of this group.

The fate of the giants and dwarfs of Salish legend is more problematic. The former group, said to be about fifteen feet tall, were relatively peaceful but mischievous. They were unable to speak Salish and simply faded into extinction in the early nineteenth century. The Salish say the giants needed a lot of food because of their size and could not compete with the growing numbers of other tribes. They disappeared, but only after several centuries of contact and stories. In the early 1930s, a Salish informant told anthropologist Harry Holbert Turney-High, "They were taller than the roof of this house, and they were strong even for their size. Once a man was thrown clear over Mount Sentinel [a prominent peak near Missoula] from Pattee Canyon into the Missoula [Clark Fork] River on the other side by a giant who just wanted to show off."

A woman then more than ninety, a member of the Kalispel, another Salish tribe, reported that a giant came to her house when she was a child, and she fed him. He wore grass sandals.

It is not known whether the dwarfs are extinct, in that they continue to play a role in Salish life. In the early stories, their role was ordinary. They were a group of dark-skinned people about two and a half feet tall. The Salish encountered them long before the Indians knew anything at all about livestock, yet report that the dwarfs kept domestic animals, specifically a three-foot-tall type of horse that was glistening black. The dwarfs were said to have every aspect of material culture that the Salish lacked but whites would later bring into the Bitterroot Valley.

The ultimate disposition of the dwarfs is not altogether clear, although the stories say they simply retreated against the onslaught of newcomers up the river valleys to headwaters and wilderness where they live today in volcanic craters and lakes. Like most tribes of the region, Salish go on quests for guiding spirits, and like most, frequently receive visions of a coyote or bear that will become a person's personal totem. On rare occasions, though, a supplicant encounters a dwarf, and then becomes forever blessed with the overarching intelligence of one of the little people. Dwarfs, however, are only accessible in the most remote and pristine places. Mostly, they are encountered by vision seekers who are fated to wield *sumesh*, a Salish word frequently translated as "medicine," but probably better called "power." Like many people, the Salish object to using "medicine" as a synonym for "power" because they had medicine in the same sense modern people do, derived from the plants hereabouts. *Sumesh* is something different, a power that is a sort of wisdom and accrues to shamans. Medicine is easy; *sumesh* is a gift, and much harder to come by, especially now when we need it so badly.

THERE IS A THEME to Salish life that sets them off from the tribes in the region and by the same token seems to make them more like those of us muddling through life in this place in modern times. They were a between people, a moving people whose ways were shaped by conflicting circumstances. Their stories and traditions were northwestern, tied closely with their relatives, all of whom were salmon people. The people of the Northwest built a culture of peace, abundance and stability, thanks largely to the gift of the salmon. The Salish name for Lolo Pass, the divide between Idaho and Montana, means "no salmon," so they were conscious of leaving their Eden for the harsher life of the mountains. Through their Montana history, they periodically wandered back to fish on the Clearwater in what is now Idaho, just as many whites do today, but they didn't move back, always returning to their salmonless adopted home.

In the early years in the Bitterroots, a new set of stories and rituals emerged to replace salmon culture. These were largely related to the plants—camas, wild onion, bitterroot, serviceberry, huckleberry—and the range of species that fed and healed them. They became a plant people, but another element arose, another conflict. The horse came, and with it a realignment of their lives along the Blackfoot River.

There is no doubt that the ponies that filtered into western Montana in the early 1700s, long before anyone in the region had seen a white man, were Spanish. Horses were a white-introduced revolution of Indian life long before the Indians of the region had seen a white face. The Salish most likely got their horses from the Snake tribe nearly a century before Lewis and Clark passed through. The descendants of Spanish horses brought to Mexico City by Cortés in 1519 worked into Indian hands in the Southwest and were traded or stolen by tribes to the north. The equestrian life spread into the Colorado Plateau, then west and north into the Great Basin, to the Snake River Plain in what is now southern Idaho, then to the Salish. Like any leap in technology, the advent of the horse cut with two edges.

Long before the horse's arrival, the Salish were hunters, taking the abundant deer, moose and bighorn sheep of the broad intermontane valleys of western Montana. There is some evidence, both physical and oral, of bison in the region around the Bitterroot before the coming of the horse, but the increased efficiency of the mounted hunter quickly eliminated bison from west of the Great Divide. At the same time, the horse allowed the Salish to travel east to the plains where bison were abundant. The way to the plains was straight up the Blackfoot River to a gentle pass at the headwaters of the Landers Fork, Cokahlarishkit.

The undeniable blessing of this leap in technology was a state of plenty. Stories and celebrations, even the seasons among the Salish—former salmon people, then plant people—shifted to honor the bison, a 1,000-pound pile of meat and shelter. The longhouse and lean-to, long the tribe's shelter, gave way quickly to the bison-hide-covered and easily portable tipi. Yet these material changes overlay what had to have been a profound change in the spirit of life, a change contained in words like "stories" and "portable" and "plains."

The shift brought on by the horse was not unique to the Salish but occurred about the same time all up and down the Rockies on the western edge of the great American grasslands, as well as all up and down the Mississippi Basin on its eastern edge. The horse enabled a nomadic hunter's life. Tribes that had for millennia survived as farmers, fishers and gatherers threw it off in a blink and took to the horse. No one went the other way; no one ignored the allure of the horse—the same problem Chinese landowners had when their peasants ran off to ride the horses of Mongol hordes.

Yet the cost of this horse life was enormous. At the north edge of the

Bitterroot Valley, where the city of Missoula now stands and just a couple of miles downstream of the Blackfoot's mouth, the Clark Fork River pinches into a narrow, high-walled canyon called Hellgate. My son went to Hellgate High School, named for this place, a name high-school students must find particularly apt, but it has nothing whatever to do with the passage through adolescence. It was named by the first white settlers, who found it filled with skeletons and rotting bodies of Salish people, casualties of war.

The Blackfoot River corridor was the path to the bison, but also the path to the Blackfeet—a fierce, forever nomadic plains people who used it to cross to the mountains to make war on the Salish. This warfare was the result of horses. Horse stealing was a mater of honor among the Blackfeet, its name synonymous with the term for warfare. They stole horses from all other tribes in the region, a way of counting coup, but also a necessity, a redistribution of wealth, the basis of their economy. Through some accident of genes, maybe, or through a skill in breeding and training, the Salish were known for owning a stock of particularly fine horses. Even in this century, the Blackfeet stole Salish horses at every opportunity.

WHEN LEWIS AND CLARK returned east from the mouth of the Columbia in 1806, the expedition crossed Lolo Pass with the help of the Nez Perce. They stopped at a place called Traveler's Rest at the head of the Bitterroot Valley, a couple of miles from where my house now stands. They split into two groups. Clark headed south and Lewis headed for the Blackfoot River. In his journal entry of July 3, 1806, Lewis wrote:

> These people now informed me that the road which they showed me at no great distance from our camp would lead us up the east branch of the Clark's River and a river they called Cokahlarishkit or the river of the road to the buffalo and thence to the medicine [Sun] river and the falls of the Missouri where we wished to go. They alleged that as the road was a well-beaten track we could not now miss our way and as they were afraid of meeting their enemies the Minnetaeres [Blackfoot] they could not think of continuing with us any longer, that they wished to proceed down Clark's River in search of their friends the Shalees.

They informed us that not far from the dividing ridge [Continental Divide] between this river and the Missouri river the roads forked. They recommended the left hand [Landers Fork].

Lewis's party headed up the Landers Fork on July 7, 1806.

I headed up the Landers Fork at the same spot on July 23, 1996. The place Lewis describes as "the right hand side through handsome plain bottoms to the foot of the ridge" is the site of the proposed Seven Up Pete gold mine. It was marked then and it is marked today with a series of rock cairns that were there long before Lewis walked through. The Salish marked their important trails with cairns, and it was their custom, when passing, to add a rock to the pile as a sort of traveler's offering to the guidance of the trail. The cairns here and another rock marker in northern Idaho are today the only physical evidence of the Lewis and Clark Trail known to remain. They are not marked or signed in any way. One must hunt for them. The guidance that was obvious to the Salish and those who walked their trails is not so obvious to us today.

A two-lane blacktop road parallels the Landers Fork North lining up on the gunsight pass through the Great Divide about twenty miles upstream, the way home as Lewis must have seen it from this spot in 1806. But it turned out to be the way to many other places, and Lewis must have had a hint of that on his trip. It was also the way to riches, not so different, really, from what it had been to the Salish for centuries, a shot at a big pile of meat that would make the coming winter easier. Foremost on the explorer's mind was not meat but fur, "soft gold," as it was known at the time. The Northwest and Hudson Bay companies had already been trapping throughout the region for many years. (At the time, trappers joked that the initials of the latter meant "here before Christ.") Explorer Alexander Mackenzie had already walked across the continent in 1793 but to the north in British territory. Lewis and Clark were drawn at least as much by commerce as by curiosity.

Their trip came but a few months before the infant nation would ship boatloads of gold to France to pay for the Louisiana Purchase, of which this grand landscape was the very western edge. It has been said the whole adventure had the feel of a prospective real estate buyer sizing up rooms and measuring lot lines before closing on a deal—and to be sure that's what it was. It was the opening foray of Manifest Destiny, that

seminal American notion that considered the perfectly settled and relatively prosperous homeland of a human culture unsettled and unpopu-
lated, land for the taking. And there was a taking, and all of the West's
history from then on, from the Mississippi through this pass to the Oregon coast and the gold fields of California, was cast in that single idea. It
was this land's job to give of itself until it was used up. Then we would
leave, head farther west to see what might be there for the taking. We
cover this with the term "natural resources" but the more accurate and
simple word is "taking."

There are, however, pockets where it is possible to pretend for a time
that the taking has not happened. In 1964, our nation passed the
Wilderness Act, under which we would inventory those tracts—mostly
in the West—that had somehow survived not visibly diminished by
logging, ranching, mining, tourism and development; in the phrase of
the law, those lands "untrammeled by man." That's not quite what we
meant. What we really sought were those lands that looked as they did
after being trammeled for 10,000 years by people such as the Salish and
Blackfeet but before white settlement. All the serious trammeling has
been done since.

The single defining idea that would govern the care of formally designated wilderness was roadlessness. There would be no mechanized or
motorized travel of any sort, as if such travel defined the difference between those who came before and ourselves. And when you think about
it, that we can mark the beginning of the end of this place by a single
expedition's travels, then travel indeed was a watershed.

The largest chunks of wilderness excluding Alaska are in Montana
and northern Idaho along the Rockies. The two-lane blacktop road
winds up the Landers Fork for four miles, crosses it, winds around to a
tributary, forks to a gravel road leading to a parking lot at a place called
Indian Meadows—and there all roads end. To go farther, one must walk,
as one may from here for weeks or even months up and down a network
of boot trails woven among the mountain streams, alpine meadows, un-
cut forests, grizzlies, elk and loneliness for as long as one wishes to go.

I parked my pickup truck in the lot and grabbed only a fanny pack,
then it was quiet except for the beat of boots that would tick off the
eight-hour walk. I meant to walk to the Great Divide, twelve or so miles
up the trail.

A QUARTER OF A MILE up the trail I remembered I had come here for something definite; it's just I was not altogether sure what that might be, something that would spring from the rhythm of walking in woods. The Salish used to come here for a similar purpose, not simply for buffalo or whatever meat or plants were in season, but for the spirit of the high mountain valleys. It was a formalized part of their ritual and was preceded by fasting, so I thought it best to drop the food, stashing the trail mix I had brought near a tree ten minutes up from the trailhead. I felt better without it.

The water may have seemed silly too, in that I would be walking next to a stream the whole way. I remember hiking along trails that hugged Lake Attitlan in Guatemala and noticing that every single Indian I met broke out laughing. I considered them an inordinately good-humored people, until I finally realized they were considering me inordinately silly. I was carrying a canteen in sight of a perfectly good lake full of water. My water bottle no doubt would make just as much sense to the Salish, but even here in wilderness, unseen microbes make it best to carry one's water. Largely spread by beaver and horses, the amoebic parasite giardia has become ubiquitous. It causes horrible stomach distress for a week or so; in severe cases it leaves some people unable to eat certain foods the rest of their lives. I carried the water.

Up trail an hour and a half, bits of clear sky began to peek between the trees, and I took the clearing to be a lake, which it was. Heart Lake. It was a flawless, sunny mountain morning, and I had this half-mile-long lake all to myself as I broke out on the bluff that overlooks it. I could see ten miles or so off west to Red Mountain, a bald hump of rock still shouldered in snow. The scene was unreal in its beauty and there came then the idea that forever nags one through wilderness, that this place is so stunning as to exist as the standard of beauty. Not a thing we could possibly do could make it more beautiful. I've read our poets, I've heard our music and I've eaten our food. I know we as a species are capable of creating beauty, but it is hard to consider its worth in wilderness. Any landscape dominated by humans is less than this. That's the painful fact of the matter, only completely revealed on a solo hike in wilderness.

The unhuman magic behind this beauty likely has something to do with why virtually all of the native cultures that lived here used these mountains for vision quests. They came here for *sumesh*. The dwarfs, a race of people who best understood this power, may still dwell in craters and beneath pristine lakes in the most inaccessible of alpine terrain. They are what we are not, just as wilderness is what we are not. We may only comprehend their power in light of this place. We have an idea of what magic is and what lies behind it, and believe it must be obtained from an approach to the supernatural.

The anthropologist Turney-High used as an informant a shaman, a Kalispel man he knew for many years. He gathered stories both about and from the shaman, Charlie Gabe, who, among other gifts, could predict when someone was about to die suddenly and unexpectedly, or even when someone was coming to visit. Turney-High gathered this story about Gabe:

> In 1931 the shaman hired two men to work for him on his ranch, one a bachelor, the other married to a pretty girl. It was necessary for the married man to spend a night away tending cattle. So just before dawn the other man rose to go to work. When Gabe arose he knew that something was wrong. At noon he went to the spring and got a pail of fresh water. Making *sumesh* over the water he gave a dipper to each person to drink, just as if he were doing them a favor. When it came turn for the bachelor to drink he found that he could not, and dropped the dipper and the water on the floor. "You cannot drink," said the shaman, "because you have done something wrong. Tell me what it was."

The man had seduced his absent colleague's wife. In the end, Gabe foretold his own death by the fact that he was no longer able to drink pure, running water. When he healed people, his advice often included drinking pure and running water. We have a notion that magic resides in a separate and inaccessible world, but magic is with us and contained in reality. It is natural, not supernatural. Power flows from the natural world and the measure of its integrity and of our integrity is the presence of clean running water.

EUROPEANS RECONSTITUTED on the American continent also have stories to explain our origins and values drawn from deep oral traditions.

We know, for instance, that we are travelers and have been finding and exploring trails for a very long time. Like the Salish who used the Cokahlarishkit trail, we have traveled to obtain riches, but probably just as much we have traveled to travel. Our history is a history of odysseys.

The Greek story of Jason and the Argonauts recounts an epic journey in the Mycenaean period, nearly 4,000 years ago. In that the whole quest was wound up in a search for golden fleece, we first think of this tale as pastoral symbolism, but the fleece and gold were real; the details of oral tradition often are real. The Mycenaeans were actively working in gold by the time of Jason, but there are no gold deposits around the Aegean Sea. They traveled for it, generally to the Caucasus and the lands beyond the eastern shore of the Black Sea where flooding streams worked gold from veins on mountains. The gold was gathered by staking sheep's fleeces in streams, because the hides had a natural affinity for the precious metal. Once laden, the fleeces were loaded on animals and packed back to Greece.

Midas, however, is the name most connected with gold in Western tradition, yet his is also a river story. Midas was a Phrygian king, ruling in an area of Asia Minor long associated with gold. His contemporary was the Lydian king and tyrant Gyges, who maintained his hold with a power to become invisible, which he manipulated with a gold ring. He is credited with inventing money; the first coins were gold rings. Money is the basis of financial transaction, which gave gold the power of producing goods, of making them visible then invisible, which is the magic of trade.

Midas, however, came to the power of gold through an accident. He entertained a traveler, who turned out to be the father of the god Bacchus. In gratitude the god granted Midas a wish, the Midas touch, which was on its reverse side a curse, the depth of which became clear when Midas touched his daughter, sapping the life from her and replacing it with gold. The god took some mercy on the greedy mortal, however, and allowed him to surrender the touch by washing it off in the Pactolus River, a real river once, now dry, but then mined for gold. The magic that ruined Midas's life did wash off in the river, where the curse stayed, and from then on it would be the curse of rivers to produce gold. It would not be the last time a river would suffer after washing away the sins of a greedy political leader.

THOSE MILES I WALKED up the Landers Fork aimed at a specific goal, not just walking. On a map, wilderness designation appears a random process, a blob of land here and a blob there, but it takes almost no time spent in mountains to understand there is an order to the process. Those lands designated as wilderness were simply those never developed, the most rugged, the steepest and the highest, the headwaters. Wilderness is upstream. The essential dichotomy of civilized life sorts the land. At the one end stands civilization and at the other, the headwaters of rivers. I was walking toward the Great Divide to find the most extreme pole. I was trying to find how far upstream one must go to escape the curse of the Pactolus.

Maybe three or four hours of fast hiking is enough to do the trick; maybe it's just a matter of the exertion, the endorphins, the deprivation of oxygen to one's brain and the otherworldly loneliness of wilderness that renders one wholly insignificant. At some point after hours of hard walking miles from the nearest human soul, all of this comes together with the realization of being lost—not in the specific, local sense, but that you have lost your way on the planet.

A long ridge wound down from Heart Lake back to the Landers Fork, rushing and rolling over the rounded glacial till, red rocks, green rocks, once the limestones and mudstones of the Rockies. The rock bottoms don't blur on mountain river bottoms; rather they glisten and shine like wood through a wet coat of transparent varnish. The trail I was on seemed little used, not one of the wilderness superhighways favored by strings of packhorses bringing in elk hunters and rich tourists. Such trails have bridges across the wider streams, but here the trail noses into the streamside gravels and disappears in the current, popping up on the opposite shore like an ouzel. I unlaced my boots and waded into a babble of water that was snow a few minutes before. The water was cold enough to make my teeth hurt and my feet as brittle as January glass. I believed for a second that a toe had cracked and fallen off when I jammed it straight into a sharp-edged rock.

Landers Fork nosed into a straight-edged canyon. It was midday and the sun was pounding the amphitheater of the canyon's walls, so I was in no hurry to replace my boots over throbbing feet. I sat for a moment, wondering if this is what it's like to be truly alive.

The Landers Fork split off a tributary, Bighorn Creek, and I split with it, up a long canyon to the Divide. I was on my own. If I twisted an ankle or smashed a toe, it would be days without food and cold nights without a sleeping bag before I could hobble out. And with this came the heightened sense of being alone and on an equal footing with the rest of the life of this place. More hours ordered themselves according to the cardiac rhythms of footfalls.

All the way in, for maybe eleven miles, the trail threaded in a thick canopy of lodgepole pine, fir and spruce, once in a while a more open slope of ponderosa pine, but toward the Divide the trees gave way to broad meadows. Then it swung around a rock face and up ahead I could see the bald ridges and ghostly white spars I know to be the Great Divide. The place has looked like this for most of the time since glaciation, with only a brief interlude that phased in during the early half of this century then broke all of a sudden in this spot on a night in September of 1988.

Wilderness is an illusion. Most of the Bob Marshall and most Rocky Mountain wilderness areas have indeed been trammeled by man. I have a late-nineteenth-century map of what is now the Bob Marshall, meticulously color-coded in pencil to record a census of the trees as these lands were being added to the National Forest Reserve system. It was not a closed canopy of forest as most of it is now, but rather, in total, only about 20 percent timbered. Its open, grassy face was the creation of lightning-spawned fires that periodically swept it clean.

In our zeal to control and protect and in our bias—especially our commercial bias for trees—we began putting out forest fires. All of them. Who hasn't heard of Smokey Bear? But fire suppression did not take into account the idea that the denizens of this place, plant and animal, had grown accustomed to what biologists label, in a rare moment of clear language, the "regime of fire." Elk and grizzlies needed the grass. A species of woodpecker evolved a black back so it could hide from predators while digging bugs out of fire-scorched trees. Lodgepole pine developed a serotinous pinecone that stays closed tightly like a pineapple until the heat of a fire opens it to release the seeds. Even well-intentioned meddling is meddling, and it destroys.

During the last couple of decades western land managers have gradually emerged from this fog and have begun to let fire reassert itself. The Scapegoat fire, officially known as the Canyon Creek fire, started in June of 1988 about twenty-five miles east of this point and burned for almost two months, harmlessly and sedentarily, but as summer dried tinder it began to stand up and walk. Then September brought some freakish winds coincident with a freakish shift of the jet stream and in a single night the fire galloped forty miles out over the Continental Divide into the plains, where it sputtered and died. In those few hours, 250,000 acres reclaimed their legacy of fire.

Resurrection is recorded there on the ridge of the Great Divide. Many of the trees are dead, but the grasses and elk have returned. As have the flowers, and on that July day I found the blooms of potentilla, penstemon, paintbrush, groundsel, geranium, buttercup, strawberry, cinquefoil, harebells, yarrow, arnica, pale yellow columbine. In the broad meadow studded with all of these lies the beginning of Bighorn Creek that is the beginning of Landers Fork that is the beginning of the Blackfoot that is the beginning. In my fanny pack was still most of the plastic jug of tap water, and I dumped it on the ground, refilled it with running creek water and drank away the long, lonely walk's dehydration.

THE NIGHTHAWKS CAME THAT NIGHT as I pitched my tent beside the Landers Fork near the blacktop road. Road or no, it was quiet, the night broken by the occasional fisherman's pickup truck laboring upstream. I lit my backpacker's stove and cooked lentils.

The Salish name for nighthawk is onomatopoetic imitation of the screech sound its wings make when it sets to dive on insect prey, then reverses course and shoots straight into the night sky. Swallows joined the rush to bugs and a white-tailed deer teetered to the stream bank just downstream of my tent. I could not imagine a will to disrupt the peace of this place.

Come morning, I walked some more, but this time without the single-mindedness of a trail. Rather I left my campsite about four miles from the mouth of Landers Fork and meandered on the route Meriwether Lewis's journal said he had walked, but in the opposite direction. The way is mostly a broad grassy plain, part of a cattle ranch that belongs to the family of United States Senator Max Baucus. One quickly reads its geology to conclude it is an alluvial terrace once a higher floodplain of a higher Landers Fork. The edge of terrace breaks sharply down in most places, thirty, forty feet to the current floodplain of the Landers

Fork and I sat for a bit overlooking its spray of cottonwoods, sedges, alders and willows. I surprised a pair of sandhill cranes and two ghostly elk.

Then I worked upslope to a second terrace across the blacktop road that parallels the Landers Fork, a mountain really, by most standards. It's open with clumps of lodgepole and aspen, but mostly a profusion of native grasses. A fawn still in spots gamboled from the aspen and I shuddered at its terrible vulnerability, which stood out sharply here against the backdrop of pipes. Pipes and little scratchings of steel tracks were everywhere on this hill. Surveyors' flags. Fresh road cuts. The roar of a tree skidder from a state-run logging operation echoed from the next ridge. The pipes are cast iron, larger than two hands can surround and sticking a couple of feet straight out of the ground, studding this hill like sprigs of cloves on a trussed and baked ham. They are the heads of test wells punched in during the past year by the gold miners. Gold mining now is hydrology because the mile-wide, half-mile-deep open pits of typical mines are dug in water, just as they are dug in earth. Groundwater must be diverted and pumped off in other directions, completely drying up springs, seeps and streams—in the case of American Barrick's Goldstrike Mine near Carlin, Nevada, for 100 square miles surrounding the mine. It is not known how that pumping will work here and because hydrology is such a mystery—a guessing game at divining subterranean streams—the effects can't be known until the deed is done. We won't know for sure whether this gold mine will eradicate the Landers Fork until it has eradicated the Landers Fork.

These wells are test wells, drilled to assess the amount of pumping that will be required, the flow rate and directions of the groundwater. They are used to prepare the best guess that will be the basis of a decision to allow the mine to proceed, a hoop the miners must jump through before winning the prize that is the mining permit. The wells went on for as far as I could see, only because the mountain of grass and aspen went on for as far as I could see. In space. But not in time. The gold deposit is under this mountain and the miners plan to annihilate the entire mountain to get at the gold beneath.

Somewhere on this panoramic scene, within spitting distance of the wellheads, there are six rock cairns. One of these ancient structures rests within a single step of where a bulldozer's blade took a bite out of a side of a hill. The 'dozer cut a new trail and had we as a people not lost all sense of direction, we could have told at a glance it was headed the wrong way. The cairns once pointed to the headwaters that are sacred and magic, and they still do, but that's not where we're headed. They once pointed to the buffalo, which was economy—a way nature sustained a people who lived here in return for an understanding of and respect for the fragile source of the sustenance. We are not headed there either. We now forgo the guidance of the cairns to get to the gold beneath.

TIMBER

FROM THE ROCK CAIRNS near the mine site, it is possible to launch a canoe—just barely—and ride, bumping and grinding over rocks down the Landers Fork about a mile until it joins the river's other spindly arm. The ride would cross under Highway 200, then through the toe of a broad meadow rimmed by mountains. From here, the course would veer west and the canoe could bounce along, fewer rocks and gravel bars, more water now, for maybe four days—depending on the time of year, the river's flow, the canoeist's inclination—for 130 miles, more or less, until the Blackfoot ends just above Hellgate Canyon and a city.

The presence of Missoula at the Blackfoot's mouth, opposite the headwaters, provides the river's opposing poles. Upstream and down. Headwaters and wilderness at one end, city and civilization at the other, pulling the river's waters forever away from a state of nature. This is not abstract. There is a real presence at the mouth of the river, images we can see, hear and smell in the roar, the diesel smoke, mountains of sawdust and rows of grimy pickup trucks bearing racks of chainsaws parked at roadside taverns at day's end. The river's last mile of banks are lined with pile on endless pile of cut logs waiting to be fed to the sawmill at Bonner. This is the present evidence of the river's history of logging on the Blackfoot. Given the damage already done, why do we bother to fight a gold mine?

In all of the northern Rockies and west to the Cascades of Washington, Oregon, California and British Columbia and on to the coastal ranges, environmentalism is mostly about logging. It is the damage most evident on this landscape. The fight against it has raised up a diffuse army of activists centered in cities but spread up every drainage into every mill town, every town. It is a war without a front or even major battles. Instead it is an unbroken string of skirmishes, each focused and specific. Each is a fight over a few acres of ground and whether it will be logged or not, and if that point is lost, then the terms of its logging are contested—clear-cut or selective, helicopters or line skidders, new roads or none. Maybe the whole stand must go, but perhaps we can save a specific clump of old growth guarding a particularly valuable stream somehow untouched by the long history of logging that has reduced many of our streams to biological deserts.

No matter what else results from each of these fights, though, one thing at least is certain, that the whole business will go on and on. The battle does not end, but advances, just over the ridge, on to the next few acres that someone plans to log next year.

The mill at its mouth testifies that the Blackfoot River has been spared none of this. Just the opposite. It flows in particular circumstances that have made its battles even more pitched and pronounced. Our river eddies in the contradiction and enigma that surround people's struggle to understand our place in nature.

On the day before my journalism job ended in 1989, I covered my last story for the paper, which was an Earth First tree sit. A common tactic by radical environmentalists, this particular event was just over the Divide at headwaters of the Blackfoot drainage on a plot of Forest Service land. Three activists had each selected a tree, and with the help of friends and mountain-climbing gear, had in the dead of night climbed the trees, attached small plywood platforms to each and by dawn had taken a lotuslike seat on each platform to stop loggers from cutting the trees. It was an aerial sit-in. My press contact with the organization was Tracy Stone, the woman who would in a year become my wife.

One of the tree sitters was Jake Kreilick, a burly, gregarious young man of around twenty-five. I knew him as a rugby player and a friendly, noisy regular at a local bar, but Jake is a full-time activist. He was arrested after that sit-in. As he was arrested in Malaysia a few years ago protesting logging there. Unburdened by First Amendment issues, the Malaysians sent him to prison to work in, of all things, the prison woodshop. As I write this in 1996, Jake is in jail again, sentenced after a protest to protect a section of wilderness from logging in northern Idaho. He intervened to stop loggers from beating up other protesters. This fight goes on and on.

IT HELPS TO REMEMBER that mining caused the logging of the Blackfoot. Mining and railroads. The drainage probably holds the doubtful honor of being the first logged in a region that would become a logger's paradise. Its first whiff of smoke and steam and its first feel of steel came early in the second half of the nineteenth century, when our taking was unchecked by even a hint of conscience.

The lands of the Salish had already been taken. The tribe's domestication had been somewhat eased by their early contact with Lewis and Clark, subsequent trade and one other peculiar development. Along with the neighboring Nez Perce, the Salish had dispatched envoys to St. Louis to request that Jesuits come to minister to the tribes. This leaning into the punch of Christianity was apparently the result of an old tribal story that foretold the coming of the black robes, but also an opportunistic alliance with the whites against their ancient enemies, the Blackfeet. In 1855, the Salish adopted the Hellgate Treaty, which granted them hunting and fishing rights on the Blackfoot, but ended their centuries-long occupancy of the Bitterroot Valley by removing them to the site of their current reservation in the Flathead Valley. The broad, flat Flathead is higher and harsher than the more agriculturally promising Bitterroot, which filled first with white farmers, and now is filling with retired ranchers and movie stars in trophy homes.

The Flathead is rimmed with the Mission Mountains, the spine that separates it from the Blackfoot drainage and the row of regal rock that makes this valley among the most scenic on the planet.

During the 1860s, the nation reorganized to reorient itself along parallel strips of steel. Like Cokahlarishkit itself, this new technology opened a road to gathering nature's riches on a scale the Salish or, for that matter, any human before could never have imagined. The railroads gathered steam as the emergent national infrastructure during the Civil War, an upheaval that was to have a great deal to do with the reshaping of the West. During the war, President Lincoln signed the first of the railroad land grants. That was the key. That law opened the West to development, and its terms can be read today from any prominent ridge in the Blackfoot drainage, written, as it were, on the land. The key pieces of physical evidence of this law are the string-straight edges of squared clear-cuts that blotch the landscape.

The straight lines predate Lincoln to the Northwest Ordinance and Thomas Jefferson. The rationalists setting the rules at the time decided that all the "vacant" lands the new nation was acquiring by rebellion, warfare, genocide and purchase were to be divided by the rectilinear cadastral survey, a system of dicing the place up in a grid of mile-square sections, not unlike cutting up a sheet cake at a wedding, as a friend of mine once said.

These rules were made by people who had never seen the West, and when the nation first sent explorers like John Wesley Powell to survey the actual landscape just after the Civil War, he (and others, but Powell especially) would build his scientific career on arguing against the squared subdivisions. Powell said the arid West is really organized by rivers and so land settlement should be based on the logic of hydrological divides. He argued that our lives should be organized by rivers. Congress, however, was in no mood to consider reality, anxious as it was to get on with the business of exploitation. It was an extraordinarily rapacious time, not unlike our own.

The rectangle stood, and came heavily into play in the railroad grants. A merchant from New York, Asa Whitney, dreamed up the idea of giving railroads a sixty-mile-wide strip of federal lands along any lines they would build into the un(white)peopled West. Whitney believed railroads were divinely ordained: "Nature's God had made this for the grand highway to Civilize and Christianize all mankind." He first petitioned Congress with the idea in 1845, but nothing came of it for nearly twenty years.

Ultimately, sixty-one railroads would receive land grants totaling 131 million acres before Congress ended the program in 1871. Almost half of that, a total of 60 million acres, an area the size of New England, went to the Northern Pacific Railroad in 1864. The plan was to build a railroad from the Twin Cities of Minnesota to the Pacific at Tacoma, Washington, and such a railroad was indeed built, completed with the driving of a ceremonial spike in Montana in 1883. Likely the spike was driven into a wood tie made from a tree from the Blackfoot. The spike was made of gold, of course, and the joining occurred at a place called Gold Creek, named for the early discovery of gold there, not for the spike. Gold was already on people's minds, but logging was more certainly on their landscape. The Northern Pacific set the pattern of the Blackfoot's life, a pattern that holds today.

Those federal lands given to the railroads were doled in mile-square sections in a strip up to seventy miles wide along the track. But an alternate section rule meant the railroads got every other section while alternate squares remained, at first at least, as federal lands. That created the patchwork that reads on the land like a checkerboard, which is what it is called. The rectilinear cadastral survey is not simply a rationalist's abstraction.

The Northern Pacific ran along the Clark Fork River right at the mouth of the Blackfoot. In 1870 A. B. Hammond, a Missoula businessman and pillar of the community, won a contract to produce all of the railroad's ties. To do this, he started the mill at Bonner that still operates today, but also set in play a second element that was to shape the face of the Blackfoot. Hammond and others formed the Montana Improvement Company, supplied the rail ties, then used the new railroad to ship timbers to the rapidly growing copper mines 120 miles up the Clark Fork at Butte. For nearly twenty years, they did all this through the simple frontier expedient of theft. Those lands not granted to the railroads remained federal lands, as were the trees, locked up as uncuttable forest reserves by an 1831 law. In 1885, a federal agent investigated the logging and accused Hammond of stealing 45 million board feet of lumber and 85,000 railroad ties.

The enduring pattern of Montana's politics also was forming in such incidents. T. S. Oakes was then head of the railroad, but also kept a great deal of money in a bank owned by Montana governor T. S. Hauser. Historian K. Ross Toole cites Oakes's letter to Hauser:

> Read this over carefully and let me know if you intend to take a position in reference to our timber interests. If we have no rights in this property you will respect, I shall at once draw our deposits from your bank . . . and in every other respect make things so hot for you, you will think the devil is after you. The Northern Pacific Company has not spent $70,000,000 to be bulldozed by you or anybody else. Let me know what your position is. The Northern Pacific Company has the right to demand of you the fullest support in every reasonable effort to protect its interests. It has never asked anything of you thus far but has done a great deal for you and your interests thus far with very little return.

Officialdom was properly moved by Oakes's prose. First, the trial of the timber thieves was stalled—for twenty-six years. Then they were convicted but on drastically reduced charges. But more important, Congress cut loose the federal timber not given the railroads, especially in the Timber and Stone Act of 1892. Patterned like the Homestead Act, this allowed individuals to claim parcels of federal land, occupy it and by logging it, gain clear title to the lands. The catch was that even then logging was a capital-intensive business, and those with capital wound up with the land. Companies like Hammond's used a widespread technique called "dummy entrymen." Employees, or even drunks rounded up downtown, were given a few bucks or a few drinks to file claims on parcels of land with valuable timber. Logging would begin. As soon as title to the claim was granted to the entrymen, it would almost immediately pass to the timber companies.

In 1898 the copper baron Marcus Daly paid $1.5 million for the Blackfoot timberlands and mills amassed by Hammond and his associates. The Timber and Stone Act transferred 663,552 acres of federal timber to "entrymen's" hands, and Daly and his Anaconda Copper Company wound up with all of it.

The way in which this history writes itself on the modern landscape can first be seen on an ownership map, with its multicolored checkerboard. There are some very narrow bands along the main stem of the river and somewhat wider bands in broad valleys like Potomac and Ovando that are white, indicating various small private holdings ranging from riverside cabins to cattle ranches. By and large, though, this strip of landscape, 130 miles long, 70 miles wide, shows on the map as being in the hands of three owners. There are green squares, land that remained federal, parts of the Lolo, Flathead and Lewis and Clark national forests. There are light purple squares with their unique history, a railroad history. After the initial rush of construction, the Northern Pacific largely ignored its timberlands into the 1950s, but as timber became more valuable, the railroad created the subsidiary of Plum Creek Timber Company, now an independent entity. Plum Creek plays on the purple squares.

Meanwhile, Anaconda held its timberlands until depressed copper prices pushed the company out of the copper business. In the 1970s it sold to a multinational timber giant, Champion International. Plum Creek and Champion each held about 850,000 acres in western Montana. Combined, it was an area the size of Delaware. And it was combined. In 1991, after about a decade and a half of what Champion called an "accelerated harvest," the corporation decided there weren't enough trees left to justify its presence. It sold all of its lands to Plum Creek and its mill at Bonner to a small independent timber company.

ONE CANNOT UNDERSTAND THIS HISTORY solely from the colors of the map. The picture is better filled by looking at the land itself, which is checkerboarded with the respective squares of the timber companies and the federal government. Both entities do log, but there is a difference. The Forest Service is the target of almost constant criticism for its logging practices, and well it should be. There have been egregious cuts. I've walked them, flown over them, spent hours and days getting the feel of them acre by acre and plant by plant. However, the Forest Service is an institution in transition, maybe no better or worse than the rest of us, and it is responsive in some sense to the rest of us. Forest Service logging is easier on the land than Plum Creek's, at least by an order of magnitude.

The best measure of this difference comes in a set of numbers. In 1986, Plum Creek and Champion owned about 11 percent of the timbered lands in my state, with most of the rest owned by the Forest Service. Still, this small minority of the checkerboard was cut hard enough then and in most other years of the surrounding decade to produce about half the logs headed for mills, according to a Montana state forester.

To understand the full effect of this, one needs to travel a couple of drainages, narrow tributary valleys of the Blackfoot similar in most ways to the Landers Fork drainage, but different in that the Landers Fork is mostly unlogged, at least that part of it we've already walked, the part that winds through wilderness. The first of these is the Clearwater River, a strip of stream that carves the Seeley-Swan Valley. The valley is lake-studded and separates the Mission Mountains from the Swan Range, which is the westernmost massif of the Bob Marshall Wilderness. The valley is less checkerboarded than most—it was chosen by the Northern Pacific to satisfy its land grant so should be a monotonously alternated patchwork of federal and railroad sections. Wilderness intervened to change this. The railroad once owned land in what was to become the Bob Marshall. To create the wilderness, the Forest Service was forced to swap land in the Seeley-Swan with the railroad, creating a contiguous domain for wilderness, but creating an unbroken loggers' domain, the Seeley-Swan, in the bargain. It is difficult today, walking in the Bob Marshall, to understand that the railroad somehow got the better end of the deal, but it's just as hard walking in Plum Creek's lands to think otherwise.

Like most Plum Creek lands, the Seeley-Swan went largely untroubled well into the 1970s, but then the company reorganized. Like most timber corporations, it figured out that money tied up in a tree growing at best at 10 percent a year, a tree vulnerable to fire and bugs, is better off "liquidated" and the proceeds set to some other occupation of capital that yields a more favorable return. Their money found better habitat in CDs than in forests, so the forests of the Seeley-Swan have been skinned from the hills, skidded off and sawed into lumber for the world's suburban houses.

I have walked an area called Jim Lakes, an alpine lake that should be heather, meadows of wildflowers and altitude-stressed white bark pine and lodgepole pine, none of it really timber. Should have been, but Plum Creek cut what trees were there and bulldozed the rest in an attempt to create a tree farm. There are strips of valley where little streams once babbled, sheltered by an overhang of trees and rich vegetation, now all slicked off, the few trees shipped to mills, the limbs and all the rest of the brush, flowers, sedges and forbs, maybe 100 species of other plants that form the rest of the forest, dozed and burned to make way for the planting of a monoculture of "commercial" species of trees in string-straight rows. Robbed of its protective canopy, the little stream goes dry, or downcuts its channel, no longer floored by the roots of streamside willows, alders, firs and spruce. Such streams once were the spawning habitat of the native bull trout or Dolly Varden, a fish beautiful, enormous and now rare enough to be considered for the endangered species list. We know who committed this assault, the evidence being Plum Creek's clear-cuts.

Occasionally in these lands—all of which can be crossed and re-crossed in a mazelike network of steep logging roads—one sees a strip or two of trees along a creek, deliberately left to protect the stream. When these stand next to a clear-cut, as they almost always do, the first wind-storm that comes—and they always do—will topple many of these un-protected trees.

Montana politics are different only in style from those that spawned the nineteenth-century letter quoted above. Such matters are handled today with more discretion, but they are handled, to the degree that the state has no law governing industrial logging practices. Just as a nineteenth-century man was free to hang Indians and beat his slaves and his wife, a twentieth-century logger is free to beat his land. There have been re-peated attempts to change this, on the argument that logging lands are woven together by rivers, as are the rest of our lands. An injury to a river, especially on the wholesale scale of logging, flows downstream to injure adjacent lands. But a compliant state legislature more interested in cash flow than stream flow has killed every attempt.

Still there are strips and tokens of compliance, behavior mostly unique to Plum Creek and the result of pressure, harangues and public-ity. One day a story in the *Wall Street Journal* labeled Plum Creek the "Darth Vader of the industry" and the next day its stock value plum-meted. Thereafter some changes came within the company. For instance, company officials announced adoption of a system called "new forestry," which respects such ideas as biodiversity. Plum Creek remains far from perfect, but it's better.

A state biologist, charged with protecting the future of the bull trout of Montana, tells of one day finding a washed-out culvert that diverted the whole of an important little stream to a Plum Creek logging road. That is to say, the road became the creek, an event that is catastrophe for all of the downstream reaches, because the creek chews up road gravels and spits them downstream. The biologists called the loggers and the loggers fixed the problem the next day, and this amazed the biologist, who was used to dealing with the old, "Darth Vader" Plum Creek and especially with Champion International, right up to the sorry final days of that corporation's rape of Montana. I've spoken mostly of Plum Creek here, but Champion's history can be read in another drainage.

LIKE THE SEELEY-SWAN, Gold Creek is not heavily checkerboarded. It is one of hundreds of so-named creeks throughout the Rockies, and is in fact a different Gold Creek than the site of the golden spike. That one is maybe ninety miles away on the Clark Fork. This one is a tributary of the Blackfoot. The first whites to arrive hereabouts were preoccupied with gold and with naming things.

The Blackfoot's Gold Creek was indeed a moneymaker. It is not checkerboarded because it was heavily claimed by the early dummy entrymen who in the mining company's service assembled an area of more than 100 square miles, mostly contiguous, of what became Champion lands and are now Plum Creek lands. That is, the federal lands that escaped the dicing of the railroad land grants eventually fell to the railroad's spin-off timber corporation.

The history of this place is visible, and most of what can be seen from any ridgetop is the work of Champion, now gone from Montana to repeat this performance anywhere else on the globe where there are standing trees.

Viewed from any vantage and scale, a mountain drainage is a series of veins, like fractal art, the dominant pattern of lines appearing the same from a satellite as it does from a few feet away. Gravity braids together streams, building from the droplet to the minute trickle to the freshet to the creek to the sweep of the river. Yet in Gold Creek, the fractal reduction as one travels upstream has been exploded. One sees this effect first from the air, progressing upstream through the normal flow of order until suddenly all the trees disappear, leaving only a series of stark, swollen veins, no longer swollen with water, but bare, scraped and desiccated earth.

What left these veins as tortured and distorted as a junkie's is a particularly vile form of forestry visited on this place. Gold Creek has a long history of logging. It was among the first drainages attacked by Hammond and his associates and had been cut over at least twice before modern times, but cut in phases, mostly cut in only its low elevations, logs skidded off by horses or aerial systems of cables. Until only very recently, the 1960s at the earliest, massive clear-cuts on this scale were unheard of, except in the Midwest and Northeast where land was deliberately being cleared for farming.

The guiding hand of forestry is something called "sustained yield," generally carried out through a system of uneven age management and selective cutting of individual trees. The doctrine is fairly straightforward and conservative. Say it takes sixty years to grow a usable saw log. That means one cuts no more than one-sixtieth of one's trees each year, a practice that theoretically can be carried out forever. Further, one slips into a stand and selectively culls out only the mature, leaving smaller and middle-aged trees to carry on, careful to do nothing that would harm the land's ability to grow trees. This system considers not only the future of the economy, but of ecology in that surviving trees provide the ecosystem services—the shade, shelter and retention of topsoil—for not only younger trees but all those other species of flora and fauna that depend for their existence on a healthy forest. It is a conservative system in the same sense that conservatism is related to conservation.

Multinational corporations have no stake whatever in the preservation of the local economy. In the late 1970s, Champion quietly abandoned the doctrine of sustained yield, deciding literally to cut and run, to liquidate all standing trees as rapidly as possible and sell off the lands. Foresters, people who make a living cutting trees, have a derogatory term for the practices that Champion adopted, the opposite of sustainable forestry. It is called "timber mining." Mark this for later use; it tells much about the difference between forestry and mining.

The grotesque veins of Gold Creek are the evidence of this abuse, in that Champion did all this with bulldozers. As far as modern logging knows, the gentlest way to remove harvested trees, a process called "skidding," is with helicopters, which is enormously expensive and impractical. Some particularly valuable trees are whisked out of sensitive areas this way, but economy demands relying primarily on other methods. The second least damaging is high-lead skidding, a system of aerial cables that lift the forward end of the log off the ground while it is being dragged. When done on winter's snow-covered and frozen grounds, this method leaves hardly a trace of its presence. It is only slightly more expensive than Caterpillars, but for the obvious reason Champion chose to log Gold Creek mostly with Cats.

In this system, the Cat, with its creaking, screeching metal tracks, clomps uphill to the site of a felled tree. The operator jumps off and sets a cable called a "choker" around the butt of the log, repeats the process at several other downed trees, then simply drags the bundle of logs straight down the slope. The wad of butts bears down into the soil like a plow, cutting a deep furrow. Because it is safest and easiest to drag the logs down the lowest point on the face of the ridge, the gouged-out skid trails invariably find the stream courses. These are the veins one sees from most any ridgetop up Gold Creek and in any drainage in western Montana where Champion once logged. They flow together in down-pointing vees, just as streams would, to intersect the winding logging roads that carry the trucks that carry the logs to mill. The skid trails weave together in a parallel drainage, but a drainage of another sort—the runoff is not water, but natural wealth.

In Gold Creek, there are vantages that allow one to see ten or fifteen miles to the horizon, and from some of these, this network of veins and roads comes together into the nightmare of one vast unbroken clear-cut.

MOUNTAIN TRAILS carry layers of motion and skid trails are no different. They carry logs to mills, downhill, because that's where the mills are, organized like everything else here according to the fall of rivers. They also carry water downhill, and with it the delicate bits of soil gouged from beneath protective cover by the tracks and blades of Cats and by the butts of logs they carry. In spring and even after the rush of a late-summer thunderstorm, but especially in spring when snowmelt sends rivers to rushing, the Blackfoot's recent history of logging prints itself on the Clark Fork River. Then, an aerial view of the two streams shows the Clark Fork clear and the Blackfoot a dingy brown stream of mud, burdened by the collective network of erosion from every skid trail and logging road up its reaches.

Montana has no law governing forestry practices, but it does have a law against degrading stream quality, and logging unarguably degrades stream quality. But try enforcing it on any one site, as it must be enforced. It's not enough to say logging degrades streams. For the law to be enforced, it must be proven that the cutting of those particular trees on that particular site along that road caused this particular problem twenty miles away. The state has only one or two inspectors officially charged with enforcing this law on thousands of logging sites spread over half of the nation's fourth-largest state. (This shortage of personnel likely is no accident. A legislature can pass a law the public demands then quietly ax the budget for enforcement of it.) To compound the problem, the damage is ephemeral. A particular cut may go months or years without contributing unduly to erosion, but in a single storm or during a single day's snowmelt, a culvert breaks or a bank gives way and a slice of a mountain falls into what was once a pristine stream.

The erosion is inexorable, insidious and virtually impossible to pin down, but it persists. One study in Idaho showed logging roads pulsing sediment from a heavily logged area thirty years after the logging had ceased. The fry—tiny, just-hatched fish—of trout hide and feed in small spaces between the gravels that line the bed of a stream. Sediment fills those spaces until there are no more.

As we work our way up this river to gold, an idea will take on increasing importance, and the idea is the power of ideas. This notion is everything to gold, but we begin tracing it now in the woods by knowing that the reality of the Blackfoot no longer matches the idea it is supposed to fill. This is recorded in simple fact. There is indeed a national idea of the Blackfoot, as there is of the people who live on it and of Missoula. It is a couple of steps removed from the real river, strained first through Norman Maclean's novella *A River Runs Through It* then through Robert Redford's film. The notion of river that dominates both is not wrong. These stories are authentic swatches of the loving of the river.

I know, for instance, that Maclean, when he was a young man, worked for the Forest Service and on a Friday night, after a full week of woods work, the crew trucks often dropped him off on the north side of Missoula near the base of the Rattlesnake Hills. Then he and his brother Paul would start walking to the Seeley-Swan, where the family had a cabin. They would not, however, walk up the highway and the Blackfoot River. That route is a long bow, and there is a more direct route along the string of the bow, which shoots north through the Rattlesnake Hills. This route would have taken them through the headwaters of Gold Creek then on north to their destination. That same place would be Maclean's until he died in 1992, when the cabin stood among Forest Service and Plum Creek clear-cuts. When they were young, Maclean and his brother would walk all night so they could be on the Clearwater and the rest of the braid of the Blackfoot in time to fish with their father on Saturday morning.

The river of Maclean's youth no longer exists. Redford decided against filming on the Blackfoot, its background now drawn in clear-cuts. It is tempting to fall for a bit of anthropomorphism here and suggest the river had aged to the point that it could no longer play its youthful self, until we remember that the river was and always has been ancient. It has no age. Of a half-million years of human culture, only ours has come to equate the age of natural features with deterioration. The face of the Blackfoot is the record of abuse, not age.

Yet the film causes the idea of a youthful river to persist, to the point that it becomes difficult for us fighting for the real river to convince the rest of the world of the peril. The image of the film is more vital than the reality.

The clear-cuts are not alone in recording this abuse. Redford could have directed his cameras from the hills to the stream itself and would have found that the fish are mostly gone. I lapse now into a bit of biological shorthand, because I am about to begin to use "trout" as a synonym for "life." Think about mines and canaries.

Some of us value this little fish, a value that can get distorted to an idea that in turn can cause great damage. This too we shall see, but later. For now, let us let the equation stand, and we can be forgiven for this. Anyone who has ever stood thigh-deep in a mountain stream toward the day's dimming and watched the swirl of rise forms work the swirling explosion of bugs knows that a good river lives. One knows this surely when a fish is hooked, and the force of its life jangles and vibrates through a tight rod so plainly that some of the river's life and fish's life becomes one's own. Through the medium of this rod we sense the life of the river.

Don Peters is a biologist who works for the state and has spent the better part of a career on the Blackfoot. He's not a guy who talks a lot, but from the little he does say, one soon understands that there is always in the back of his mind what biologists call a baseline, what the rest of us would understand as the idea of the way things must have been. It is a measure of our society's attitudes toward rivers that there is no good account of the baseline on the Blackfoot. Until only very recently no one ever bothered to takes its pulse, to count its fish. When they did, only during these last couple of decades, it was only in response to some enormous threat, first a proposal to build a dam on the Nine Mile Prairie near Roundup, later mining and logging. This is almost a morbid impetus for science, like taking the "before" pictures of Nagasaki.

Yet the question of what once existed is idle. It is the measure of biological potential, which is what might be. The difference between potential and actual is the measure of abuse.

Peters has been forced to assemble this baseline haphazardly, mostly by interviewing old-timers for the anecdotal bits and pieces that might someday add up to a picture. Sometimes this has paid off, such as occasions when some longtime residents reported there were once hordes of spawning fish in a small tributary that had long since been written off as dead from abuse. Peters puzzled over this, checked out the tributary he once thought unimportant, found some glaring and obvious problems such as culverts placed badly so spawning fish couldn't get through, and he fixed them. A section of creek deemed dead has been revived, because someone remembered.

But from time to time, something emerges that speaks to how far we have strayed. Maclean's description of fishing the Blackfoot is one example. Here is another. By happenstance, someone sent the state a cramped, two-page typed and neatly ruled fisherman's diary from 1911.

FISHING NOTES For The YEAR 1911

During the summer of 1911 I spent eight weeks fishing on the Blackfoot River. I was with the folks at our place just below the junction of Landers Fork and the Blackfoot. Being so located makes for almost ideal fishing as we always had three options of water to fish in: up the Blackfoot, up the Landers Fork or down the Blackfoot, all being equally good in those days. We were also only about 4 miles from the Flesher and Holter lakes where my cousin and I used to go nearly every Saturday for a day's fish.

Date	No.	Wt. lbs.	Lgth. ins.	Kind of Water	River	Kind of Fish	Upon what Caught
July 3	16	1	—	Hole	D	Native	Coachman
4	12	$1\frac{1}{4}$	$15\frac{1}{4}$	SW	B	Native	Bull-head
5	7	$\frac{3}{4}$	—	SH	D	Native	Rube Wood
6	11	2	$17\frac{1}{4}$	SH	B	Bull-trout	Bull-head
7	17	$1\frac{1}{4}$	$14\frac{3}{4}$	SH	L	Native	Bull-head
8	2	$\frac{1}{2}$	—	SH	L	Native	Coachman
9	61	3	$20\frac{3}{4}$	SH	B	Bull-trout	Bull-head
10	11	$\frac{1}{2}$	—	SW	B	Native	Coachman
11	25	$1\frac{1}{4}$	$17\frac{3}{4}$	SH	B	Bull-trout	Bull-head
12	1	$\frac{1}{2}$	$12\frac{3}{4}$	SH	L	Native	Coachman
13	1	—	—	SH	D	White-fish	Snagged
14	11	1	—	SH	L	Native	Coachman
15	12	$1\frac{1}{2}$	$15\frac{1}{4}$	SH	L	Native	Coachman
16	26	$\frac{3}{4}$	—	SH	L	Native	Coachman
17	1	1	$14\frac{1}{4}$	Hole	JB	Native	Bull-head
18	13	$\frac{3}{4}$	—	Ripl	B	Native	Coachman
19	28	$1\frac{1}{2}$	17	SW	B	Bull-trout	Bull-head
20	3	1	$14\frac{1}{4}$	SW	B	Native	Bull-head
21	14	—	$10\frac{3}{4}$	Hole	JB	Native	Coachman
22	69	$\frac{3}{4}$	—	SW	La	Native	Queen of Water

Date	No.	Wt. lbs.	Lgth. ins.	Kind of Water	River	Kind of of Fish	Upon what Caught
23	4	—	10½	SH	L	Native	Back of Fish
24	2	1¼	14¾	Ripl	D	Native	Bull-head
25	—						(Shot a cub bear)*
26	2	—	—	Ripl	D	Native	Grey Hackle Red
27	6	2¾	19½	SH	B	Bull-Trout	Bull-head
28	2	—	—	Hole	D	Native	
29	22	—	—	SW	La	Native	Coachman
30	41	1	—	SH	L	Native	Royal Coachman
31	4	1	—	SH	D	White-fish	Grasshopper
Aug. 1	4	1	14¼	SH	D	Native	Small fish
2	—						(Didn't fish)
3	16	½	13¼	SH	L	Native	Grizzly King
4	2	—	—	Hole	D	Native	Royal Coachman J.
5	43	—	—	SW	B	Native	Royal Coachman J.
6	8	1¼	14¾	Hole	D	Bull-trout	Back of Fish
7	4	1¼	15½	SH	JB	Native	Bull-head
8	—						(Didn't fish)
9	40	1¼	13½	SH	B	Native	Grizzly King
10	24	2	16¾	SH	B	Native	Bull-head
11	6	1¾	18	Hole	D	Bull-trout	Bull-head
12	36	1	—	SH	D	Native	Coachman
13	37	¾	—	SH	JC	Native	Grizzly King
14	9	½	—	Ripl	B	Native	Bull-head
15	7	—	—	Hole	L	Native	Grey Miller
16	7	¾	—	Ripl	B	Native	Bull-head
17	8	1¼	—	SH	C	Native	Bull-head
18	6	—	—	SH	C	Native	Bull-head
19	4	½	—	SH	L	Native	Bull-head
20	4	½	—	SH	L	Bull-trout	Bull-head
21	1	—	—				
22	—						(Didn't fish)
23	5	¼	—	Hole	JB	Native	Bull-head

Date	No.	Wt. lbs.	Lgth. ins.	Kind of Water	River	Kind of Fish	Upon what Caught
24	7	1	—	SH	L	Native	Bull-head
25	—						(Didn't fish)
26	1	¼	—	SH	B	Bull-trout	Bull-head
27	—						(Left for Home)
	703						

Hole—Open hole

SW—Still water

SH—Shady hole

Ripl—Ripples and Rapids

B—Blackfoot

D—Down below camp

L—Landers Fork

La—Holter Lakes

JB—Junction of the Blackfoot

C—Copper Creek

JC—Junction of Copper Creek.

★The bear was a spring cub and measured three feet ten and one-half inches.

The above data was set down by myself faithfully every evening in a little note book and altho the notes were not transcribed until this year—1924—I know that they are accurate in all particulars with the possible exception of weight. It is to be regretted that we didn't have a pair of scales with us and the weights are all merely estimates. By the length of some of the fish they must have been exceedingly thin to weigh as little as we estimated.

This was the best years fishing I had ever had and it was not until 1924 that it was surpassed in number or average size.

There still are anglers who pay such scrupulous and compulsive attention to their catch; there are none, at least in Montana, who catch this many fine fish to record, in that most of the life has left our streams. By this I mean that streams are no longer mostly alive.

IF WE RETURN for a moment to the sediment between the rocks we may venture into this issue of "alive" much as all those who have tackled it before have done, which is to say, in error. We have a simple, obvious and true answer to the cause of the lack of fish on the Big Blackfoot, which we take as a rough measure for a lack of health in the stream and, accordingly, even if we don't care about fish, a lack of life in general. We can point to an obvious cause for this problem: the logging visible all around. Cause and effect, the straight line that leads to a solution. Curtail the logging, and meanwhile, do something about the sediment.

Erosion and the resulting sediment are not at all new to Rocky Mountain streams. Water is the creator here, and the whole face of this valley is the work of glaciation, which is nothing if not an enormous ice bulldozer that scraped and reworked this geology for literally hundreds of thousands of years. We worry about a few trees missing from clearcuts now, denuding topsoil and allowing the erosion, but it is safe to say there was virtually no vegetation here during the hundreds or thousands of years it took for the glaciers to recede. Further, the salmonids—the trout, char and salmon that are the signature of high mountain streams—blossomed and flourished throughout the region *before* the glaciers were gone. These rivers and these fish can deal with erosion on a scale far more vast than anything we can imagine.

Streams flush in the seasonal flooding cycles. As soon as someone figured this out, we made an early error in oversimplifying streams. A few decades ago, logging drew the blame for the decline of fisheries throughout the Pacific Northwest, but not so much through erosion. The streams became choked with limbs, stumps and logs—debris from logging—that created long unbroken series of dams. These slowed water flow and caused the sediment to deposit heavily in the rocks and prevented annual floods from washing it back out. The solution was to clean up the streams by removing the debris, and literally hundreds of do-good groups—conservationists, anglers, Boy Scout troops and the like—fanned into streams.

Some were even paid to do so, unemployed loggers and salmon fishermen paid through federal programs for "displaced" workers. In 1996, I talked with salmon fishermen—young men in their thirties and relatively early in their careers in western Washington state—who had been paid once to take wood out of streams and now, in the last couple of years, to put wood back in. The earlier generation's fad of cleaning streams has been directly reversed and now those same do-good groups fan out to load on the debris, now regarded as shelter and habitat for fish. When one reengineers nature, one commits to an eternity of reengineering nature.

This second effort, putting debris back, was based on an assumption that we understand rivers, and only after literally millions of hours and dollars flowed to this effort in the Columbia River Basin did a few scientists start counting fish to determine whether it did any good. There is simply no evidence that it did. One study on the Clackamas River in Oregon showed no result whatsoever from an investment that was enormous, hundreds of thousands of dollars on a single small stream. And still there is no restoration of fish.

T. C. Dewberry thinks he knows why, and much of the answer boils down to cables. Dewberry, a biologist, does his work on Knowles Creek, a tributary of the Siuslaw River on the mid-coast of Oregon. Dewberry uses scuba gear to study fish. He noticed something curious: Juvenile coho salmon on the Siuslaw were about half the size they should be. They were stunted by a lack of food, despite the fact that coho populations in the system were about 1 percent of their historical levels. This implied there was considerably less than 1 percent of the food there once was.

He dove some more, especially observing a stretch of stream in old growth, and came up with the notion of a stream as one big digestive tract. The key to the process is holding water in pools along the stream's route. This in turn traps organic material, such as decaying leaves, which in turn draws insects that eat that material. Young salmon and trout eat the bugs.

The effort to artificially restore these dams and pools relied on cables to anchor the debris that was put back in the streams. The natural old-growth pools, however, are different from the cable-anchored structures in a key way, a difference that is everything to our concept of rivers. Dewberry says natural pools are dynamic. All pools age, and as they age, they stabilize and lose their ability to digest material. Dewberry says any fly fisher understands this immediately by remembering that the first few years of a new beaver pond's life produce tremendous fishing, but it wanes to nothing as the pond ages.

We have known since Heraclitus told us in 500 B.C. that we never step into the same river twice, but still we fail to realize the literal truth of this, that rivers are dynamic and alive. We fail to restore them if we do not allow them to change. Nature accomplished this with large, old-growth trees that died and fell into streams, then came to rest against other trees. These structures created a series of flats or pools along a run of stream.

"I think of these flats as a series of beads on a string," says Dewberry.

This array, however, was an open invitation to catastrophe. In fact catastrophe is what makes it work through periodic, massive, sweeping floods. The floods break loose some of these huge logs and roll them downstream, but not far, resetting the series of ponds and revitalizing the whole system. Ponds are reborn and begin digesting again.

Dewberry did an experiment on Knowles Creek, by building unanchored debris dams out of very large logs. Before restoration, smolts were typically eighty-five millimeters long. After, they were close to double that size at the same age, hearty smolts with a head start in the competitive world downstream.

Unlike many biologists, Dewberry doesn't worry much about the sediment from landslides. A healthy stream channel with its normal load of large woody debris and a protective flank of mature conifers can digest a lot of flood-borne sediment. The key, he says, is conservation of old-growth riparian vegetation where possible, and reestablishing mature conifers along streamsides where necessary.

"You've got to get the conifers coming back. We're going to have to wait decades," he says.

The importance of Dewberry's ideas extends beyond the trees, though, in that he points to a view of nature that is unsettling but necessary. He speaks of the creative forces of upheaval and catastrophe. Stability is not normal—change is. The riparian community is a culture of sorts, and its resiliency absorbs the shocks of this upheaval. Once culture is lost, so is resiliency, and with it the life of a river. That's what all of this has to do with the Blackfoot. Logging destroyed the streamside culture that gave the Blackfoot a life of its own.

The Blackfoot's biologist, Don Peters, says the big trees are gone from the river, most gone 100 years ago. The Blackfoot still is at the putting-in-wood stage. Peters and others do what they can by felling the biggest logs into the most likely stretches of the river; by doing what they can—absent an enforceable law protecting streamside vegetation—to jawbone loggers into leaving streamside trees. One deals. Threaten when it might do some good. Buy a forester a beer when that might work. Write a letter. Pass a petition. The war in the woods is waged in imperceptible increments.

I KNOW WHERE there are trees big enough to save the Blackfoot along the banks of some of its tributaries, and anyone hearing this claim will say, "That's easy—such trees stand in wilderness," which is true enough. But I have another place in mind. Wilderness is not good enough. Only the headwaters are there, and we must care for the life of the whole river. Besides, if we say the only way to shield the lives of our rivers is wilderness, to fence lands from human activities, then our rivers are defeated and so are we. We and our rivers must learn to coexist, to share health.

This place I have in mind has been logged; in fact it is a small parcel of land, maybe 160 acres, resting smack in the middle of the Gold Creek drainage, a sort of island in a corporate sea. It was homesteaded—likely under the provisions of the Timber and Stone Act late in the last century—by Frank H. Parker, and today there is a small gravestone with his name on it that sits within a small wrought-iron fence set amid towering ponderosa pines maybe 300 or 400 years old, trees two sets of linked arms cannot reach around.

In many ways, these trees are testimony to the soundness of an idea that went so wrong in execution. Parker was apparently the sort of homesteader Congress had in mind in passing the Timber and Stone Act. He lived with the land, and after him, so did his successors, the Primm family, which held the land until 1977 when Mahala Jane Primm died. Her name is on the opposite side of the same stone that bears Parker's. They say she's buried there, and so is her husband, but he's in an unmarked grave. A man I met up one of Gold Creek's logging roads told me that the couple had split up when the old man grew crotchety in his declining years, and so Mahala Jane lived on the old homestead alone, without electricity or a phone or neighbors until she died. The old man died elsewhere, but friends lured Mahala off the property long enough to slip her husband's remains into the homestead's soil.

For ninety years people lived on this land raising crops, building buildings and cutting trees as they needed, but only what they needed in lives governed by the constraints of the land and wrapped by a river. Such lives leave more than they take.

After Mahala Jane Primm died, her heirs sold the land to Champion. I first found the place in 1990 after hearing about it from a friend who had stumbled on it while elk hunting. It's not easy to find, isolated a couple of miles up a gated logging road. I didn't know then that Champion owned it, but a trip to the courthouse's property records quickly told the tale, so I called the corporation to see if the threat of the glare of publicity might hold back the chainsaws and Cats. A company man said Champion had already decided not to log its acquisition, to maintain it as a preserve. What about an easement on the deed, I asked. That would make the good intentions legally binding, especially if the company should sell its holdings. No, said the company man, you'll have to take our word on it.

On a hot August afternoon in 1996, I revisited the Primm place for the first time in six years. In the interim, Plum Creek had acquired those magnificent and valuable trees, single trees big enough to build whole houses. I jumped the gate at the head of the logging road and headed up it, afraid of what I might find at the other end. The Primm house was gone, as was the main barn, both disassembled board by board during the six years since I had visited last. A second and older log barn seemed to lean a bit more. But otherwise, all was the same. Those trees still stood.

This, then, is how it is with the loggers. We fight and now and again we win and for another day a few trees stand, but looking to their towering tops one quickly realizes the sense of timelessness is illusion. In a second, in the time it takes to trade stock, a decision can be made and logged into a computer in a cubicled office half a continent away in Stamford, Connecticut (Champion's headquarters), or in Seattle (Plum Creek's). Such a decision may already have been made. And these trees too will fall.

WITH THIS INFORMATION about logging covered, we return now to the site of the proposed mine, to a set of bulldozer tracks there I have already mentioned. It is difficult to imagine how much was imperiled by that casual cut by a Cat, so very few feet from the rock cairns that mark Meriwether Lewis's trail and the Salish going-to-the-buffalo trail, wrapped as that value is in intangible human values. That we cannot put a price on it maybe is enough of a valuation. Because these tracks stood within sight of well caps and pipes that were the exploratory work of the mine, we immediately assumed that the cairns were threatened by gold, but it turns out this is not the case. In the nineteenth century when the checkerboard was diced up, the Forest Service and the timber corporations drew the bulk of the squares. There were a very few sections left over that now appear as a light blue on color-coded maps. Those are the property of the state of Montana, ceded by the federal government to support state activities such as education. Like all the other players on the map, the state logs its lands, but unlike the federal government, the state makes no pretenses about balancing that logging against preservation of wildlife or recreation. The goal of managers, by law, is maximizing profit off the land.

Those Cat cuts next to the rock cairns are the result of the state's logging. A state archaeologist reviewed the project and allowed the loggers to proceed, despite the fact that the mine's archaeologists had already identified and marked the cairns. The loggers were oblivious to their presence, and only luck saved the cairns from destruction.

MY FRIEND ANNICK SMITH called me one summer's morning mad as hell. Annick is a writer too, and has just finished a book about restoration of tall-grass prairie in Oklahoma and has written much about her home, which is in the Potomac Valley. She and her late husband, David Smith, moved a century-old hand-hewn log cabin from farther up the Blackfoot, and it sits isolated amid a grassy meadow rimmed by fir and pine and hills. Elk are her neighbors most of the year, but her unnoticed neighbor has been Plum Creek, which owns one wall of trees at the far edge of the meadow along a little creek that is a tributary of the Blackfoot. Don Peters has done some of his restoration work there.

Annick was angry because Plum Creek, after years of ignoring its trees along the edge of her meadow, had begun logging. She wanted me to come up and see what could be done, which was, of course, nothing. The cut was still active as we walked it that day, with huge piles of logs yarded up along the road waiting for trucks to haul them to a mill. From the road we looked downslope 100 yards or so to the creek then up the opposite bank where a crane's boom was swinging and banging, its cable snaking downed logs. We cut down the bank and walked along the trees and stumps, below the skidder, and the loggers stopped working, flustered a bit and worried that civilians might get hurt if a cable snapped or some such. They were polite and offered us hard hats and then a forester came and chewed us out a bit for blundering into the work, but he was polite too.

I was supposed to be sharing Annick's anger but felt oddly at home and comfortable walking amid the downed logs along the stream. The truth was I had seen many far worse cuts. It wasn't a clear-cut, not even close. It had been selectively logged and some big trees had been properly left rimming the stream, even a few larger trees upslope. The skidding was being done with the high cable of the crane, which keeps the butts of logs from ripping up the soil. It was not perfect. Some very old ponderosa pine had been cut, and they could have been left to tower over the rebirth of the place, especially since they were already dying. Their centers had already begun to rot, decreasing their value as saw logs, but enhancing their value as elders in this community. Left alone they may have died and fallen over the course of another century, decayed over the next and brought a new generation from their detritus a century after that.

Not perfect, but so much better than has been the rule. And although Annick was mad enough that day not to see it, most of what was good about the cut resulted from her work and the work of others like her. She knew the cut was coming and had written the letters, made the phone calls and kept the pressure on the right points. Bit by bit, drainage by drainage, this is how it is done. This war with loggers is a series of never-ending battles, to the point that it has almost become a relationship, a partnership of adversaries.

The truth is, Annick and I and all of us are implicated in this; we do not stand solely on one side. We're writers and our work comes to you on dead trees. In living among the trees, there is the possibility of understanding the burden that each of us shares for this destruction of life for the sustaining of our own lives. This is what sets logging off from gold mining. It is wrapped in life. There is a chance for regeneration, for incremental gains, for coming to grips with the consequences of our lives in logging.

Don Peters puts it to me another way, that no matter what the battles he has had with loggers, he would much rather deal with a state-sized drainage full of loggers than a single gold mine. Whether they like it or not, loggers live in the life cycle. Living there ultimately corrects excess. They have to stop and wait for the life cycle to reassert itself, for the trees to regrow, and in the interim, there is no logging.

There is no such possibility with mining. From the outset, the miners plan to dig their hole, grab the gold and run. There is no possibility of rebirth, nor do they need one. Gold has the built-in Midas curse of being immortal.

Cows

I will always remember a week spent in wilderness with an old friend from Michigan. We left finally and reluctantly and walked out, down Monture Creek from the Bob Marshall and back to my truck parked at the trailhead at the edge of the Ovando Valley. As we pulled out onto the highway, past the trees, and onto the great, open grassy bowl of valley, the sun was setting, splashing late-day light on the snow-shouldered peaks at valley's edge. The friend was awestruck, and said so: "This has to be the most beautiful spot in the world."

I believe it was the first such superlative I had ever heard him deliver in the thirty or so years I've known him, which made me think he may be right. Even from the highway, the panorama of this valley can stun. At its center is the Blackfoot River, but noting only the river understates the role of water here, a problem that could be somewhat corrected by seeing the valley from the air, or better, from a mountaintop along its rim. There is no shortage of these.

From above, a network of potholes, unnoticed at ground level, snaps into sharp relief. When the glaciers' mass pressed this valley flat, their enormous weight pushed globs of ice and mud deep into the surface, like candles into a cake. This buried ice persisted for many years after the glaciers left, but the soil slowly warmed and the subterranean deposits of ice melted, leaving voids, potholes. From the air, it looks as if a giant had gamboled through a muddy field, leaving footprints, which is sort of what happened. The holes now are full of water, providing a scattering of ponds and lakes frequented by the valley's considerable collection of geese and ducks. In all, though, they remind us that the water's role is bigger than the rivers and streams. All of this valley is underlain with an aquifer, which is really the underground expression of the larger river, the dialogue between mountain and valley expressed in water. Punching a hole in the valley floor is like punching a window into this unseen world.

These potholes also are geology's foreshadowing of rancher Jon Krutar's ponds. Krutar's days seem preoccupied by legacy, geologic and otherwise, and his diverse heritage seems to condense to a single scene on his 500-acre ranch: The hatchery ponds form a series of slits in a tree-lined meadow. They were cut by an ancient backhoe, a wheezing D-9 Cat and his old man's and his own stoop labor, then vivified by mountain water. The meadow is back to grass now, but an arm of Kleinschmidt Creek trickles perpetually through the series of rectangular ponds, even though the fish are gone. The commercial trout-rearing operation that once was the business of the ponds has gone belly up, just like most enterprises of ranching country, but the ponds remain. So does the issue of what to do about them, a far more layered question than one might think. Much is woven in a rancher's relationship with water.

Fish aside, the issue before us now is cattle ranching, and it is my habit to freight such discussions in anger. That day, however, I could not get mad, especially not on Krutar's place where there is so much room for hope. It was the first day of October on Kleinschmidt Flat, a broad alluvial plain at the head of the Ovando Valley, halfway between Missoula and the Blackfoot's headwaters. The day was flushed with fall sun of the sort one wishes could be canned and set on shelves in a cellar against the threat of January, especially here in Kleinschmidt where frost can pierce all months. Of course, it being October, frost had long since come. The river birch, the cottonwoods and quakies had raised a golden glow of their own to rival the sky's.

To the north the peaks of the Bob Marshall rim Kleinschmidt, the flattest corner of the larger Ovando Valley. It is so flat because the mountains are so steep. The glacial soils of the wilderness canyons are only precariously smeared to the rock peaks, like a sloppy coat of stucco on adobe bricks. Gravity abetted by water periodically rips the smear of gravel off the rock faces, dumping it into the North Fork of the Blackfoot River, which threads the wilderness canyons. The river's mountain-propelled rush allows it to bear heavier loads of soils, but as soon as it pushes beyond the mountains to the flatter country, it slows. Slower water is weaker water, and it drops its sediment load like a bushed backpacker. The flat gets flatter. The sediments fan to the alluvial ooze that becomes a plain, a tabletop as far as one can see.

Once I watched two sandhill cranes grazing in the middle of this plain, in spring, when the wildflowers bloomed in range not yet grazed to perdition, ancient birds in an ancient landscape.

On an October day when there are no clouds, the sun lights all creatures from valley rim to valley rim with an equanimity that includes cows. In this light it seemed forgivable to believe the cattle a part of the landscape just as the cattlemen believe. Krutar descends from such cattlemen, who are wrong about this. Cattle do not belong in Montana. Their importation has wreaked a terrible havoc on every turn of the Blackfoot, not to mention virtually every square inch of ground between the Mississippi and the Rockies. "Every inch" is overstatement, but not nearly the overstatement one might believe.

Understanding this requires first a grasp of the creator, which is evolution, or more to the point, coevolution. An entity does not exist in, nor does it rise fully formed from, a vacuum. The turn of its jaw, the sheen of its hair, the pout of its flower and the shade of its spots all issue from an unimaginably long and tortuous trail of trial and error, with the trail's course set by all the other beings that make up the creature's environs. A bison has a big shaggy coat because a bison eats cold-weather grasses, an antelope is fast because there are fast wolves, a hummingbird long-beaked because nectar hides deeply. A creature out of its context then becomes, at best, dead, or at worst, a menace (a predatory insect without coevolved enemies, for instance).

At its finest of settings, coevolution means there are species of birds evolved to feed on the seed of only one species of plant, and plants in turn wholly dependent on a single species of bird to spread their seed. There are coarser settings. At the other end of the scale, there are the generalist species, the opportunists able to exist across a wide range of climates and conditions, existing on a broad range of forage. Humans are the best example, but black bears, coyotes and white-tailed deer are nearly as adaptable.

The laws of coevolution are constantly ignored by humans. Paradoxically, this is part and parcel of our own adaptability. That is, we, especially we here in the United States, quite consciously set out to reengineer the landscape. We mostly did this by moving creatures around, always believing what we found could be improved. Thus, in the 1870s fish hatcheries were already at work in the San Francisco Bay turning out trout to replace the trout already living in Rocky Mountain streams. The Bureau of Plant Industry (a subset of the turn-of-the-twentieth-century Department of Agriculture) sent plant explorers around the world gathering species to replace "inferior" natives. (One imagines the racist subtext that made people believe this was a good idea.) As a consequence, the grassland region of the nation, the area between the Rockies and Mississippi, now hosts some 4,000 species of exotic plants—as much as a third of all plant species. Many have become a pestilence absent any coevolved native enemies to keep them in check.

One of our most dramatic feats of engineering came in the extinction of the native bison and their replacement with cattle. Superficially, at least, this was not a great stretch, which showed so clearly on that October morning when those cattle seemed to settle into the panorama as softly as the stream and its frizz of fall-gold willows. The West, all of it from the prairies of Illinois and Missouri west to the bunchgrass and sagebrush plains near the Rockies, is a place of grass, a distinct biome. The world is blessed with only a few great grasslands—the pampas of South America, the steppes of Siberia and Mongolia and the sub-Saharan grassland of Africa—but they are the world's most productive biomes, known mostly for raising hordes of great hoofed beasts. Why not cows?

Fossilized remains of horses in Nebraska showed a dramatic shift in their teeth occurring 60 million years ago: The grinding molars of large grazers showed up. Grasses are abrasive and wear out skinny little nipping teeth. Grasses are best attacked with molars. Sixty million years ago the Rocky Mountains erupted and molars were simulacra erupted in the jaws of resident plant eaters. Great grasslands couple with great mountain ranges in that mountains create rain shadows, arid reaches, too dry to be forests and too wet to be deserts. These are the places where grass grows in black topsoil, bringing great hordes of meaty beasts and the great predators that follow them. In such a place in Africa humans evolved, so it appears the relationship between man and grazers is every bit as deeply wrought as that between mountain and molar.

Bison, and to a lesser degree elk, evolved to fit the plains, both of them distinctively large piles of meat. The bison arrived at its supremacy in fits and starts. A predecessor species called *Bison antiquus* with a broader, bonier head, shared the landscape with a whole range of great grazers including camels and woolly mammoths—elephants. All of those disappeared when humans entered the continent about 12,000 to 15,000 years ago across the Bering Land Bridge. The disappearance of these beasts coincident with the appearance of spear-wielding humans is thought more causal than coincidental.

A set of creatures came with the humans, including elk and a species of bison that looks very much like our present-day specimen. The American bison's closest relative is the steppe bison, of which a few remain in Poland, but cattle branched off further back in the family tree. Ice-Age Europeans were in the business of hunting bison too, but their chase finally produced a domestication, and in short order, a couple of dominant strains of cattle: a dryland, rangier, wilder beast around the Mediterranean and the more familiar shorthorn cattle whose lineage, like that of many western cattlemen, centers on the British Isles. Taxonomists once emphasized the separation of the two by labeling the American wild cow as *Bison bison*, but in recent years, they have changed the American bison's genus name to *Bos*, the genus of bovines, including domestic cattle.

In coevolution, however, occupying the same genus is no guarantee of a fit to an alien ecology. Prairie restoration experts, for instance, have found that even an exact species is often not close enough, and have learned to rely on what they call local ecotype. This means that in restoring a given species, say big bluestem grass, it is often not sufficient to simply obtain any seeds of big bluestem. Specimens from only hundreds of miles away often die or do not do well, so finely does evolution tune a genetic package to local conditions.

Cattle, especially the British strain, evolved in the wet regions of the British Isles. Their genes were tuned by an abundance of water; the bison's by water's scarcity, guaranteed by that 60 million years of rain shadow. Transplanted to the arid West, cattle adapted by seeking out the closest analog they could find to their evolutionary roots. They, like humans, bunched up along the streams and rivers and chomped off everything in sight.

Bison, on the other hand, not only were easier on the soggy reaches around streams, but were far more adapted to surviving harsh winters. They migrated great distances to avoid the worst of it, a habit evolution had not programmed into the sedentary cow's software.

All this meant that many cattle adapted to their introduction in the West by dying. There was a series of massive die-offs, 50 to 80 percent of herds in a single winter, shortly after cows moved into the West in the last quarter of the nineteenth century. Drought followed by fierce winters drove home nature's point. The Europeans responded by reengineering the landscape. They imported wetland grasses and plants, pumped the streams into irrigation ditches to make the land wet enough to grow them and raised hay to feed cattle during the tough winters.

The eastern tier of grassland, that strip of states from Minnesota on the north, south through Missouri and west even into Nebraska, was simply plowed up. Now it raises grain, not cattle, but 70 percent of this grain goes to feed livestock.

This grain land, plowed land, by far suffers the worst because agriculture wipes out all possibility of ecosystem. Iowa, for instance, has about one-half of 1 percent of its native habitat remaining, once tallgrass prairie and oak savannah, once the most productive in the world. The more arid lands farther west are less hospitable to the plow—although plowing has been tried with disastrous results—so it is grazed. Virtually all of it. States like Nevada and Idaho are more than half publicly owned federal lands and virtually all of that land is leased to ranchers at below-market rates. All the studies and surveys of these lands, your lands, since the turn of the century have shown them severely degraded by overgrazing. A 1989 report by the Forest Service, "An Analysis of the Range Forage Situation in the United States," sums this up. So does the 1987 National Rangelands Inventory.

National Wildlife Refuges are grazed. The Charles M. Russell National Wildlife Refuge in Montana has been grazed to the point where it is a high-plains desert. A biologist I know told me he was hired to assess the damage and when he went to do so, the rancher holding the lease threw him off with threats of violence. The federal range managers told the biologist to leave it alone. In some cases, federally designated wilderness is grazed, the Aldo Leopold Wilderness in New Mexico, for instance.

Hydrologists can mark the advent of cattle in the late nineteenth century by a change in the stream profiles, a mark of upheaval generally reserved for geologic cataclysms. The Big Blackfoot is no different. Pick a stretch along Kleinschmidt Flat or through the Potomac Valley and see how this plays on the land. From a distance, all appears well in the morning light with the sun on the mountains and the little meander of a stream babbling its way through a meadow, the cows peaceful. Such scenes can convince one that cows can work, especially those of us who have seen much worse. They are spread all up and down the Blackfoot and visible to anyone who cares to float the river—stretches of streams where the cows have stripped all the vegetation from the banks then turned it to a hoof-churned quagmire of cowshit that becomes what's left of the river's banks. The damage is obvious, but the problem extends deeper than the obvious.

Streams erode, a fact as inexorable as gravity. They run downhill, but if allowed, will downcut their own channels so that the water runs in a deeper and deeper slit in the meadow. What prevents them from doing so in many cases is bedrock, but absent that, it is the life within and along the river that preserves the river's own life. The Blackfoot Valley is arid like the rest of the West, but will support a profusion of lush vegetation in those places where the flooding waters of creeks and streams braid out to feed a strip of riparian vegetation. This is an up-by-the-bootstraps operation. The most common streamside residents are clumps and canopies of willows, now yellow in October. They rest on a dense footing of roots where they grow, and these roots brace the bottom of the stream to prevent it from downcutting. This in turn keeps the water level high enough to saturate the adjacent grounds with water, creating a band of naturally irrigated vegetation along the stream. The willows hold the stream just as the stream raises the willows. During spring floods, the stream quickly spills over, creating broad swales where water rests, slows and settles sediment, pulling the teeth from the flood.

Cattle overgraze and kill streamside vegetation, especially willows. The stream downcuts, drying the riparian zone and killing more vegetation, but also precluding the possibility of recovery. The downcut means the same volume of water flows in a narrower, deeper channel, so it must flow faster, and it does, downcutting further still. Fast water bites harder. During floods, this effect multiplies by several orders of magnitude, and the sediment load goes on downstream, the willows' natural provisions for flood control now absent. The speed of the sluiced water now causes it to chew away at the river's meanders and bends. It straightens, picks up even more speed and downcuts even more.

Couple this now with logging. The hillsides above the stream have no cover of trees to ration out the snowmelt when the first sunny days of spring arrive, so the snowload comes off suddenly, making an even bigger flood and creating more downcutting. Further, a significant portion of the runoff, a majority in some cases, once did not leave as runoff. Trees take water up their roots and trunks and breathe it to the atmosphere in a process called evapotranspiration. Now that water is added to the flood.

AMONG THE RANCHERS of the Ovando Valley, Jon Krutar is a newcomer, always will be, and he knows it. This fact was impressed upon him as a child in a one-room schoolhouse that served the ranching families of the Blackfoot. He and his brother and sister were not allowed to use their sleds on an established sledding hill, a run the other kids reserved for long-timers only. His father, after all, had only bought his ranch in 1949, a few years before.

Krutar's father came from ranching stock but was orphaned at nine and grew up landless, working his way back to land by raising a down payment selling heavy equipment in the building boom after World War II. His relatives told him not to buy near Ovando. "There's not much topsoil, the winters are tough and all you got is the water," they said, but he believed in the power of water, and he bought. So Jon grew up a newcomer, a Swede among the string of Irish around Helmville who had settled their places as homesteads generations before. He's still a newcomer when he deals with those same kids from that one-room schoolhouse, middle-aged, but still on their home ranches.

Krutar is more suspect still because his tenure is not continuous. He studied economics at the University of Montana, got a graduate degree from Michigan State University, taught economics at the Air Force Academy and finally at Carroll College in Helena. He has retired now, but is still fit and vital, thin, his bright-eyed face topped with a thin shock of gray hair. He came back to live on the ranch only a couple of years ago, but has been running it remotely since his father's death in 1986.

Krutar hands me a handwritten letter he found in a sealed envelope after his father died. In it, the father tells Jon where to find a check for funeral expenses, that he is to be cremated and where there is a key to a file cabinet that will contain the records for the ranch. The letter says: "Please try to hold the ranch against all future economic & social intrusion so that you will always have an 'ace in the hole.'"

There is earned wisdom behind the discrimination against newcomers in ranching country. Contrary to the impression offered by bucolic scenes on October mornings, this is not a settled landscape, but a place constantly in upheaval and churn. Newcomers come and go. It is said they "starved out." A ranch really doesn't begin to come into its own until it has accreted the learning of a couple of generations. The information of survival accrues like genes in cattle. Krutar's generation is making big changes on its ranches, but cautiously, slowly, always mindful of the memory that their fathers did not starve out, but those who made big changes often did.

All of this can be read in Kleinschmidt Creek, a meander that winds along the highway side of Krutar's ranch before joining the North Fork of the Blackfoot. Like almost all western creeks, Kleinschmidt has been punished by the cattle that allowed the survival of these ranches. Krutar and I walk a clean-mowed hay field past long barns and sheds that were part of the ranch's original structures. He grew up in a log house that overlooked this creek, but it burned down, and he now lives in a suburban-style house his father built in 1974. We cross the creek first on a thumping plank bridge that rings underfoot like good, old wood, but this bridge is new.

Krutar says his father hated bridges because they were rough and planks were always rotting out or breaking loose. It was a mark of progress when the old man let go of enough hard cash to buy a couple of culverts to replace the old bridge. From a rancher's point of view, culverts are better, but from a creek's, worse. They back up, clog and constrain the life of a creek into straight-line steel. Water pools, sediment drops and fish abandon the silted-in stream. Krutar ripped out his father's hard-won, paid-for culverts and built the plank bridge as part of the general resurrection of the creek that now is in his care.

Mounted on a farm tractor parked near the creek is a hydraulically powered tree-spade, a device that plucks small trees from the ground, root ball and all, for quick transplanting, like hair plugs on a rich bald guy. At this point, you need to know that ranchers make their money from grass, which is a function of treeless places. Most ranchers earned their toehold in this country by whacking down trees and clearing and flattening land, the better to raise cows. Ironically, virtually every ranch has a woodlot, a wild brushy place. Often this is a vestige, a place that because of weird water table or steep aspect simply could not be defeated, tamed and cleared. These woodlots stand as blots on an otherwise faultless record of order, but secretly become a source of pride for some ranchers. Against all reason they protect them through the years, even when improved techniques might allow taming. Krutar puts his tree-spade to work in just such a plot, digging native shrubs like river birch and trees like Engelmann spruce and cottonwood from the wild place. He transplants them along the creek branch to rebuild the canopy of vegetation wiped out by an earlier generation's grazing. He and his hydraulic tree-spade are reversing civilization.

All of this he does with the cooperation and even some money from the state and federal government. His advice comes with a fishery biologist from the state and another from the U.S. Fish and Wildlife Service. A backhoe has pulled out the debris from some stretches of Kleinschmidt Creek, and added some debris strategically in other stretches. Headgates and other obstructions have been pulled. Sod cut and laid. Cows have been fenced off almost all the way along the stream except a short "watering break" located on a rocky site where their hooves won't wipe out the bank. A natural wetland is taking on floodwaters once again and has pooled a large pond where ducks hide, dropping in from a nearby lake. Krutar is resurrecting a small segment of the Blackfoot's veins, which makes him something of an eccentric here. It's a luxury he can afford. He has his retirement income and his education; his neighbors have only their cows, which are at once their income and education.

GARY SULLIVAN IS TALL, well over six feet, affable, bright eyed and boyish, an effect only slightly tempered by a big, black mustache. He is 90 percent energy, with that sum equally divided between constant motion and constant patter. He is, and this is unmistakable even at first glance, a man with a mission. When he mentions real estate, the term is spun with a salesman's zeal, so one could be forgiven for making an 180-degree mistake as to what that mission might be. Sullivan is selling nothing more than a big idea. He is by training a biologist, and biologists don't often talk real estate, or talk much at all for that matter, but he has evolved to meet the demands of his time.

Sullivan is a wildlife biologist with the U.S. Fish and Wildlife Service, an agency drawn to the Upper Blackfoot serendipitously in 1989 when bankruptcy sent a ranch pocked with degraded glacial wetlands to the land market. The Nature Conservancy—following its traditional modus operandi—moved in and bought the land, then gave it to the feds. The wetlands were restored and the ranch became a 1,500-acre wildlife preserve. In the old days of the Fish and Wildlife Service, however, this land likely would have remained not much more than a duck farm. Back then, the service was not above eradicating certain natural predators that downsize the "yield" of "harvestable" waterfowl. And in the old days, this preserve would have become a target of ranchers' anger, something to grumble about: land pulled from the tax rolls to attract hunters, birdwatchers and fern-feelers to tromp down fences, leave gates open and give perfectly good grass to ducks when it could be going to cows.

Federal land management agencies like the Forest Service and Fish and Wildlife Service evolve too. A generation of well-trained and committed wildlife biologists is percolating into the ranks, a movement formally called conservation biology, but an informal term rings truer. Sometimes they say they are doing "combat biology." If so, the tactics are those of guerrilla warfare.

To begin with, these biologists have gone a considerable distance toward reforming those agencies that employ them, which explains a good part of the change in the Fish and Wildlife Service. The agency is now less concerned with turning out ducks and more tuned to the health of the total ecosystems under its control. Ecosystems include the entire network of life—flora and fauna, predator and prey. And humans.

Under this ethic, setting aside a wildlife preserve in isolation from the ranchers is not a victory, but a failure to consider the human role in nature. For Sullivan, this means good biology is no longer practiced exclusively in the lab and peer-reviewed publications; good biology is practiced on the tailgate of a pickup truck, and especially at a place like Trixi's Bar. Trixi's is a red-painted wood tavern set on a hill in a ring of red-painted cabins just outside of the village of Ovando. The inside is wrapped in cheap paneling, mostly fake, and a zoo of stuffed heads that are not. There is an elk, a moose, a bear and a bighorn sheep. Plastic beer signs complement the menagerie. A woodstove glows and a rack of men in ballcaps line the bar, where a person can get a decent bowl of bean soup and a ham sandwich for a couple of bucks. When a customer says put it on the tab, he means the one that's been running for a month. The bathrooms are labeled "Bucks" and "Does."

Lacking a city hall, Grange hall or church of any consequence, let alone one that everyone can agree on, Trixi's serves as the social hub of Ovando. Sullivan understood this early on, so he and his fellow feds cruised the bar for ranchers.

"We decided this was going to be more like a marriage than a date. We were going to become a part of this community over here," he says. "We did more good work by walking into Trixi's Bar and going toe to toe with those guys. We drank in there in uniform and we broke all kinds of rules. I've logged hundreds of hours in there."

Krutar was an early convert to the cause of wildlife conservation and signed on with Sullivan, who put together a package of federal and state money to help pay for stream restoration on Krutar's private land. The plan was to use the refuge the Nature Conservancy had bought as an anchor, as sanctuary, really, for an idea, but to spread that idea upstream and down. Habitat does not stop at fence lines. Sullivan used the social contacts made at Trixi's to work on ranches like Krutar's to restore cow-damaged land and spread habitat from the preserve to the nearby ranches of the larger valley.

Sullivan says other ranchers were more resistant than Krutar, but there were methods for cracking that resistance. Like goose boxes. He often carries goose nesting boxes in his pickup, and he would simply visit a reluctant rancher and offer to set a box near a creek. The geese would come and nest, and a ranching family would enjoy them, and Sullivan's pickup would be welcome again for another visit and another idea.

A gaggle of geese will not reform a ranch, but as Sullivan and I bounced along in his pickup on the back side of the refuge, he pointed out a wetland where rare red-necked grebes visit and an upland where rare Columbian sharptail grouse nested. The habitat that drew them developed on a ranch adjacent to the refuge, once overgrazed, now a thriving native grassland. It worked like this: The refuge is mostly grassland that the feds wanted mainly as habitat, but grassland evolved with grazing. Sullivan did not want to turn the federal land into a cow refuge, as indeed some are, but he did want cows to hit it lightly and strategically in alternate years. This sort of judicious tinkering with cattle can make them mimic bison in their grazing, not a perfect fit, but certainly better than the status quo and also better in some ways than no grazing. He offered this grass to the neighboring rancher, but instead of charging him for it, as is standard practice, he made a deal. The neighboring rancher owned 600 acres that were continuously grazed, the worst of management practices for native grasses. Sullivan got the rancher to agree to divide his land into three 200-acre pastures. The government paid for the fencing to divide the range. The rancher in turn agreed to rest one 200-acre parcel every year. The grass the rancher lost in this bargain would be made up by lightly grazing the 1,200-acre refuge.

The deal meant a 600-acre increase in viable habitat for wildlife, an increase benefiting both grebes and grouse. The rancher, meanwhile, has reported that the improved range conditions have led to faster weight gains for his cattle.

"He's been good and the main reason he's been good is we've got a big carrot over here on the refuge," says Sullivan.

In a similar fashion, Sullivan has paid for the fencing that keeps cattle off banks along Monture Creek, a tributary that joins the Blackfoot just downstream of Ovando. That creek sends a pristine thread of riparian habitat threading through the Bob Marshall Wilderness and an area that is managed as wilderness from its headwaters twenty or so miles downstream before it crosses onto private land. That upstream stretch is perfect in all regards except one—the stretch on private land downstream is so degraded that spawning fish have been unable to migrate through it to get to the good stuff. The publicly held habitat was degraded by private use miles away.

A redd is a nest of a spawning bull trout, the native fish so imperiled as to be eligible for the endangered species list. Young bull trout spend their first year hiding among stream-bottom gravels, and, as a consequence, redds can only exist where subsurface waters boil up through those gravels to join the streams, constantly refreshing the surroundings of the hiding young. Like all of the Ovando Valley, they depend on the unseen river that appears in the windows, the potholes. Because of this dependence, spawning can only occur in a very few places where springs join the creek bottoms. Monture Creek once had many such places, but grazing killed them. Sullivan's fences brought them back. In the 1980s, before fencing out Monture Creek, biologists found seventeen redds on a sample stretch of stream. After fencing, there were eighty.

SULLIVAN AND I bounce along a stretch of state land, once badly overgrazed because state officials had written a bad grazing lease.

"This used to look like Uganda, like they had elephants grazing in here," he says.

The range of Uganda, the real Uganda, in some ways is in better shape today. A few days after rattling around Montana with Sullivan, I happened to hear Jon Hutton speak. He is a conservationist working in Africa and argues for hunting as a way to save elephants and other African wildlife. He said African people kill elephants "because they have no choice. . . . This is not academic. This is the reality I live with."

The idea, one now being adopted by an increasing number of conservationists, is to give local people both responsibility for managing wildlife and an economic stake in its continued well-being. We have forgotten, especially in our society, that nature sustains us and "us" includes our economy. Economy is the very definition of sustenance. If we are to revive the memory of that connection between nature and economy, then we must shorten and localize the link. This is another way of asking, "What is a bull trout to a rancher?"

IN CONTRAST to the manicured farms of the Midwest, working ranches show so little evidence of human intervention that every board, wire and ditch is a significant artifact. In these we may read a legacy of aspirations, design and failed design that is the record of this enterprise's struggle to find its niche. Jon Krutar's, like all ranches, holds the hay sheds, ricks, ditches, diversions and always the fences that are primarily the record of engineering the landscape to accommodate cows. The bison that once roamed Kleinschmidt Flat fed the people hereabouts and required none of these things, inflicted none of this damage, at least on a scale that our damage-jaded eyes would call damage. Now we fence and hay to accomplish essentially the same end, and call this progress.

Unlike most ranches, Krutar's also has that plank bridge and three braids of stream inching their way back to health. If we are lucky, these restored streams (now they are artifacts too) flow in the direction of our future. His ranch, however, holds a couple of other creations far more enigmatic than the other two. Krutar and I leave the creeks (in Ovando it is a "crick," not a "creek") and we walk a managed pasture. We come to a bit of a ditch that siphons off a chunk of a small creek and sends it in purposeful course across a grassy meadow. We follow the ditch to where it empties to a series of rectangular pools that are the above-mentioned fish ponds. Think of a football field with each of the lengthwise and crosswise white lines being a strip of sod and each of the spaces between being a four-foot-deep pond of water. These are artificial trout-rearing pools.

They were Krutar's father's idea, an attempt to move his ranch away from strict dependence on cows back into the flow of the Blackfoot's waters. They were designed to raise trout commercially for table from hatchery stock imported and raised like chickens in cages. Jon and his father dug this grid themselves and set the diversion that would channel the string of water that would make it all live. It did not. The enterprise ultimately failed. Now the water trickles through, apparently sterile.

No biologist would mourn this demise. Trout farms take water from real trout in streams. Because of artificial feeding, they create unnatural concentrations of fish, trout cities sort of, with the attendant problems—especially of waste, trout shit in such magnitude as to upset the balance of nutrients downstream. Captive trout, "rubber fish" some people call them, are a peril to the genetics of native populations. Hatchery-bred diseases for which hatchery-bred fish have some tolerance race through native populations in epidemics analogous to the smallpox that raced through native human villages hereabouts a century and a half ago. In this fashion, the Madison River, a blue-ribbon trout stream of southwest Montana, lost 90 percent of its young rainbow trout in 1995 to whirling disease, which is caused by a parasite of hatchery fish imported from Europe.

Yet Krutar tells me he cannot bring himself to finally bulldoze and close the ponds. Maybe they will be of value someday, maybe in resurrection. Maybe they can be used to raise native bull trout to restock restored streams. Mostly he is thinking of legacy, of his son who will wind up with the ranch, and he doesn't want to foreclose any options his son might have by filling the rack of ponds.

His attitude toward the ponds only makes sense when considered against one more artifact, a pile of hand-hewn logs at the edge of the meadow. They are past logs; it is Krutar's habit to travel around the region disassembling old log buildings ranchers want razed. He brings them to his place. They are logs of the future, though, in that Krutar intends to reassemble them into rustic cabins that he will rent to fly fishermen who will pay to fish his repaired streams. Like the commercial trout ponds his father made, Krutar thinks he has hit upon a way to tie the economy of his land back to the natural flow of waters.

Krutar tells me now the story of one of his neighbors, who, during the last big game season, was approached by a city-based hunter who had spotted a herd of mule deer grazing the rancher's hayfield. The hunter offered the rancher $1,000 for permission to shoot one deer, and the rancher refused. Krutar laughs now and says that what the hunter didn't know and never found out was that the rancher would have let the hunter shoot the deer for free had he bothered to ask. All of which speaks to the difficulty ranchers have in entering what is for them the wholly alien bargain of tourism. Fee hunting and fishing is anathema to the local concept of freedom. And besides, most of these guys plain don't like strangers on their land. It is beyond economics. Nursemaiding rich tourists is simply not as honorable as raising cows.

Yet it is the future, or at least a part of it, a future that will be attained only through the evolutionary change of attitudes. What will speed that evolution, though, is the same principle that is aiding African elephants. The ranchers must have an economic stake in the future well-being of the wildlife of this valley. That's not a great stretch. After all, part of the environmental health of the place raises grass, so they already are in-vested in the ecosystem's integrity.

Krutar's log piles juxtaposed against his now useless but preserved ponds speak to this. These ranchers have seen new ideas come and go. They can tick off by name their neighbors who have tried new ideas, and most of those names are no longer lettered on mailboxes in the val-ley. The bedrock value of ranchers is the same as any species evolved to stick to its niche: survival. In this context the legacy of knowledge that has ensured survival of preceding generations is held in far more esteem than anyone's new idea.

KRUTAR SPEAKS in measured sentences, with an academic's habit of weighing and analyzing conflict dispassionately. Through the day, I only hear him bite off angry words a couple of times and both are directed at neighbors. One has diverted streams to make ponds so that he might ad-vertise his land as having both lakes and streams. Of this neighbor, he says, "He's a subdivider, not a rancher."

Another, a newcomer, not in Ovando's but in absolute terms, has bought a working ranch and is using city money to build a mansion, a log monstrosity with a red steel roof that Krutar calls the "Pizza Hut." The battle of the Blackfoot is often oversimplified to one between recreation and ranching, but there is a more logical schism that Krutar sums thusly: "Recreation won't have shit once it's all subdivided."

What he means by this takes some telling.

WRETCHED EXCESS

I CAN THINK OF no worse assignment than accounting to the Salish people for our care of the
river valleys of western Montana, their former
home. Whites have used this place badly; that's the
reality, but a good part of this reality rests on ideas.
It is tempting to blame materialism and mourn the
loss of idealism, but the truth is, idealism has
wrecked the West. We have destroyed the nature of
this place, its reality, for the sake of imagination.
The West is like a drugged-out, fame-addled fashion model, unable to bear the burden of her image.
Gold is the epitome of this destruction, but there
are other examples.

Now we must leave the Blackfoot River and
travel downstream along the Clark Fork just one
drainage to the Bitterroot Valley, which is a vision of
the Blackfoot's future. The Bitterroot joins the
Clark Fork only about ten miles from the mouth of
the Blackfoot, on the opposite side of the city of

Missoula. The Salish ranged throughout the valleys of western Montana, but the Bitterroot was their center place until a treaty drove them away. Now it is "settled" with a strip of major highway, U.S. 93, shot down its center like a stripe down a skunk's back. Like everything else that is human in the West, our highways first followed rivers, simply because rivers had already found or had made the flattest and easiest going. When they held only horses, wagons and travois, these roads were not much more built-up than Cokahlarishkit, so the rivers could hold their own against them. The roads flowed with rivers, but the machines came and the machines grew in power sufficient to remake the landscape in their own image. The roads that are the habitat of internal combustion upstaged the rivers as vital forces. The life forces that flowed on rivers began flowing on roads. Now one may drive these roads oblivious to the founding river wending nearby.

Especially one may lose track of the Bitterroot River along its 100-mile run from the Idaho state line and Lost Trail Pass almost straight north to where it joins the Clark Fork at Missoula. The valley's west rim is the granitic massif of the Bitterroot range, the leading edge of a designated wilderness area that runs almost across Idaho, the largest contiguous wilderness in the lower forty-eight. The valley, river and range are named for the bitterroot, a squat native plant with a shining face of flower that spreads in a pink sunburst in early summer. Its root was important food to the Salish, but now it is scarce.

The eastern edge of the valley is walled by the Sapphire Mountains, a somewhat gentler range that in ancient times was a part of the Bitterroots, but broke off and walked the twenty or so miles across what is now the intervening valley. The Sapphires also hold a small wilderness area, and both ranges are majestic and breathtaking as major mountain ranges ought to be. One's eyes are drawn to these and tempted to stay as long as possible, as much for their beauty as for the contrast they offer to the foreground, the valley floor itself. The highway strings together a series of towns and small cities its whole length, in recent years coagulating to a single blur of commerce, a horizontal junk heap of convenience stores, Kmarts and Wal-Marts, trailer courts, subdivisions, truck stops, antique shops, country western bars, used-car dealers, flea markets, fruit stands and Kampgrounds. Yet in this cacophony, there are counterpoints and themes that, like the eddies of a river, tell the river's story.

First, it is unique, unlike the strip sprawl elsewhere and forever in the nation. It is western. There are those towering mountains as backdrop. There are working ranches among the Circle Ks and used-car dealers. On plain display everywhere is that brutally pragmatic western disregard for aesthetics that places a welding shop and ramshackle trailer court next to a meadow full of elk and a mountain stream. The highway is crowded with shit-spattered four-wheel-drive pickup trucks driven by hatted men with big belt buckles and lips wadded with chew.

Western color notwithstanding, this strip's main lines still are drawn by the same rules of strip sprawl that form a general plague on the nation. The chain stores are here serving up the same stuff as they serve the rest of the country. No American would feel lost or alien here. A McDonald's is always nearby. A subdivision is a subdivision.

This sameness is relevant to the Blackfoot in that the Bitterroot is like the rest of western Montana, only more so. It is the harbinger for the rest of the place, the Blackfoot included. It is what the Blackfoot will become and already is becoming. Which brings the questions: Why do we bother to prevent a gold mine on this river's headwaters if this is its future? What good is saving the waters of a river if we cannot save everything else around the river from becoming what the Bitterroot Valley has become?

THE DISPARATE ELEMENTS of the western landscape are not so much disparate as they are an organic outgrowth of a story that is consciously attempting to write itself. Check out the snoose-chewing, hat-wearing, buckle-polishing driver of that shit-spattered pickup back there and like as not you will find a guy who was a year ago writing code for software in Silicon Valley. We think of him as a newcomer or interloper here, but we are all newcomers here. He is the norm. He is the new westerner and the future of our place. It is a future enslaved by an idea. The rampant growth of my town is not an expansion of the old West, nor is it the same suburban sprawl as every other place. Rather, it is the same sprawl crossbred with the old West, and it is a horribly virulent combination. An example is in order, one I will fabricate. Let's take our programmer here in the pickup. We will reconstruct his recent history as well as his present.

Our guy is from California, which, according to stereotype, makes him to some degree typical. The mountain West, especially in the northern reaches, is viciously anti-Californian, a tradition bolstered nearly a generation ago when then–Oregon Governor Tom McCall—an enlightened Republican who, like all of his breed, is now dead—openly and amusingly waged battle against the "Californication" of his state. In Montana, one may read bumper stickers suggesting that residents of the Golden State entering here be "gut shot" at the border. Scratch the surface of one of those displaying such a bumper sticker and you will likely find the tooled Tony Lamas he's wearing only recently replaced Guccis that once slapped marble at the Palo Alto mall.

The truth is, our newcomers are only "Californian" because the label is convenient. Just as likely, they are from Seattle, Portland, Denver, the Twin Cities and even Billings, retired ranchers fleeing the abysmally cold winters east of the Great Divide to live in "Tropical Montana" west of the divide, where it's only 30 below for no more than a week at a time, two tops, in January. Whatever their disparate backgrounds, however, they have in common a couple of elements: a firm idea of some sort of western tale—mountains, wide-open spaces, pistols, saddles, bad paintings, nut-case politics and Appaloosas—and a disdain for overcrowded places with insufficient headroom to accommodate this story. They are not necessarily from California, but lots are, deft as that place is at the creation of and living in imagery, and overcrowded as it is in the sprawl of more than 33 million people. (California and Montana are almost exactly the same size in land area. Against the former state's population, Montana hosts fewer than 900,000. We have managed to fit an entire state, the nation's fourth largest, into a single telephone area code. Try that anywhere along the Atlantic seaboard.)

So they are not necessarily all Californians, but our guy is, a relevant fact in that we know this: When he first buzzed his dusty Acura into the Bitterroot Valley it was bearing a trunkful of money. (No, most emphatically he did not and has not traded the Acura for the pickup. It's still in the garage and still has the California plates.) He might have been an ordinary schlump back in Mountain View, but we know he's now cash flush, and this, for the purposes of our river, is the single most relevant fact. He's going to spend that cash, and the river will suffer in direct proportion. Midas lives.

We know about the cash because our pal is fleeing sprawl, he and every single one of his counterpart newcomers. Sprawl means outrageous real estate prices, astronomical numbers unheard of in Montana, numbers we locals still whisper to one another at gatherings the same way nomadic shepherds would whisper totals of a potentate's stock of camels and wives.

Local interest in this goes beyond our age's ceaseless fascination with the rich, because this trunkful of cash in the Acura is about to impoverish many of us. It works like this. Our guy sells his California house in a hyperinflationary market, a three-bedroom bungalow that Silicon Valley types call a "scraper," as in "best call in the bulldozers and start over with a fresh, clean lot." He got $500,000. A half million bucks will buy the biggest house in western Montana, and it always does, because it has to. Newcomers here are known as "equity refugees." Because of the nation's tax laws, our guy has no choice but to sink his cash into a house or pay a hefty part of it off to the IRS as a tax on capital gains. His deal is this: He can either spend $130,000 to match the $500,000 house he had in California, and tithe to the IRS on the balance, or he can live in a mansion on a fresh-carved new mountainside overlooking a panorama of snowcapped peaks and rolling meadows of gamboling elk, moose, grizzly bears and bighorn sheep. What would you do?

In their collective impact, the ceaseless stream of incoming cash-laden Acuras translates as the subdivision of Montana, but it is warped by the persistence of the nineteenth century. First, because we are rugged and independent here, we do not cotton to such as the known communists who staff planning offices and zoning offices telling us what we might do with our land. Specifically, our legislature has encoded in law an odd notion only repealed in 1996: Parcels larger than twenty acres could be developed with complete freedom from the subdivision laws that govern the dicing of smaller lots. The practical effect was to guarantee the dividing of whole valleys into parcels of twenty-acre "ranchettes," a term that unites real estate agents and newcomers in that both are able to use it without embarrassment.

Our guy might be perfectly happy to live on an acre lot—a spread of land synonymous with wide-open spaces to any recent refugee of suburbia—but the law means he'll take twenty times as much, which to the collective welfare of the state means suburban sprawl canters across the valleys twenty times faster than anywhere else.

Valleys. Remember that. And remember free of government controls, which means free of government's rules regarding sewage treatment, which means every cradle of every flowing body of water in the west end of the state is checkerboarded with septic tanks. Water, the major ingredient of sewage, runs downhill. That's what valleys are all about in their geological essence, which precedes and preempts subdivided essence.

Now our guy has his twenty-acre slice of heaven. It cost him $50,000. What does he do with it? Because he still has $450,000 to spend, mansion planning begins in earnest, but like as not this particular mansion—not to mention every other one in sight—will show the distinct architectural influence of our guy's having watched one too many episodes of *Bonanza* during his impressionable years. Ben Cartwright raised fine strapping lads like Hoss and Little Joe in a log lodge. Real westerners live in log cabins, preferably with heads of dead animals on the wall.

We return now to the strip of flotsam along Highway 93. Beginning around the town of Stevensville and running south there are, slipped in among the convenience stores and subdivisions, maybe a couple of dozen plots of industrial operations. These are the valley's log home builders, factories for prefabrication of what amount to life-sized Lincoln Log sets. They export log houses as far away as Asia (the Japanese are particularly anxious to cast Ben Cartwright's shadow), but judging by the profile of the subdivisions surrounding the factories, much of these factories' issue does not go so far. Nor does the raw material come from afar, which is why—in this setting so near our river—this amounts to a great deal more than just one more example of peculiar American middle-class silliness.

Log homes once were logs, which science tells us is the root word of "logging," a fact one need not ponder long to connect them to those very clear-cuts visible on the horizon lines all around the Bitterroot Valley and the Blackfoot. So were, of course, all other houses for that matter, those of newcomer and native alike. Houses here and in subdivisions from Connecticut to California are born in these clear-cuts. A couple of other factors, however, make the connection even more onerous in the case of the newcomers' log mansions.

First, log construction developed in this country in a time of nineteenth-century excess, imported especially by Scandinavian immigrants to the Northeast. At the time, forests were regarded as impediments to agriculture, and loggers were trying to eradicate them as rapidly as possible. As settlement moved farther west and wood became scarce, builders developed the technique of balloon framing, which is how most houses are built today. A log house, square foot for square foot, probably uses triple the amount of wood of a conventionally built structure. Further, because a balloon-framed house's walls are hollow, they may be filled with insulation, making them many times more energy efficient, not a small factor in a place of subzero nights and howling mountain winds. As a practical matter, a log house is a truly awful idea.

The second factor, however, goes back to the trunkful of money our tax laws say our newcomer must spend. This and the general mindset of the late-twentieth-century American bourgeoisie popularized the concept of the trophy home, the notion that made it of logs, but also made it big. My nearest neighbor's new house is of logs and easily 3,000 square feet. Rattling around in this space are an elderly couple, retirees, who spend half a year in the house. This size and configuration is typical of our newcomers, a sin they might expiate by annually writing a check to the Nature Conservancy or some such release valve of well-earned environmental guilt.

Understand that by comparison, the average Japanese house is less than 1,000 square feet, a third the size of my neighbor's. More to the point, this is not simply a factor of American culture but of *recent* American culture. During the 1980s, the Reagan years (and we shall revisit this decade in a similar discussion of the consumption of gold), Americans somehow got the idea they were cramped. The size of the average new house then rose dramatically from about 1,400 square feet in 1984 to more than 2,000 square feet by the end of the decade, according to the American Association of Homebuilders. We of the West know these as the timber war years, an escalation of battle we blame on the greed of Plum Creek, Champion and Weyerhaeuser, but those above numbers are sufficient to explain the escalation. Somehow or another Americans, suburban Americans at that, who had been raised for decades in the largest homes on the planet, suddenly seized the idea they were cramped and in service of that idea, suburban America dispatched its timber corporations to clear-cut the West.

OUR GUY'S LOG HOUSE has been built. The land under it, what builders call its "footprint," perhaps a fifteenth of an acre of his twenty-acre parcel, has been consigned to biological oblivion, along with the roads leading to the manse, and of course the clear-cut that built it. So far, though, all is not lost. There are still 19.93 acres out there to be dealt with. Because the buildable land in the region is on valley floors, there are few trees on this parcel. Forests here grow on mountain slopes that hold snowmelt. Valleys are relatively open.

Typically, valley floors were savannahs before settlement, large grass-lands treed at a rate of maybe ten trees to the acre, and those accessible ten trees were the first to go at settlement. The dominant vegetation was and is grass, mostly native bunchgrasses. There is a sort of magic in these plants that tells us their role in creation. The dominant species like blue-bunch wheatgrass and Idaho fescue have the ability to cure, that is, to grow luxuriantly in May and June then go dormant in August and on into the winter. Their trick is carrying all of their nutritional value, the energy they stored in growing, into the winter. Most grasses can't do that.

The value of this trick only appears in a relationship. The elk herd resident on the ridges around my house will typically wade through belly-high bunchgrasses all summer long, ignoring the forage in favor of shrubs and buds. In January, however, the elk return to the site and strip it clean of cured grasses, a relationship honed through 10,000 years of coevolution.

The valley floors in which we insert log-home subdivisions and cat-tle ranches have another purpose: winter range. The elk and mule deer herds of my region are vertically migratory. They spend summers high in the mountains, where all of the wilderness areas and most of the healthy national forests lie. This summer forage, partly because of our preservation of it, is abundant and in no way limits the number of bear, moose, elk and deer, but because our wilderness derives from a headwa-ters strategy, valley forage—winter forage—has become scarce. Winter is the season of starvation, now more starvation among newly snugged-in log homes, smoke issuing from their chimneys in a picturesque curl.

Much of this could be avoided, even in subdivisions. The trophy homes could be clustered all at the point of pie-shaped twenty-acre plots, leaving an expanse of open space all around. This practice is com-mon in deference to golf courses, for instance, but almost never used to preserve wildlife habitat. Instead, we fractally replicate the rectilinear idea that carved the West in the first place, and each lot becomes a squared twenty-acre simulacrum of township, section and range. We subdivide the checkerboard into a smaller checkerboard.

The typical homeowner landscapes the immediate area around the house by planting a lawn made of exotic grasses and shrubs, with no nutritional value for wildlife. They fertilize, and the excess fertilizer runs off into the rivers. They water it by pumping groundwater that would otherwise support the flow of rivers and streams. Still, the lawn is only about an acre. The remainder of the ranchette, of course, is reserved for horses.

The horse revolution rebuilt the western landscape in the early years of the 1700s and restructured it again with the brief period of open range covering about thirty years in the late nineteenth century. This thirty years gave us the cowboy, who as a working model disappeared with the fencing of the range. Ranchers by the 1890s began growing hay to feed cattle, depending far less on grazing open range, and ranching became tamed, a form of farming.

Range or no, the idea of the cowboy persists with a vengeance vicious on the land. Back to our hypothetical newcomer. His log house is in, and sprinklers sputter and whir across the new-mown lawn through August afternoons. He has bought his pickup truck. It is a four-wheel drive, enormous and gets eight miles to the gallon. So far he has used it only to haul a kid to violin lessons and once to transport a chainsaw wood carving of an elk to adorn a lawn that was once elk habitat.

Before we go too far in casting this fellow as a local phenomenon, however, understand that it is likely he owned his truck (or some other enormous gas-guzzling four-wheel-drive monster) long before he moved from California. The most popular-selling new vehicle is a Ford half-ton pickup truck, a weird development that swept the nation during the last decade, much as oversized homes did the decade before. Veneration of cowboys is widespread, and any self-respecting accountant from Santa Clara needs a decent rig, the better to cast a long shadow over the parking lot of the line-dance bar on Saturday nights. Because of this new image of ourselves, the nation's fleet mileage dropped from twenty-two to about eighteen miles per gallon, according to the Federal Energy Information Administration.

Through whatever path, our guy has wound up owning a truck and probably a Stetson to go with it, a condition known locally by its detractors as "cappuccino cowboy" or the more rustic "all hat and no horse."

Our guy, meanwhile, has been around long enough to be aware of these jabs and has decided to do something about them. He's got the eighteen acres not surrendered to log house and Kentucky bluegrass lawn. So he buys a horse. More likely several. Horses are to the rivers of the West what sacred cows are to the Ganges.

It takes about twenty acres of grazing land to support a cow and calf here, and it takes about half again as much to support a horse—a figure all ranchers know better than their hat sizes, and a number most suburban horse owners have never heard. Thus, the two horses our friend has now hauled to his ranchette need sixty acres and have less than a third of that. They overgraze until the spread is mostly dirt dotted here and there by a few unpalatable weeds, overgrazed to the point that would have embarrassed the most rapacious of nineteenth-century cattle barons. Which is to say our newcomer fits in fine, and his land looks just like his neighbors' and his neighbors' after that—a valley tiled with the hammered dirt squares of twenty-acre ranchettes, the new West.

Beyond the subdivisions there are a few remaining ranches. These now have been converted to growing hay that our newcomer buys and hauls in his pickup truck to feed the horses that have run out of grass. Horse hay is irrigated, which explains why in dry years one may walk across what in spring had been a river and hardly get one's boot tops wet. Certainly not enough water to wet a fish, the trout that brought our friend here in the first place, as much as did the memories of Ben Cartwright and the lure of wide-open spaces to serve as habitat for one's pickup truck.

MY PLACE HAS AT LEAST one prominent story, and I am thankful for that; it is fine and finely wrought. Norman Maclean's *A River Runs Through It* seems almost geological, layered and accreted with the deep history of the place. He lived most of his adult life away from here, teaching at the University of Chicago, but still this was his place, the Big Blackfoot. He spent summers at the family place at Seeley Lake. He stayed in close contact with many people here until he died in 1992, just before publication of his only other book. *Young Men and Fire.*

In many ways, the story itself is testimony to an indissoluble tie to the place, particularly the river. He never really left his boyhood growing up in Missoula early in this century, walking these valleys and ridges, the very ridges that roll along outside my study windows as I write this. Most appropriate, his story is about love to the point that the love driving the human relationships in his family becomes the same as love of place. I wonder what then he would make, sour curmudgeon that he was, of his story's role in the perversion of that love.

The novella lived its book life quietly, walking, in book publishing parlance, on its own legs. It never received much national note, but that was not Maclean's goal. He shied away from a big-name New York publisher. It was his story, and he wanted it handled his way, which was to keep it in print for a long time. The University of Chicago Press published it in 1976—its first fiction project ever—and did indeed keep it in print to allow it to age and weather into its audience. It was still in print almost twenty years later when it had sold about 100,000 copies to a quiet, appreciative audience. It was the sort of book a person read every four or five years and closed almost prayerfully at that last sentence, long before memorized and just as likely lived: "I am haunted by rivers." Then one went about one's business more quietly for a couple of days, sadder and more fulfilled.

William Kittredge and Annick Smith knew Maclean well and worked to make *A River Runs Through It* into a film through the 1980s, spending years drawing out details of the real lives therein, fleshing it out for a script. I remember years ago Kittredge showing me copies of a newspaper column Maclean's brother, Paul, had written for the Helena *Independent Record*, then owned by the same corporation that owned the paper that I worked for. But it would not be until nearly twenty years after publication that Redford became interested (Maclean himself had turned down other producers, including the actor William Hurt after taking Hurt fishing and finding his casting unconvincing).

Redford made a fine film, true as could be expected to the book. We cannot fault the original story, fine as it is, nor Redford's handling of it for the perversion, but understand now that it was not long after the release of the film that a phrase became popular here. It was and is "a realtor runs through it."

Shortly after the release of the film, the switchboard at the Missoula

County Courthouse flooded with calls. The courthouse. Never mind the chamber of commerce. The callers wanted to know but one thing, how they could contact a real estate agent and move to the Big Blackfoot. The little town near my home, Lolo, is not on the Blackfoot, but represented Missoula in the film and is now indicative of what is happening throughout western Montana. In the last twenty years the town has grown 231 percent. I've already told you what the development looks like.

In Missoula itself, the price of a typical house has doubled in the past ten years, meaning many of my neighbors can no longer afford to live in their own community, especially those who had not yet bought houses. Our wage rates are below national averages, but our cost of living here is above.

The newcomers either brought the pile of money that was the equity in their old houses or brought independent incomes, retirement accounts and trust funds—and increasingly telecommuted to existing jobs in the Silicon Valley and other cyber hubs. The growth here was not the result of a general prosperity in the economy; it brought few new jobs. Realtors and carpenters made money, but not everyone did. Meanwhile, trendy boutiques and shops sprung up downtown selling goods most people here had not heard of and could not afford. A row of galleries sells watercolors of splashing trout taking dry flies and of cowboys, plus cowboy mugs, cowboy shirts, cowboy gear, cowboy boots and gear for cowboy boots, all rendered as some boutique manager might imagine essential western accoutrements. You can buy any sort of hand-hewn log furniture you might happen to need.

A while back, the local newspaper took measure of our trendiness by censusing the celebrities who had taken up residence in western Montana. The list included Carol Burnett, Michael Cimino, Emilio Estevez, Steve Howe, Kiefer Sutherland, Jack Nicklaus, Liz Claiborne, Charlie Sheen, Shecky Greene, John Lithgow, Jan-Michael Vincent, Polly Bergen, Huey Lewis, Christopher Lloyd, Charles Schwab, Charles Kuralt, Jane Fonda, Peter Fonda, Ted Turner, Meg Ryan, Dennis Quaid, Michael Keaton, Brent Musburger, Brooke Shields, Mel Gibson, Jim Nabors, Hank Williams Jr., Hoyt Axton, Jeff Bridges, Glenn Close, Tom Brokaw and Andie MacDowell.

As you might imagine, a small town with these names in the phone book has a somewhat distinct nature.

I know of a place untouched by trends, a bar that is really something of a hole in the wall, probably unchanged, or unwashed for that matter, since the 1930s. It serves cheap beer and greasy burgers. Loggers, lawyers, tree-huggers and reporters crowd on its narrow, fluorescent-lit row of stools. It is loud, grimy and there is neither fern nor chablis glass on the premises. The bartenders are two big guys from Anaconda. Once my wife asked for a brandy glass and was asked in response: "Where the fuck do you think you are?"

It is a small corner of refuge in an otherwise shifting world, and one afternoon I sulked on in for a breath of stale air, sat down on a stool and noticed Andie MacDowell sitting on the next one.

WE SAY we are "loving it to death," but this isn't love.

The people moving here are motivated by an image, or a series of images: the independent cowboy and his horse on wide-open spaces, the silence of a fly fisher on a still-clean mountain stream. Behind these images lies something real and undeniably valuable and desirable. They seek silence, solitude, independence and purity. Yet translated through imagery, this seeking becomes a curse, and every bit of silence they touch becomes noise, everything clean, unclean. The curse derives from the relationship between ideal and real.

All of this has nothing to do with love, in that love implies a relationship and giving. Love implies an awareness of the needs of that which is loved. It implies giving, sacrificing to protect those needs. It is true that we can cast what has happened to my place into a sexual metaphor, but the proper analog would be a term confessing more force and violence than making love.

The popular pastime among people here like me, people who have been here ten or fifteen years—a sufficient interval to allow us to forget we did pretty much what the newcomers have done—is to complain incessantly about the trashing of our valley. To a degree, some of this can be constructive. For instance, absent any real will of government—both state and local—to do anything but take the cash all this growth generates, some people have been forced to come up with creative solutions to protect a bit of land here or there. Private groups, as we shall see, have worked with ranchers to establish easements that grant them tax credits that can save their land from developers. Others have banded together to buy land outright, including a bond issue to assess Missoula's taxpayers to buy and leave vacant the two most prominent mountains adjacent to the city. This can save small bits of habitat, and now Missoula is one of the few cities where one may watch elk herds wintering on nearby hills while walking its central business district.

These easements and some other measures, especially and ironically the enormous concentration of industrial logging land, have kept the worst of the sprawl from invading the Blackfoot Valley. Most of the worst of it is along the Bitterroot, but as I float the Blackfoot and watch the inexorable pressure build, I begin to grasp the implacability of what is to come.

Thinking about this and hoping it was all borne of innate pessimism, I sought out another view and stopped to visit a friend, Tim Hall, a county planner. I asked specifically about the Blackfoot Valley. Was there hope? He showed me Potomac. I have seen the valley many times, a picturesque run of ranches like the Ovando Valley, but a bit more closed in. It lies about halfway between Ovando and Missoula, very much a Blackfoot community. Hall showed it to me in a new way, on a computer screen, an instant aerial view that was really not much more than a good map of the place rendered in pixels. It appeared as I knew it, especially in the detail he chose, which diced and color-coded the valley according to land ownership. The pixel lines corresponded to fence lines I knew, and a face I could live with.

Through the years of the twenty-acre subdivision loophole, a few people quietly sliced up their land, but never sold, so subdivision does not read on the real face of the place. That process accelerated especially, in that when repealing the law, the legislature left a gap between passage and implementation that created a rush to subdivide.

Hall hit some keys on his computer telling the software to add the lines to land under a single ownership, but already legally subdivided to ranchettes and ready to sell. The computer instantly drew the future: an order of magnitude leap in the number of straight, squared lines on what was once a smooth, rounded place. In this new version, the Potomac Valley looked like a butcher's diagram of a beef cow. More lines. And how could it be otherwise in the Potomac or anywhere else? More people. Same amount of land. More lines.

We who live here complain loudly, often and shamelessly, as if all this were simply a matter of building better borders, or fencing out the Californians and their ilk, convincing them to go elsewhere. We believe we are being singled out and picked on with this plague. The truth is, the plague is fair, even equitable, a just consequence of what we have become.

Remember that Montana, even with all the growth I describe, has fewer than 900,000 people and is almost exactly the same size as California with its more than 33 million. During the first years of this decade, Montana was worried about a growth rate that would have brought maybe, just maybe, another 20,000 people to the state. During that same period, California was growing by about 2 million a year, more than twice Montana's total existing population added to the same land area each year. About half of California's growth came in the form of immigration to the United States, legal and otherwise, a phenomenon that has the residents of that state doing what the residents of mine do: looking to stronger borders to keep outsiders out. Also during that same period, India added 100 million people.

The force of these numbers is the perspective that sends the mind racing straight up the Blackfoot to the refuge of the wilderness. That is what it is, a remaining refuge from the world that is crashing down around us in unsupportable numbers, the sheer crushing weight of human biomass. The truth is, my neighbors and I—the people bitching about all of this—live lives of inestimable privilege. We live lives cast in the gold standard, a firm line dividing the world's population.

There are nearly 6 billion humans on the planet, twice as many as were here thirty years ago, a doubling in half a lifetime. But more interesting is applying the gold standard to these people, essentially what Alan Durning did in his study for the Worldwatch Institute (*How Much Is Enough*, W. W. Norton). We can divide the existing total world population into the 20 percent—1 billion—who are the richest, the 20 percent who are the poorest and all the rest, a world middle class. It turns out the dividing line for this, the number that sets the standard of poverty for the poorest 20 percent, is an income of $700 a year per person. The dividing line setting off the richest 20 percent is $7,500 a year, placing virtually everyone in this nation above the gold standard, in the richest category, most of us well above it.

During the last thirty years, the size of that richest group has increased not at all. There were a billion of us a generation ago and there are a billion now. That is to say, all of the people added to the planet in the past thirty years have been born to lives of poverty we cannot imagine. About a quarter of the world's population views a glass of clean drinking water as an unobtainable luxury; I worry about sediment-free water to float my raft. These are the huddled masses, and weighed against their yearnings we have gold and subdivisions and wilderness.

The explosion of the population of poverty has resulted in an ever-widening inequality in the distribution of income in this nation, the gulf between rich and poor, and correspondingly, a drive by the rich to protect themselves from the poor. This is the not-so-subtle push of the Republican politics to dismantle a government that might redistribute wealth or provide services to the poor by taxing the resources of the rich. This is the drive behind gated communities and the explosion of subdivisions and trophy homes, and in this sense, Montana is becoming not much more than a large, gated subdivision where the new rich can escape the crime, poverty and race problems of the cities that created their wealth.

It is the same drive that is propelling the wealthy to buy gold, which is a hedge against chaotic economies that surely will result from overpopulation. At the same time gold jewelry marks status, which is how the rich distance themselves from the poor. All of this we will examine in detail later, but the present setting makes me consider the desire of gold in context of my own desire of wilderness. Both are indulging in luxury.

I do not wish to draw this analogy too closely, because I can defend wilderness's existence on separate grounds. It is more than sanctuary for humans fleeing the tortures of an overcrowded world. In fact, one can argue that this overcrowding and the inequity are in violation of nature's rules and if we are to have any future at all, then we will learn it from reading nature's laws more perfectly in places like wilderness. For this alone we need wilderness, no matter how we might use it.

But in defending it and in fleeing to it, I realize that I am indulging in one of the world's rarest luxuries: silence and solitude. These become more precious and unavailable, more goldlike, with each human birth.

Many of us would gladly trade all the world's gold for a silent, wild place. There will come a time when all of us will feel that way, but by then, there will be no silence left, only gold. It endures.

Easement

THE TWO CRISP, blue eyes that are the focal point of his open face suggest one is looking at facets of heritage more significant than an expression of the Scandinavian allele for crisp and blue. He tells it like this: There are ideals in his genetic code, from his mother's side a longstanding and unavoidable affinity for public service and from his father's, maybe a commitment for defending nature, but just as likely an affinity for wading into controversy and speaking his mind. His paternal grandfather, a congressman from Minnesota, once was hanged in effigy for his unpopular notions, an event his own father witnessed and remembered, but it did not stop his father from speaking ideas during World War II that almost instantly turned the world's most famous man into a pariah.

Land Lindbergh mentions all of this in our conversation over coffee one late fall day in Missoula while mentally I tick off a few attributes that his words leave out but that register just the same in those eyes. I think of the tenacity that kept his father flying alone, for whole days in subzero cockpits across unpeopled terrain, sometimes with no greater cause than to deliver the mail on time. Through nature or nurture, some of that must have come to Land. But more pertinently, as I sit scribbling in a reporter's notebook, I think of the family's longstanding and justified animosity toward reporters, stemming mostly from the famous kidnapping and murder of Land's oldest brother, when the yellow press staged a circus and a raid on the family's privacy that makes the O.J. trial seem serene and dignified in comparison. The ensuing flap over Charles Lindbergh's Nazi sympathies during World War II did little to ameliorate this, and the prying has persisted through generations. Land himself was born in England because the Lindberghs had gone there to escape the howling mob of journalists in the United States. Nonetheless, when it comes to the Blackfoot River, Land is willing to say what he has to say. And he speaks for maybe an hour, openly, thoughtfully and honestly.

And modestly—a trait of his that needs to be overridden at the outset. The truth is, much of what is right about the Blackfoot River Valley, much of the success in preserving its natural integrity, its wild character and its sense of human community, can be traced to Land Lindbergh. He won't admit to this and will only confirm the details, so up front I say it for him.

IN LEONARD MOSLEY'S BIOGRAPHY of Charles Lindbergh, there is a flat black-and-white photo of the aviator and a skinnier, even more open-faced Land poring over maps of the Blackfoot River Valley. They were becoming ranchers and on April Fools' Day of 1965, Land, then a twenty-seven-year-old kid fresh from school, took charge of 10,000 deeded and 30,000 leased acres that would be the Lindbergh ranch. It is a great, sweeping reach that spans the entire valley just below Clearwater Junction. Land (his given name is fortuitous and eponymous, deriving from his paternal grandmother's family name) no longer owns it, having sold it only a few years ago to live now on what he describes as his little place, a square mile of wooded lands and canyons threaded through by the Blackfoot River. He lives there with his adult children, quietly, as is his style.

His charge is inadequately expressed in acreage, although 40,000 acres in the hands of a twenty-seven-year-old seems plenty descriptive of "tall order". Beyond the numbers, though, is the fact that the purchase of the ranch came late in the more famous Lindbergh's life as he was throwing all of his energies into environmental causes.

Mosley's biography contains a thought Charles Lindbergh recorded after a late-1960s trip to Indonesia:

> Surrounded by wilderness, representing the human lifestream with diverse competing lifestreams close at hand, I start doubting my superiority. I am struck by the perfection of competing species in contrast to my own. I'm amazed at the beauty, health and balance nature has achieved through instinct's influence. I ask what intellect has done to warrant its prestige. As earth's most messy, defective and destructive animal, man's record gives him little cause for pride.

And a few years later on his visiting Minnesota, where he had grown up:

> Few men have seen with their own eyes, as I have in the past fifty years, how serious is the breakdown of America's land surface. I have seen fencing pushing westward, enclosing once open land. I have seen bird and animal life disappear. I have seen towns and cities spring up where there were none before. Forest land converted into agriculture, farm land in turn become suburban subdivisions, mountains slashed through with power lines and super-highways, rivers and lakes fouled by pollution, the skies over even small towns hazed by smog—all evidence of human thoughtlessness about their environment. But there is still hope if we take measures in time. The situation is in many cases reversible.

If anyone heard this message, it was Lindbergh's rancher son.

THE BLACKFOOT VALLEY has never been lacking for newcomers with big ideas; just ask the Salish about this. Likely as not, however, the outsiders create more trouble than they settle; again this may be confirmed by the Salish. What has allowed Land Lindbergh to contribute as he has is his quick learning of an idea that settles so slowly in many. He puts it simply: "The landowners had to lead. Anything proposed from the outside is automatically rejected."

While many see ranchers' native suspiciousness and obstreperousness as an impediment, Land saw it as a deep expression of the values that drive conservation. He believes in the fundamental connection between "conservation" and "conservative." This belief manifested itself first in Land's selection of allies.

In the 1960s, the threats to the integrity of the valley were expressed somewhat differently, but they were fundamentally the same. The issue then was trespass and encroachment, especially by hunters from nearby cities, the harbinger of suburban sprawl. Wrapped in this seemingly simple problem was an emerging change in attitudes toward Montana's landscape that is hard for an outsider to understand, especially those who consider public land a park. Public land in the West was to a certain degree considered waste land. Ranchers homesteaded the valuable parcels along river bottoms like the Blackfoot, then more or less treated the uplands—the public lands—as if it were their own. This idea drew practical reinforcement from the layout. Highways ran along river bottoms among ranches, so to get access to public lands—uplands—hunters and everyone else needed to cross ranches.

Montana grew up with this to the point that most land, even private, was considered open. To cross, one simply opened the gate, and there were no problems as long as one closed the gate. Ranchers, hunters and especially federal land management agencies were used to this, and really had no system for doling out access—as would become necessary when cities pumped in ever-growing numbers of hunters. Some behaved badly, and the ranchers locked the gates.

When Land first settled into his ranch, this problem was beginning to express itself, but as an outsider, he also understood this as simply the beginning of what would become a larger threat that would necessarily entail a well-planned response. Ultimately, dealing with trespass was a way to begin dealing with the future.

Land needed allies, and he found two in particular, Hank Goetz, a forester, and Bill Potter, a tough-as-nails rancher. It is thirty years later and the three men, all past sixty, still get together to kick around ideas. Land calls them the "three old buffalo."

In many ways, Potter was the more important discovery. Goetz is an academic and the sort who can be expected to dabble in land-use decisions and ideas; Potter is not, and his work with Lindbergh made him a bellwether.

To begin with, Potter despises environmentalists and spends more than an average share of time "moaning and groaning" about them, according to Lindbergh. Potter, however, is a survivor of the tough conditions of ranching, something one does not achieve without being mindful of the care of the land.

"He's a genius," says Lindbergh. "He'd never admit it, but he's the original conservationist. It kills him to cut a tree unless there is something wrong with it."

Part of Potter's ranch is timbered, so he conducts a selective logging operation. Foresters and environmentalists see it and invariably label it a model of sustainable logging, a modern buzzword but an old idea. He logs selectively, trying to mimic the natural culling effects of fire and age. He leaves large old trees, and takes the diseased and dying.

"He views that land and the resources on it as a savings account," says Lindbergh. "When he needs a tractor, he goes out and picks out the trees to pay for it."

Commitment to the land and a sense of independence have become the guiding factors in a series of decisions that produced a strong core of protected land in the Blackfoot. It began with the trespass problem, when landowners and government officials simply got together and worked out a plan that included access corridors for hunters. This cut the pattern that would later come into play in the evolution of the Blackfoot's best tool for conservation.

This is not to say the Blackfoot and its ranchers suddenly were swept into an era of five-year plans, peace, harmony and prosperity. The valley retains its reputation for irascibility, especially where government planners are concerned. Lindbergh once did propose something like a comprehensive land-use plan, zoning and all, and was shouted down, and that is exactly the treatment one could expect today for similar ideas. Yet planning and community effort is occurring in the Blackfoot under the ranchers' own terms. The tool is the conservation easement.

The land trust movement runs nationwide and is used to set aside everything from East Coast parks and bikeways to desert habitat to farmland to California's coastal vistas. Some of the early work on development of this tool, certainly the earliest in Montana, came in the Blackfoot, pushed along by Land Lindbergh and a few friends.

Conservation easements are relatively simple and come in a variety of flavors, but generally are designed to restrict development. Legally, they work just like a more conventional easement for a road crossing or a power line. Property rights are really layers of rights and an easement is the giving up or selling of one of those layers. In the case of a ranch, the owner generally gives up the right to develop the land. He can continue present use and continue to live on it, even build a new house to replace his old one, but that's it. No subdivisions. No condos. The agreement attaches to the deed and passes to all subsequent buyers.

Besides conservation, the agreement has spinoff advantages to the rancher. The easement usually devalues the land, because it can't be sold to developers, so its value for property taxes drops. That shows up as a lower tax. Often, the difference in value of the land can be claimed as a donation to a nonprofit group, so certain owners can then take the value of that donation as a deduction on their federal taxes. Also, easements make it easier to pass on ranches intact to heirs because of reduced inheritance taxes.

This is how an accountant might view it. Ranchers might view it as a way to beat the government out of a few bucks and at the same time keep the land the way it is—a good deal for them. They also view it as a neat method of dealing with a nasty phenomenon of ranching communities. In some cases the heirs are simply biding their time until the old man goes to the big roundup and have already penciled in papers with a developer and picked out the new Jaguar. A conservation easement can dash those plans. More than one hard-boiled ranching type has used them to ensure he'll be laughing in the grave.

The problem with all of this was Montana had no law allowing these easements. In 1973, Land called some lawyer friends and friends in the Nature Conservancy. Land's father once sat on the Conservancy's board. A law was drafted, the legislature was lobbied and the easements began. Among the earliest in the Blackfoot were those reading "Land M. & Susan M. Lindbergh to the Nature Conservancy," "Anne Morrow Lindbergh to the Nature Conservancy" and "Lindbergh Cattle Co. to the Nature Conservancy."

"WE'VE GOT FORTY-SEVEN THOUSAND ACRES so far," he tells me right up front, because a hard number connected to acres is what resonates to a man raised in ranching, and Jim Stone was. He's thirty-six, wiry and taut and smiles perpetually, talks easily. As he sits at a coffee shop in jeans, a cowboy shirt and clean new running shoes, no hat over his close-clipped red hair, most wouldn't take him for a rancher. Most real ranchers wouldn't be taken for ranchers.

Stone was mostly raised on the ranch he now works near Ovando, called "Stone's Throw." His father bought it. His father worked for Bill Potter. Jim and the valley have been together most of his life except for high school when he went away to a sort of cowboy prep school in Colorado and to college at Montana State University in Bozeman. His course work was in agricultural business and fine arts.

"Jeez. Don't put down that fine arts part. Put down 'metalsmithing.' 'Fine arts' makes me sound like a flaming liberal. I went into silversmithing. Now I weld a lot of our own stuff on the ranch."

There is further incriminating evidence for Stone's alleged liberalism.

"I guess I'd call myself an environmentalist." Were that not enough, he holds an even more seditious view: "It's a whole lot easier to work with a group than to do it yourself."

That last is, of course, anathema to the rugged individualist image of Hollywood oaters and of radio talk shows. The notion of independence among ranchers has always been complete bullshit. Ranchers have survived against some of the worst odds on the planet. To do that, they cooperate.

Stone's main task these days is steering that cooperation. He is the next generation. He says he took his lead from guys like Lindbergh, Goetz and Potter, "a lot of people I knew and respected." Stone heads up an organization called the Blackfoot Challenge, a grassroots group formed by the valley's landowners. It spearheaded the drive for the 47,000 acres of new conservation easements Stone mentioned at the outset, continuing the work Lindbergh began, but evolution has occurred. Besides the easements, the group has become a sort of clearinghouse, bringing together corporate landowners such as Plum Creek Timber, as well as federal land management agencies like the Bureau of Land Management and the Forest Service. It has become a means of coordinating and deciding the relative importance of a variety of land-use efforts.

For instance, the BLM is interested in carrying out an attack on a couple of species of exotic weeds that are seriously threatening wildlife habitat in the valley. These same species threaten rangeland, and ranchers have been fighting them for years. During that battle, they have learned there is much to be gained from coordinated efforts—hitting seed sources, problem areas and vectors of spread like logging roads first, regardless of who owns the land in question. They have developed a ranchland epidemiology, so Stone's group became the vehicle for coordinating the attack. The BLM is putting $120,000 a year for seven years into the project, while the Blackfoot Challenge provides detailed mapping of the spread of weeds to design an effective strategy of attack that includes both spraying of herbicides and biological controls.

In this fashion, the Challenge has racked up a record of achievements besides the easements. It has a hand in outright purchase of 3,700 acres for conservation; it restored, improved or established 1,500 acres of wetlands; improved 13.5 miles of streamside habitat; restored and rebuilt 17 miles of stream channel; reseeded 430 acres of native prairie; removed barriers to fish migration in 150 miles of streams; and controlled erosion along 17 miles of roads.

The real measure of accomplishment, however, may be in the evolution of the way the place thinks of itself. I was at a meeting just before interviewing Stone, one at which he spoke, but the meeting was held by a collection of soil conservation agencies and attended by the ranchers of the valley. "Valley" is at once a geographic and political term, a subdivision of people as well as a pocket of land cut by a glacier. It defines a community, simply because it defines lines of sight and of travel. One knows nothing of the people over the ridge, but those on this side of the ridge are one's neighbors.

The term and idea have always come into play, one way or another, but now the ranchers speak in a more precise and meaningful term. They call themselves residents of a watershed. A valley is, of course, a watershed, in that it is defined by a river, but the use of the term places a new burden of responsibility on our politics. It is acknowledgment that community is organized by rivers, that the water from my ranch runs to yours. When the water leaves the valley, its quality will be the measure of ours. By simple association with one's neighbors it is no great stretch to decide that because we wish to receive good water, we will wish to give good water. It is a river people's golden rule.

During the fall of 1996, an event occurred that told just how far this might go. We worry greatly about the effects of ranching on the Blackfoot, as we should. The cows have taken their toll. But an intact ranch keeps back the subdivisions, which are the greater threat to the river. This idea, however, needs some perspective, again on the scale of watershed. Only 24 percent of the land in the watershed is in private ranches. Another 56 percent is either federal or state land, with perils of its own to be sure, but subdivisions are not among them. The remaining 20 percent is held by the timber corporation Plum Creek. What's worse, that portion is heavily concentrated in a corridor directly along the river between Bonner and Potomac, the stretch closest to Missoula and so therefore most attractive to developers. Further, Plum Creek got that land from Champion, which had logged it mercilessly. It is not worth much as timbered land. And even worse, Plum Creek has created a real estate arm and has announced it is in a mood to sell.

In October, the Bureau of Land Management, Plum Creek and the Nature Conservancy, which began the easement process in the valley in the first place, announced a deal. The Conservancy would pay Plum Creek $18 million for 11,730 acres of land that formed a ten-mile-long corridor on the most valuable stretch of the river. The BLM would later buy the land back from the Conservancy after raising money from the sale of parcels of less sensitive landscape elsewhere. The land would become public, and be set aside for recreation and wildlife habitat.

Land can be protected.

JIM STONE GETS a little antsy with one particular line of questioning, because he's heard it before, and he knows where it's heading. His neighbor Jon Krutar responded much the same because Jon too is involved heavily in an association of locals, the Blackfoot Legacy. It is less geared to on-the-ground ranching problems than the Challenge and more to the broader range of landowner issues, but still not a competing group. The line of questioning that unsettles both of them has to do with the gold mine.

For similar reasons, both groups decided not to take a stand on the mine. Phelps Dodge is in fact a member of the Challenge, but only technically. Stone says the miners take no active role.

Both groups will remain neutral on the issue to preserve the common ground. Both seek to serve as neutral clearinghouses, forums, places where everyone can exchange views. Taking a stand would undermine their political effectiveness. That's not to say any of the principal figures are overly politic, if one asks the right question. For instance: Forget the politics of the group, how do *you* feel about that mine?

Stone: "I definitely oppose that damn thing."

Land Lindbergh drops his chin when he begins talking about the mine. When he first heard about it, he thought it might not be such a bad idea. He understands the plight of people around Lincoln, the unemployment that has long been a part of their existence. A few jobs could help.

Then he got a look at the mine's detailed plans.

"It would be a catastrophe," he says. "I don't think any of us could possibly comprehend what it would do."

And then he watched the miners go to the state legislature and arrange quietly for some special laws that weaken state water quality rules to benefit the mine and hurt the Blackfoot. "My valley," Lindbergh calls it, and he deserves to—but he cannot call the state's government "my legislature," as the miners can.

"It's getting harder and harder for me to believe there's a reasonable compromise out there," he says.

For a man who has built a life of integrity on reason and on accommodating the needs of both neighbors and community, that is a considerable statement. The mine removes common ground, the place once occupied by reason.

Driving down the valley from Ovando and Krutar's place through the broad plain the glaciers worked, then past Stone's and down toward Clearwater Junction near Land's quiet "little" place, I think now of the Alamosa River, which I have never seen. It is in Colorado and had the misfortune of draining a heap-leach gold mine.

In 1986, Galactic Resources Ltd., a Canadian firm, began to leach gold at the Summitville Mine at 11,700 feet in Colorado's San Juan Mountains. No doubt, the phrase "state of the art" appeared somewhere in the list of promises the company made in trying to sell the project to regulators and residents. Galactic worked its ore by spraying it with a solution of cyanide, just as Phelps Dodge plans to do on the Blackfoot. Six days after the first cyanide hit the heap of ore in 1986, the liner designed to contain the poison began leaking. The problems multiplied and were complicated by high-mountain precipitation and avalanches. By 1991, cyanide and acid drainage had ended life in seventeen miles of the Alamosa River downstream of the mine. Farmers who drew the water found their irrigation pipes corroded and full of holes. Galactic went broke and abandoned the mine, but only after reclaiming a third of its $7.2 million bond from the state. The Environmental Protection Agency intervened and at one point, according to its figures, was spending $33,000 a day from the federal treasury to stabilize the site. The EPA ultimately expects to spend as much as $150 million on cleanup.

Damage like this is readily apparent, and this is what causes our nights of tossings and turnings as we think about the possibility of this mine. But it occurs to me that something very human and real has been built here in this watershed, a commodity that the environmental impact studies ignore, something increasingly valuable in this Tower of Babel of American politics, this ziggurat topped with gold. The Blackfoot is a community built by a river, and imperiling the river threatens that as well. The intangible quality we call "community" does not automatically sprout from aggregations of people. It is built. The heart of the cooperation and sense of common good that drives the protection of this place has a clean river at its heart. What will happen to the sense of watershed when the river no longer flows clean?

Truth Is Butte

It is wrong to say a river ends, yet there is a sense of the Blackfoot's end as one rafts its last few miles, a stretch that pinches together with the highway into a claustrophobic bit of canyon. The bends of river bob and weave in synch with log trucks and tanker trucks busting downward to centers of commerce below. Pinched, but lazy, this stretch is usually empty of rafts and kayaks, but on a summer day awash in giggling kids, young and otherwise, in inner tubes, a flotilla of family outings. This cackle of human joy bouncing off rock walls is the sound of us making this our river. In its last mile, it pools wide and silent along a pullout where the floaters de-tube just upstream of the mini mountain ranges of log piles at the Bonner mill. No one floats the last stretch past the mill and under a bridge to the confluence with the Clark Fork, which is technically the river's end.

It is wrong to say rivers end because their waters

go on renamed as another river. The Blackfoot, however, does not go immediately on, but pauses with the Clark Fork in a reservoir behind Milltown Dam. Layered in the mud below this reservoir is evidence of another river's beginning, the very reason it is appropriate for us to stand right here to consider the Blackfoot by considering its mirror-image limb, the reaches of the Clark Fork upstream of Milltown Dam. This place is the necessary vantage because it is the very spot that has formed the locally held and deeply held horror of mining.

The reservoir is ringed by ramshackle frame houses fitting the name Milltown, all with a brand-new supply of piped-in fresh water. Their old wells were condemned after infusing these people with arsenic, cadmium, lead and copper dug up deliberately 140 miles away. Milltown is a federal Superfund site. The Blackfoot ends in a Superfund site, a formal designation reserved for the nation's most foully polluted places. It is the nation's largest such site, or part of it. The map of the terrain along the Clark Fork from here upstream to Butte is dotted with polluted spots together called a "complex," by which the bureaucrats mean an array, but the sense of the word as applied to disease also works. So does "complicated." (Bureaucrats should always be so deft in their naming.) It is also among the nation's oldest Superfund sites, simply because after decades of study and experiment, no one seems quite able to understand or even convincingly propose how to undo what mining has done.

From Milltown, we may look up the Clark Fork to a copper mine and our past and up the Blackfoot to a gold mine and our future. This vantage tells why we often hear a comparison in discussions of the gold mine, that the dimensions of the proposed open pit almost match the dimensions of the Berkeley Pit at Butte, the hole that killed the Upper Clark Fork and left this reservoir underlain with toxic muck, wastes that must inevitably be dealt with—to use the phrase that federal regulators use but that no one can comprehend—"in perpetuity."

JIM KUIPERS LIVES in Butte by choice, a preference difficult for an outsider, especially a near outsider from elsewhere in western Montana, to understand. Once a tourist hailed a friend of mine on the street in Missoula, a friend who had grown up in Butte. The tourist mispronounced the name of the town: "How do I get to Butteee?" Answered my friend: "Boy, have you got that wrong."

The town is as ugly as they come, but it didn't start out that way. It sits in a broad valley that tips up against roiling rock peaks that form the Continental Divide. Its treeless rush of openness is breathtaking until one realizes there are a few trees, but they are stunted and twisted, atypical for their species, even at this altitude of 5,000 feet. These mountains were deforested, much like those around the Blackfoot, for timbers and fuels for copper mines. But unlike the Blackfoot, the forests did not return because pollution from smelting copper settled heavy metals and other poisons into the landscape. Around the turn of the century and on into the 1950s, the air here was lethal.

The valley's fate was cast in 1864, when prospectors, whose appetites had been whetted by the California gold rush, fanned through Montana combing every wash. They found and began working a gold vein at Butte. It wasn't much, but it led to a vein of silver in 1867, which also wasn't much, but it led to copper just as the twentieth century jolted into the electrical age—which runs on copper wires.

Since 1879, Butte has been a copper mining town, and it still is. That's why Kuipers lives there, thirty-something and outgoing, a compact man with a beard and a ponytail—he is a miner. His grandfather was a miner, working gold deposits just over the Great Divide from Butte. Kuipers trained as a mining engineer at the Butte School of Mines. He has run gold mines for the major players in Nevada, Colorado and Utah. He's worked at copper mines in Arizona. He's mined in Butte, but he mines no more, working now as a consultant and contractor to the state on cleanup of abandoned and problem mines.

In 1994, Kuipers traveled to Siberia to investigate American involvement in gold mining there. Existing Siberian mines were operating under notoriously lax Russian regulations, and it was as if he got to see mining distilled to its essence.

"You see people drinking tailings pond water [waste water from mine processing] coming right out of the smelter. You can and do see people who are dying of metals poisoning," he says. That trip was followed by what he calls the "last straw," work on a gold mine in El Salvador, where a mine manager, to avoid the relatively minor expense of impounding toxic tailings water, let the poisons run directly into a river that was the drinking water supply for a city of 500,000 people nineteen miles away.

Kuipers's language reveals something of the culture of mining when he says he was always a "latent environmentalist, but I finally came out of the closet.

"I'm not going to tear down any more mountains. I just can't do that," he says. "I'm just to the point in my life when I think we don't need another mine."

He says those foreign mines that were his life's watershed only vary from their counterparts in the United States by degree. At every mine he has known, American and foreign alike, poisons have escaped. So Kuipers came home to do cleanup, but he came home to Butte. All around there are other mountain towns, unpolluted and undug and still close to the wilderness where Kuipers backpacks for weeks on end, but Butte was his choice.

"I like Butte. There are no false pretenses here," he says. "They [Buttians, yes, that's what they're called] don't view what has happened here in any negative sense. They just view it as what has happened."

And what will happen. At the very edge of the city, under what was once the center of the city, sits the Berkeley Pit, a mile-wide hole that is slowly and inexorably refilling itself with water made toxic by flushing the ground of poisonous metals. In the winter of 1995, in what was a well-publicized but undoubtedly not unique event, 342 geese landed on the lake that is forming in the pit. They all died, poisoned almost instantly by the water. Everyone agrees the water is rising. Everyone agrees there is no stopping it. Eventually it will reach and flush into the aquifers that are Butte's drinking water supply.

"It's only a matter of years until that water is going to be a part of our daily life," says Kuipers. It seems that mines, like rivers, do not end.

ONE MAY BEGIN to gather a sense of enormity of the Berkeley Pit far away and well out of its sight. From Milltown's slackwater that had settled out the metals when water slowed, one heads upstream past Rock Creek and the cow town of Drummond. Somewhere between Garrison Junction and Deer Lodge, the traveler begins to see the slickens. These are barren patches in the floodplain, an area that otherwise produces some of the region's most luxuriant vegetation. The soil in slickens appears crusted with powder. Some of it is the telltale ghostly green of oxidized copper, which is precisely what it is.

Slickens are now a part of the geology of the Clark Fork basin, and they are wholly artifice. Periodically, the river was so laden with heavy metals that floods, traditionally the source of nutrient-rich silt along riverbanks, became the source of heavy-metal wastes. Because this has occurred for a century, the slickens are layered and braided into the plain and now pose a hazard of their own. Thunderstorms, spring floods and scouring walls of ice chew at the terrain to bust loose the metals, once laid to rest, now back in play in the life of the river. That is, the riverbank has become so polluted as to become itself a source of pollution. Farther upstream fish biologists labored long and hard to restore trout to a stretch of about ten miles, but during several years, sudden summer thunderstorms pried loose mining wastes layered in the geology of the floodplain. Every fish went belly up, a stream rendered lifeless in a matter of minutes.

There is no way to deal with this save digging up and replacing 140 miles of streamside geology, and then where do they put the diggings? How do they move the wastes out of reach of water on this planet?

At the town of Deer Lodge just downstream of Butte, there is a historic ranch for the tourists, and there is the old territorial prison that once held notorious real-West bad guys. The tourists seem to like that too, but none seem to tour the slickens. K. Ross Toole, a fine historian who knew our state better than most, said: "Everywhere the Montanan is surrounded by his real heritage. Almost nowhere will he recognize it." Our heritage is mining.

AT THE TURN of the century, opera companies touring the booming West scheduled stops at Denver, San Francisco and Butte. From this, we understand how well the diggings paid. The groundwork for all of this was laid by the state's most famous oligarch, Marcus Daly, an Irish immigrant who had honed his pickax in silver and gold strikes at Calaveras County, California, and in Nevada's famous Comstock Lode. Forget images of grizzled prospectors, gold pans and mules; capital did the mining, even then. Daly sold interests in Nevada for $100,000, which set him up to buy an unimpressive silver mine at Butte called Anaconda. The accident of nomenclature meant the name of a big snake would eventually become synonymous with copper mining, monopoly capitalism and hardball politics from Butte to Chile to the Upper Peninsula of Michigan.

Daly became convinced his silver mine was really a copper mine and recruited a list of backers from San Francisco that included George Hearst, scion of the newspaper family. They built a company town near Butte. It's still there, and it's still called Anaconda, and it is still in the shadow of an enormous brick smokestack now dormant but once the source of exhaust from the world's largest copper smelter. According to K. Ross Toole, by 1885, Butte and Anaconda were turning out $7.3 million a year in copper, $3.3 million in gold, $10 million in silver and another half million worth of lead. Less than a decade into its life as a mine town, Butte was an international force. Between 1880 and 1890, Butte's population jumped 265 percent, to 142,924. This is more than triple Butte's current population and more than double the current population of Billings, the state's largest city now.

The mines and Butte inhaled the fuelwood and timberwood from a 200-mile radius to frame their works and fuel their smelters. The smelters exhaled the exhausts that killed the trees as the wind settled metals and toxic dust on the land. The tailings piles from a honeycomb of adits and shafts, once exposed to rain, leached the metals that became the geology of the Upper Clark Fork. The mines inhaled the immigrants: Irish, Cornish, Slavs, legions of workers who would become the Wobblies, the Butte Miners Union, the Western Federation of Miners that fought against conditions such as those that caused a mine fire that killed 162 men in 1917. When that fight escalated, Wobbly agitator Frank Little was dragged from his room and hanged.

Then the mines raised private armies, the notorious Pinkerton men, of which the novelist Dashiell Hammett was one, and class warfare joined tailings as a part of the landscape.

The mines raised a body politic as raw and ragged as a hole in the ground. By the 1890s, the snatching up of independent mines and claims had coagulated largely to two sets of hands, those of Marcus Daly and his rival, W. A. Clark. This tight little oligarchy produced the period Montanans call the War of the Copper Kings. The two hated each other, and when Clark decided to run for the U.S. Senate, Daly joined the battle, then fought in the statehouse, because the legislature elected senators. It ended with legislators taking the floor and waving envelopes containing as much as $30,000 in cash bribes. Daly's men "investigated" this bribery by paying $100 each for "affidavits" testifying to Clark's perfidy. Judges and legislators were bought wholesale, as was a complicit press, literally so. Daly owned the Butte *Standard*; Clark the Butte *Miner*. Clark later escalated the press war by raising $1.5 million to buy papers all over the state, which in turn became a part of the legacy made even more significant when the War of the Copper Kings ended.

It ended by consolidation, with Daly dead and Anaconda heavily capitalized by Standard Oil Company and reconstituted as Amalgamated. The new structure quit fighting Clark and bought him out, acquiring as well the holdings of F. Augustus Heinze, an ally of Clark's and another copper baron. By 1915, Amalgamated dissolved and again became Anaconda, but now Anaconda stood in complete control. It began an era that we called and still call the Copper Collar, a hold on the conditions of life in the state that was absolute.

For instance, in 1903, when the legislature refused to pass a civil trials bill Amalgamated backed, the company simply shut down all of its operations in the state except its newspapers, a sort of capitalist's strike. The governor, faced with a crippling of the state's economy, caved in and called a special session of the legislature, which quickly did its duty—which meant doing Amalgamated's bidding.

The company prosecuted its interests by owning the legislature and the rest of the state's politicians, as well as strategically placed judges, well into this century. The record of outright bribery is lengthy and well documented. Newspapers, and not just those in Butte, wore the Copper Collar, at least visibly and formally, until the late 1950s. Anaconda owned and operated the only daily newspapers in Butte, Missoula, Helena and Billings, four of the state's five largest cities and four of the six daily newspapers that are responsible for all of the daily circulation in the state. This situation is without precedent in American journalism. Working as a reporter in Missoula, I have worked with journalists who have worn the Copper Collar.

The railroad that drove the golden spike at Garrison, and made the transportation of copper possible, bought its ties from the timber company that would eventually belong to Anaconda Copper. The copper company held those trees until the early 1970s, when it was sold to Champion International, which we have seen was sold to Plum Creek Timber Company, the railroad's timber corporation. And when I was a reporter for a former Anaconda Company newspaper and wrote a series of stories critical of Plum Creek's and Champion's timber practices, Plum Creek executives reached an understanding, acknowledged in *Audubon* magazine, with editors of the corporation that owned my newspaper and my bosses pulled me off the story.

When the mining industry needed relaxation of clean water standards in the state in 1995, it quietly went to the legislature and got them, without a ripple, arguing it would have to otherwise shut down its mines. In that particular statehouse that is not an argument; it is an echo.

If one could see the political stream as one can see a real stream's bank, it would appear layered and folded with slickens, a landscape rebuilt with mining's residue. This river's history is summed in a single color photograph I once saw, a picture of the Clark Fork River in downtown Missoula. One is used to seeing evidence of the wholesale corruption of mining in sepias or in jerky stark newsreels from archives from the turn of the century. We believe in progress and believe these matters must be visited in history, but that modern color snapshot says this history is not deep. The river was red with metals pollution. It ran red.

There was a strike in Butte in the early 1970s, just before Anaconda left the state. The union shut down a treatment operation at Warm Springs Pond, a man-made pool designed to settle out metals in slack water near Butte, at the point where the confluence of Silver Bow Creek from Butte and Warm Springs Creek, running down from the old smelter at Anaconda, join to form the Clark Fork. With that operation shut down, which is to say, with the river running unimpeded, as it was meant to run, it sucked up enough copper-laden sediments to turn it red and it ran red as a brick 140 miles downstream to Missoula.

All of this degradation is blamed on turn-of-the-century technique. This has become the mantra of modern miners, that gold mines such as those at Lincoln cannot be held accountable for Butte, just as they claim their political machinations have nothing to do with the bribery by the Copper Kings. There are problems in mining, but technology has solved them, the miners say. Technology's alchemy turns mines to "good neighbors" just as it turns bribes into "campaign contributions." This claim ignores the fundamental reality of mining.

THE BERKELEY PIT is not a creature of jerky newsreels; like the red river, it is a thoroughly modern development. The hill that became

Berkeley Pit is known as the richest on earth and there are grounds for that boast. It has produced about $25 billion worth of copper. It accounted for about a third of the nation's copper supply—a sixth of the world's—during the first half of this century, when copper carried the electrons that turned the shafts driving the industrial age. The world's industrial economy is built on copper and steel, so it is built on a hole at Butte.

A series of holes, actually, because until the 1950s, all of the ore came up on headframes and giant pulleys that stood at the top of mine shafts and drew it all to the surface. The adits and shafts of the richest hill hummed and rocked with explosives until 1975 and by then there were 10,000 miles of shafts, stopes and tunnels tracing the richest veins, all chewed in with drilling and explosives. This history can be seen today on street corners of Butte when people routinely wish each other well with a hand signal: a vertical fist, thumb up then tapped down over the hole formed by the roll of fingers. "Tamp 'em" is the greeting that goes with this pantomime, reliving the tamping of blasting powder tight in a hole—the town's idea of well-being.

Mine shafts are not a necessary condition of mining, but of a specific part of mining. They mark mines that are particularly rich—fat, dense veins that justify the labor-intensive business of sinking shafts to especially deep veins buried under a lot of just plain dirt and rock, what miners call "overburden." One shaft at Butte is ten feet deeper than a mile. Or more often, shafts simply mark mines that are old. The decades since World War II have brought a quantum leap in industry's ability to move dirt and rock cheaply with the advent of massive electric shovels with buckets that can hold a pickup truck and with ore-hauling trucks capable of driving off laden with ninety tons of dirt. Ninety tons is a pile the size of a house. I once saw a box from one of these trucks—not the whole truck, just the dump box—being hauled down an interstate highway, which had to be closed because the box spanned both lanes.

All of this has meant it is no longer necessary to sink shafts, but easier to simply haul the overburden away. This is especially true of deposits where the richest veins have played out, but the overburden still contains small amounts of mineral, too small to be mined of its own right, but a plus on the balance sheet when one is moving the overburden anyway. The easiest pickings were gone, but the demand for copper was not, so we go to greater lengths to feed the copper into the wire that is our economy's grid of energy. Increasing price drives increasingly invasive measures. Shafts disappear into very big holes. In the 1960s and '70s, when this technology was applied to Appalachian coal mines, with considerable controversy, they became known as "strip mines," but industry prefers to euphemize the accurately implied violence by replacing this with the term "open pit."

The Berkeley Pit is a strip mine, a creature of modern technology just as computer-driven trucks and "soft" campaign contributions are. Anaconda began strip mining at Butte in 1955, and immediately a dozen old mines closed. So did much of Butte. The city's downtown was underlain with the old honeycomb of shafts and tunnels that were about to disappear into one huge hole. Writing in *Harper's* in October 1996, Butte native Edwin Dobb said of this:

> The Berkeley Pit had come into being—rather, nonbeing—an ever-expanding void on the east side of the Hill that had swallowed the Irish neighborhood known as Dublin Gulch; Meaderville, where the Italians lived; and most of Finntown; along with the sections where the Serbs, Croats, Montenegrins, and Albanians had settled; as well as the McQueen Addition, whose original residents were Austrian and Hungarian. In all, about one-third of the Hill was depopulated. Destroyed too were the Columbia Gardens, a seventy-acre refuge of shade tress, large dance pavilion, Ferris wheel, merry-go-round, and elaborate wooden roller coaster—Butte's version of Central Park and Coney Island joined together, treasured no less.

What copper gives, copper takes away, or more to the point, does not take away. Most of the stuff that was the hole was not copper. It is still here, still piled up around Butte, the issue of greatest significance for the Blackfoot and any place staring down the gaping barrel of a strip mine.

The Berkeley Pit, before ceasing operations in 1982, was the nation's largest strip mine. It is a mile wide, a half-mile long and a quarter-mile deep, numbers that only make sense standing on the edge of what is now tough, ugly Butte and staring into its incomprehensible mass of nothing. Then try to imagine all of that nothing as something stacked up in piles all around. The copper was an infinitesimal percentage of the material removed. The rest stayed. Sort of.

The biggest problem of open-pit mines is sulfide, or more to the point sulfide exposed to air and water cycles. Mineralized areas of the earth naturally contain large amounts of sulfide, and have for all time, but as long as it remains buried, it remains harmless. Exposed to the air, however, sulfides oxidize, then water—rainwater, river water, leaching aquifers—wash it from the rocks as sulfuric acid. Some of this acid simply runs off the waste rock or tailings piles like rain off a mountain, downhill to rivers where all water goes. Some of it is waylaid by intervening chemistry. Besides sulfides, waste rock and tailings contain a range of minerals, either some of the copper that escaped extraction or associated metals like lead, arsenic, cadmium and zinc. They are inert, but the acid changes that, leaching them from the rocks and adding them in various compounds—each with its own unique set of toxic implications—to the broad-based chemical soup. This too heads for rivers.

Our national consciousness of toxic chemicals formed in places like Love Canal, and we fear complicated and esoteric organic compounds, pesticides, herbicides and industrial solvents hatched from petroleum and chlorine. Yet nature, given no more help than a gaping hole in the ground and a simple sprinkle of rain, can manufacture a vicious brew no more complicated than high-school chemistry.

The problem, however, is only simple in concept, only simple on a small scale. The massive size of open-pit mines, not the chemistry, makes it intractable. Consider for a moment the very existence of the Berkeley Pit, still gaping like a newborn fifteen years after the last shovel shut down. Strip mines developed in Appalachian coal country, but the landscape is less significant to their final form than is peoplescape. The East called them strip mines because calling a thing by its name is the beginning of facing its reality. They were controversial. Not long after strip mining spread in the 1960s and '70s, there came a series of laws that forced reclamation, and reclamation meant something quite simple. When, in the words of folksinger John Prine, "The coal companies came with the world's largest shovels, and they tortured the timbers and stripped off the land," they could not simply complete the verse and forsake the land by writing it off "to the progress of man." They must fill in their holes and restore the land to its original contours. This is not complicated technology. Even house cats grant the planet this simple courtesy.

Hard-rock miners do not. The law distinguishes hard rock or mineral mining from coal mining and imposes requirements for reclamation on the latter. Hard-rock miners will proudly announce in op-ed advertisements and in panel discussions that they reclaim the land, but that generally means they shape tailings piles and seed them to grass (which won't grow because of metals in the soil). They do not fill in the holes. The reason is very simple. Mineral strip mines operate on a razor-thin profit margin, especially gold mines, for reasons we will discuss in the next chapter. It costs an enormous amount of money to fill ninety-ton truck after ninety-ton truck to dig a mile-wide hole. Refilling the hole would cost twice as much, shooting the profit margin. Collectively, the strip mines raise to all western politicians the same threat Amalgamated raised in Montana in 1903. Do it our way or we close.

This threat resonates in a thinly populated peoplescape, where, unlike the East, there are not enough people free of the mining company's direct and indirect payroll to pressure the politicians.

Significantly, a leading proponent in Congress for reform of these laws has been Rep. Nick Rayhall of Virginia, a coal mining state. Rayhall is no screaming environmentalist. He simply believes it is unfair that coal miners in his state are forced to jump through the full gamut of reclamation hoops while western miners pocket the disparity in the law.

THE GAPING HOLES REMAIN, a practice that leaves the hole, any groundwater it contains and the tailings and overburden exposed to the inexorable chemistry of oxygen and water. The toxic legacy of open-pit mines is not a function of technology, but of will. No amount of modern technology changes this elemental fact of chemistry. True enough, this acid could be neutralized, but at an enormous cost on the scale of a mile-wide hole, more cost than the copper would bring, and the companies' only mandate is to bring us copper as cheaply as possible. Given the choice of charging off some of the real costs of this copper against the future, we do so.

It is the scale of strip mining in both time and space that ratchets this simple chemistry up to astronomically devilish proportions. This emerges clearly even through the mask of terse and precise prose of a federal document prepared for the Environmental Protection Agency by ARCO, the corporation that bought the Berkeley Pit from Anaconda in 1977:

> These past mining activities and disposal practices in the Butte area have resulted in groundwater injury. Injury is demonstrated by, among other things, the fact that groundwater exceeds state and federal drinking water standards for various substances, including arsenic, copper, zinc, cadmium, sulfate and manganese.
>
> Disposal of tailings, process water, and other waste products in the Butte area also cause surface water contamination. This occurs in two ways. First, Butte Hill groundwater that is not captured by the Pit flows downgradient and discharges to Silver Bow Creek. Thus, contaminated Butte groundwater is a source of contamination for Silver Bow Creek. Second, surface runoff from tailings and waste products transports these materials directly and indirectly to Silver Bow Creek.
>
> A unit of the Silver Bow Creek/Butte Addition NPL site known as Area One demonstrates the complexities of the interactions between various resources. At Area One, buried tailings and waste products at the former site of the Parrot Smelter have contaminated groundwater, which subsequently discharges to Silver Bow Creek. At Lower Area One, tailings and waste products at the former site of the Colorado Smelter and the Butte Reduction Works are located immediately adjacent to Silver Bow Creek. Groundwater, Silver Bow Creek and waste materials are intimately [*intimately?*] related at Lower Area One, causing contaminated groundwater to become contaminated surface water. Also tailings and waste products in the floodplain are continually being rereleased to Silver Bow Creek as a result of runoff and streambank erosion.
>
> This pattern of sources releasing hazardous substances to resources, which in turn become sources that rerelease hazardous substances to other resources is typical. Indeed, this characterization depicts the Upper Clark Fork River Basin—from the upper reaches of the watershed in Butte downstream some 140 miles to Milltown reservoir.

It is as if the Berkeley Pit raised a tidal wave of toxins that has rolled over enough landscape to make a small state. Except that this analogy places the crest in our past, when really the crest is yet to come.

THE BERKELEY PIT is but the biggest hole in a hill of holes, and deep holes find water. In the beginning there was water, which had to be moved from the holes just as surely as the dirt and rock did. Water is easily moved, especially when the copper is flowing to market in sufficient quantities to pay the price of pumping, but in 1982, ARCO "closed" the Berkeley Pit and shut down the pumps.

From the hills around Butte, the pit still looks open enough; open is exactly what comes to mind when one stares across this chasm and tries to make some sort of sense of its scale, to understand that a terrace that looks the size of a stairstep on the opposite side has a run and a rise to accommodate an ore truck highway. It looks open as it must have to the geese flying by, and it is an open question.

The surrounding terrain is rolling sagebrush hills, so the lake at the bottom looks as out of place as do all thoughts of water in this arid place. Yet water is everything.

Butte trashed its water a long time ago. Underlying the entire valley is a deep-water aquifer in heavily mineralized rock, permeated again and again by the shafts designed to dig up the rock. The deep aquifer's water is laced with cadmium, lead, copper and arsenic. It's probably better off left where it is, and that would be Butte's fondest hope, long since dashed. This aquifer flows to the pit and is the biggest source of the 28 billion gallons of water that has made the pit half a lake. That and a now diverted source of polluted surface water that sent 2.5 million gallons a day into the pit.

As of 1996, the pit had become a lake 876 feet deep at its center—876 feet of water in 13 years. The EPA predicts the depth will hit the critical point, 1,147 feet, by 2021. At that level, this water that is sufficiently lethal to snuff geese will begin flowing to the surface, alluvial aquifer. Butte long ago began drawing its drinking water elsewhere, so that's not why the point is so critical. Alluvial means flow, in that this surface aquifer flows from and back to streams, part of the unseen life of a river. This means roughly 2.5 million gallons a day of miner's waste will begin flowing to the Upper Clark Fork drainage. This would be an "injury" on an unprecedented scale for a river whose precedent is built of "injury."

Given this looming deadline, the EPA has decided a treatment system will be in place by 2021, a target that breathes new meaning into the word "deadline." Nonetheless, the EPA's goal is more a profession of faith than projection in that no one has devised a method for treating 2.5 million gallons of groundwater a day. There are cost estimates of $7 to $10 billion to build such a system, which is an interesting set of figures, given that no one really knows what the system will look like. Nor does anyone have any real idea who will pay for its construction (care to guess?), not to mention its operation, projected to be necessary for as long as water flows, which, judging by past experience, is forever.

THE BACKERS of the Seven Up Pete gold mine on the Blackfoot say they will make a gift to the state. The hole they will dig there will generate a rock pile of 900 acres, just more than a square mile. The plan is to hire landscape architect Lee Anderson, who will bulldoze this rock pile (he calls it an assignment to "co-create with nature") into an "earth sculpture." In a brochure on his work, Anderson said the goal is to create "a world filled with natural beauty, peace, harmony, love, stability, abundance and prosperity." All this from a pile of rock, acid and heavy metals. There are those who might suggest taking this asset that is the pile and combining it with another asset—the hole—to put the whole business back as it was, but there's the issue of profit, not to mention depriving Anderson of his canvas.

As to the asset, the hole, the miners at nearby Lincoln are already calling it Lake McDonald and raising visions of prosperous, loving and harmonious families boating, fishing and sunning on the open pit's terraced beaches. (The vision makes no mention of fall goose hunting, but it seems a natural.) They say their pit will become a nice lake, and they will donate this lake to the state. I imagine there will be a plaque and a photo-op ribbon cutting with the governor.

On hearing this offer, one activist who has spent the better part of his career wrestling with problems flowing from the existing Lake Berkeley said, "No thanks. We've already got one of those."

WHEN CONTEMPLATING THE LANDSCAPE that holds the Berkeley Pit at its center, it is best for a second to lift one's eyes to the hills, as, no doubt, some of the people of Butte intended. To the east, the mountains rise steeply to the Continental Divide and on a ridge overlooking the pit is a curious sight in a city of odd sights. Arms outstretched as if forgiving all this—it stretches even a deity's sense of charity to believe she is blessing it—stands Our Lady of the Rockies. She is a statue of steel welded together by retired miners and such folks hereabouts, and painted blue and white and set by helicopter on a ridge above the city, lighted twenty-four hours a day and beaming like a plastic Jesus on the dashboard of the continent. That the town saw a need for a mountain-top Madonna is at first glance simply a commentary on the florid Catholicism of immigrant miners.

But where else? Where is a place more in need of forgiveness? In this sense, the Madonna is not necessary to Butte, but to the continent as a whole, perched on the Great Divide and facing west, seeing first the Berkeley Pit and then everything beyond.

Our Lady is the testimony that Butte confesses its sin and probably has much to do with why the ex-miner Jim Kuipers lives there. He says this to me not amid Butte's proletarian grit, but in a trendy little cafe in Missoula, a new hangout of the new cappuccino cowboys. He wrinkles his nose a bit and announces that the air stinks in Missoula; it gives him headaches. He's right. The air in this adopted home of glitterati does stink—Missoula lies in a bowl of mountains, and while the chamber of commerce will tell you they hold elk and deer, they also hold back cleansing winds. The air stagnates, especially now that our river valley floor is threaded with strip malls strung together by five-lane highways of Acurae and Lexi.

Warts and all, Butte is still about understanding who we are and where we came from. Like the layers of metals laid down in the watershed, mining has layered human culture, and now bits of it put down generations ago are being busted loose by shifts in the stream of public consciousness to remake the political landscape. As one might expect, much of that is simply a resurrection of poisons better off buried. Kuipers has examples. He took his training at Butte's Montana Tech, more traditionally and more accurately known as the School of Mines. Kuipers had grown up working summers in his grandfather's mine, so was born and raised to mining. The truth is, he liked the work. But he was also a bit of a hell-raiser and had spent a few years in the Southwest, where he had encountered rigid Mormon authority and the writings of Ed Abbey. Both shaped him. Montana Tech made no room for such ambiguity, and his first year there was big trouble.

"Tech only allows one attitude: that of the industry," he says. It is a state-funded machine to perpetuate the attitudes that made the Berkeley Pit, a situation that has produced one of the bigger ironies, not of Butte, but of the Seven Up Pete gold mine. Remember that the proposed mine would sit on state land near Lincoln and that state land is dedicated to raising income for schools. Over its life, the Seven Up Pete mine would pay an estimated total of $60 million to the university fund, which in a state of 800,000 people is very big money indeed. There's a quirk in the system though, in that individual parcels of state land are earmarked to raise income for particular schools. The mine's land is tied directly to Montana Tech.

In the main, on the straight line, mining perpetuates mining and that is Butte's culture, but it must be remembered that Butte and Montana Tech helped form Jim Kuipers. That's the other aspect of Butte, and the one that keeps him living there, he says. There is no bullshitting a Buttian. When the mining companies flood the state's airwaves with slick PR videos showing deer frolicking next to ore trucks and showing public officials drinking water from a mine's discharge pipe, the average Buttian knows better. He is not opposed to mining—heaven and Our Lady know—but by the same token, he is not deluded enough to believe it happens without enormous damage. Just as he carries a symbolic load of blasting powder in his hands, he carries a real load of mining's effluvia in his bloodstream. Mining is literally in a Buttian's blood; he knows it just as he knows it will likely shorten his life. Copper was enormously important, crucial to the creation of the industrial framework of this nation's economy. It was crucial enough to justify paying a price, and Butte paid it. The town knows the price of the Acura better than the guy who is driving one.

Kuipers is looking for a bit of land now, something a little remote and quiet where he can raise a garden, but he has a particular requirement. He wants to live on an abandoned mine. He wants to use what he has learned in mining to restore and resurrect a hard-used piece of land.

He is under no illusions in this, and understands full well the land will never again be pristine, maybe not even perfectly healthy, but maybe healthy enough to hold a small house for him and his wife and maybe with enough unpoisoned soil to raise his vegetables. In this fashion, he hopes to become a vanguard in a new sort of homesteading movement, a twenty-first-century pioneer.

"I'm just to the point in my life when I don't think we need another mine," he says. It seems that there is no way this notion can translate to public policy. Literally, it is impossible to decide we will not pay the price that Butte has paid.

"There is no way to say that in the United States," says Kuipers.

Understanding what he means by that and why that is true, however, requires that we now examine gold.

GOLD

I STRUGGLE not to be completely dismissive of
gold, a matter of values. The ultimate word of that
sentence generally implies ethics, preferences and
personal rules, but in fact value is most often measured by price. On this measure, there can be no
question that gold has value. That's not the argument.
The problem is, its value now must be weighed
against that which is priceless: clean rivers, peaceful
days, free thought, love. The juxtaposition jars and
jolts me to anger, even arrogance. How can you ask
me to trade clean rivers and my mountains for your
Rolex watch? I cannot imagine someone willing to
make such a trade, yet the undeniable fact is that
the trade is made daily, is made in favor of gold
more often than not, to the point that I cannot dis-
miss the bargain as aberrant, deviant and diseased.
The love of gold is not unique to our present
psychotic culture of greed, nor is it unique to the

psychotically greedy through the ages. Gold is an element of the human condition.

The cursing of rivers did not begin or end with the Pactolus; Midas has a long string of heirs, even to the Copper Kings who called on the Clark Fork to wash away their sins. The Midas story has survived across cultures and time; modern schoolkids know the story, and that is enough to make it real. It is a real story, its value assayed in time's crucible.

Midas, too, was real, as was the Pactolus River, real in immortal story, but also real in the historical sense. He was a Phrygian king ruling more than 2,500 years ago in an area eventually absorbed by Persia, as was the neighboring kingdom of Lydia, which during the same era was ruled by two other kings, Gyges and Croesus. Gyges is regarded as the first tyrant; he established control over his subjects by manipulating a gold ring that would make him either visible or invisible, as suited his purposes. The real source of his power and his place in history is encoded in this legend, in that he is credited with inventing money—the first gold coins, which were rings. Money can make goods appear and disappear, make them real or abstract. Croesus survives today in the simile "rich as Croesus."

At the bottom of all three of these guys' stories lies gold, no accident since all ruled in an area where the streams drained Mount Timolus and washed from it alluvial deposits of gold. This region of Asia Minor was where the Greeks gathered both stories and gold. Midas married a Greek. In trade for gold's eternity, the wandering Greeks gave the kings literature's eternity.

The allure of gold spans all recorded human time, but the breadth of its appeal is as impressive as its depth. It is in our time fashionable to condemn the Western culture we inherited from the gold-gathering Greeks as the source of the world's diseased greed. Against the notion, there is this: In 1963, the government of India grew tired of that nation's passion for gold that was draining currency reserves. The government decreed that jewelry's purity was to be reduced to fourteen-karat gold. There were widespread demonstrations and riots, and 100 goldsmiths committed suicide rather than work with the less pure gold.

True, there are cultures that had no ancient tradition of gold, but only a few, isolated from the mainstream. As isolation waned, the passion for gold waxed, a development that makes, not breaks, the case for the universal attachment to gold. In 1706 the Japanese finance minister petitioned the Shogun:

> A thousand years ago, gold, silver and copper were unknown in Japan, yet there was no lack of what men needed. The earth was fertile and produced the best sort of wealth. Gangin was the first prince who caused the mines to be worked diligently and during his reign so great a quantity of gold and silver were extracted from them as no one could have any conception of, and since these metals resemble the bones of the human body, inasmuch as what is once extracted from the earth is not reproduced, if the mines continue to be this worked in less than a thousand years they will be exhausted.

Since these metals were discovered the heart of man has become more and more depraved.

THE FIRST GOLD was not mined, but gathered, a skinny pebble of pure gold deposited on a gravel bar and snatched up by a passerby. Its unique properties engendered a primal fascination. It might be enough to say it was attractive, in the same visceral sense I express when I say a woman is attractive. Beyond that, there are layers of value. It is a metal that works easily, but it is not hard enough to make tools, unlike the copper and iron people were also beginning to pick up here and there. But also unlike these other metals, it doesn't tarnish. It gleams like the sun and holds its shine forever, a combination of uselessness and illusion of eternity that would naturally bind it up immediately with religion, as religion was bound up with the sun.

Gold is available on our planet almost anywhere there are mountains or folds in the earth to conduct the hot water that brings it to the surface. Gold is the burden of waters even before those waters are rivers. It exists on all five continents: In the Americas from the Yukon south through the Rocky Mountains cordillera into Mexico, in the Sierra Nevada of California, in Quebec, to a small extent in the Southeastern states, the Black Hills, the Andes and Brazil. In Europe, it's in the British

Isles, France and along the line of the Alps and the Balkans. It's in central and southern Iberia, Asiatic Russia, Anatolia, Armenia, India, Korea, China, Japan, Australia, New Zealand, South Africa and the Upper Nile.

Its ubiquity creates a cultural history that is not, to use the term in vogue, Eurocentric. We know, for instance, some details about the Incan attachment to gold, although not nearly enough. The Spanish conquistadors were more interested in collecting gold than cultural artifact. They melted most of the finely wrought sculpture to cold, hard ingots. In this fashion they took 190 tons of it from a single Incan city. It is estimated 500,000 pounds of gold flowed from the New World to Madrid. We do know, however, that gold was woven into Incan hierarchy and religion. It was said to be the tears of the divine sun and its ownership was forbidden to commoners, a practice universal enough to have a name. The British too would later have sumptuary laws forbidding commoners to wear gold. Inca, Spaniard and Brit all displayed the several facets of attachment to gold.

In her history, *The Magic of Gold*, Jenifer Marx teases out three themes, three strands that weave human culture to gold, and identifies each with a particular culture. They are religion, aesthetics and commerce. It seems to me that it is the first of these that resounds so thoroughly into the present, the strand that has ensnared the Blackfoot. In any event, though, the model is an abstraction. In reality, each of the three strands is woven together in each of the cultures, in each human for that matter; it's a useful abstraction, nonetheless.

In fact, this blending of the layers of values was common, and began early in history. The Phoenicians were skilled goldworkers and traders hired by the Hebrews to gild Solomon's temple. They tricked it out with gold right down to the nails. The Hebrews seem to have caught on, however, in that their scriptures wound up containing more than fifty references to gold. The Phoenicians traded in Transylvania, Bohemia, Africa, Iberia and Britain at a time when the height of achievement in most other cultures was herding sheep. As traders, their attachment to gold was commercial, just as they invented writing not so much for literature as for a way to write contracts and receipts. Nonetheless, common people in Phoenicia wore gold rings, chains and nose rings, so the aesthetic applied.

A blending of values occurred in all cultures, but it's helpful to consider Jenifer Marx's three pure values—religion, aesthetics and commerce—in the context of three cultures. We may begin tracing this with the religion of the Egyptians, who, like the Incas, identified gold with the divine sun. In the beginning, gold was god. The structure for this was the obelisk, towers erected in Egypt, especially at Karnak, and throughout the Middle East. In Babylonia, the obelisks became ziggurats, but the idea was the same. Obelisks and ziggurats were towers elevated over surrounding terrain and they were gold tipped. They were a link between heaven and earth. The gold gave the sun god a familiar lighting point, a sort of god decoy. They served mortals as well, giving leaders a tool to at once invoke elevation and the sun. The obelisks plugged god directly into the guy with enough power to make people build towers, the guy with the power to organize labor to his bidding.

The Egyptians established full-scale gold mining at Nubia and Kush 4,000 years ago. Notably, the mines were so far distant from Egypt on the Upper Nile that supply lines were difficult, at least for such matters as food for slaves. Accordingly, it was cheaper to work the slaves to death and catch or breed new ones than to feed them, an expedient the early miners gladly accepted to preserve the profit margin.

This need to recruit labor probably explains a prominent Judeo-Christian myth. The Babylonians' towers, the ziggurats, were broader than the obelisks and tiered. The top tier alone was tipped or coated in gold, the color of heaven. Some of these structures ran to heights of 300 feet and each of their bases were the length of a football field. Laborers to build such a structure would necessarily need to be recruited from far and wide, many nations and many languages. The Tower of Babel was a ziggurat.

The Greeks were the aesthetes of Marx's analysis. Their anthropomorphic pantheon was not so much interested in invoking the sun, and their somewhat more egalitarian political norms steered them away from amassing legions of slaves to build towers. They sought gold simply because people liked to look at it. They were fond of jewelry and traveled extensively to obtain the everlasting luster. The earliest stories of Western culture recount epic travel and much of that travel was for gold. We know this from mining methods. Lanolin, like cyanide, has a natural affinity for gold, a fact that was understood by the ancients and remembered by the more modern. The practice of capturing alluvial gold by staking sheep fleeces in gold-bearing streams survived into the nineteenth century.

Jason and his Argonauts bore a load of these golden fleeces, probably from the Caucasus Mountains beyond the eastern shore of the Black Sea. The Mycenaean Greeks gathered gold from that area 3,600 years ago and even then understood it was not all luster and beauty. Jason brought Medea back from that neighborhood, but settled later for a political marriage to the daughter of the King of Corinth. Medea sent her a gold robe that caused her flesh to melt. We can only imagine what sort of metallurgical accidents and horrors lie behind that story of melting flesh, but here's a hint from 1745 in the *English Book of Trades*, which in speaking of using mercury to process gold said this: "It is dangerous to the constitution: few guilders live long: the Fumes of the Quicksilver affecting their nerves and rendering their Lives a Burthen to them. The Trade is in a few Hands most of them Women."

Adds Marx: "The ancients knew this process caused loss of teeth and hair, tremors, mental disorientation and death."

The Romans carry the third thread of gold—their attachment to the stuff was neither religious nor aesthetic; it was almost strictly commercial. It was a medium of exchange, a way of amassing wealth. Says Marx: "The Romans did not share the superstitious regard for gold which enhanced its value for the Oriental. Nor did they have the Greek appreciation for the metal's intrinsic beauty. The pragmatic Romans adored gold, craved gold for its tangible value. With gold, power and prestige could be purchased and maintained. Roman avarice was notorious."

Marx goes on to quote a mosaic found on a cloth in a Roman merchant's shop: "Salve Lucrum." Hooray for profit. Supply-side economics has an ancient history. This thread of gold's history can be traced in the etymology of our word "crass," so useful these days.

Marcus Crassus achieved public office but was not first known as a politician. He was a fireman. He organized a fire-fighting brigade that would speed to the scene of a burning tenement and demand payment for services about to rendered. If no payment was forthcoming, he would put out the fire anyway, then claim the building as his own.

When Phelps Dodge moved into Lincoln, it donated equipment to the local fire department, so at least the methods of Crassus have undergone a certain refinement. Other methods are less evolved. Crassus bought up state-owned mining lands that Caesar denationalized, just as mining corporations today buy federal land below market prices. Rome by then had also not worked out all of the political pitfalls of campaign finance, and Crassus became Caesar's prime source of loans for bribes and public games. At one point, Caesar was into Crassus for the time's equivalent of $3 million. Never mind. Crassus had the state gold mines, and the shape of that deal has not changed in 2,000 years.

Mines, however, were not enough. Crassus invaded Parthia to steal gold. The King of Parthia captured Crassus, and had him killed by pouring molten gold down his throat, so that the story ends happily. But not—and there is ample precedent and antecedent for this—for rivers.

The Roman passion for gold was not nearly as important as their technology. Their hunger made gold scarcer, causing them to work far afield for it, just as the Phoenicians, Egyptians and Greeks had done. But no longer did they seek out surface nuggets and placer deposits. They made the curse of the Pactolus epidemic.

By the third century B.C., Roman gold mines were already plagued, like the Berkeley Pit, with seeping water. The mines at Sicily had begun to fill with water and the inventor Archimedes, known for doing most of his heavy intellectual lifting in a bathtub, invented a screw for lifting the water out of the mines. That bought some time, but only some, before the mines were used up and the Romans moved west into Spain.

By the middle of the second century B.C., southern Spain, specifically in the Guadalquivir River basin, was producing most of Rome's gold. They sunk shafts as deep as 750 feet and pumped seepage by having slaves haul the water out in tar-covered baskets. So far, minor variations on a common theme. But as B.C. rolled to A.D., the Romans invented hydraulic mining. That's a euphemistic name for the wholesale vandalizing of a landscape.

Hydraulic mining uses vast amounts of very rapidly flowing water to erode away hillsides, ridges and even whole mountains. The soil washes downstream in rivers, while the water-carved slices in the earth reveal veins and nuggets of gold. We think of landscape-altering technology as a modern twist, but it is not. The Romans deforested Spain and North Africa for lumber, and they moved mountains into the Guadalquivir River.

Marx says of this, "As early as the first century A.D. rivers carrying the wastes were clogging up at their mouths, the coast line was altered and harbors filled in completely, turning port towns into inland settlements."

The systems used as much as 800 feet of hydraulic head to undermine a mountain, allowing the mountain to simply collapse. By 79 A.D., Pliny was writing of "gold gained by the destruction of mountains."

IT IS TEMPTING NOW to conclude that the Romans and their commercialism and methods were the last word in the matter, sufficient to fast-forward us to present-day Crassi and the undermining of mountains. That is more true of method than of idea. Hydraulic mining was the driving force behind the California gold rush. The Sacramento River and San Francisco Bay would eventually come to inherit the disease that had plagued the Pactolus and Guadalquivir. The idea driving this was crass, the commercial attachment to gold, but especially toward the end of Rome's Iberian adventure, new impulses morphed out of this purely commercial attachment, bred of hard times. "As the empire slid into a morass of bankruptcy and bloodshed, gold was often the only acceptable medium of exchange," writes Marx. And now, just as the religious quest for gold marked an attempt by mortals to appropriate its eternity, chaos created a longing for the security its universal appeal could grant. Its value transcended any sanction it might gain or lose from government or fashion, and in this power, men saw a satisfaction of the longing for economic security that is every bit as powerful as the need to transcend the physical laws of death.

Although it seems the Romans were not religious in their attachment to gold, it would be wrong to think that element died with antiquity. Religion provided not only the need, but the power to build the ziggurats; religion was the power to organize labor. A tower is the physical manifestation of real hierarchy that invests a leader with both religious and political authority. Gold would stay woven into the mantle of authority, even as it changed hands among religious, political and religious-political autocrats. We can trace this by watching gold change hands; follow the money to follow power.

As power moved from priests to kings, gold moved with it, maintained as the symbol of authority, literally so in crowns and scepters, the minitowers that turned their wearers and bearers into gold-tipped ziggurats. But more interesting, as Europe's medieval era waned and power began to spread further to a rising merchant class, so did gold, and there came a sort of counterrevolution, an attempt to prevent the transfer of gold parallel to the attempt to prevent the transfer of political power. This took the form of sumptuary laws, which as we have seen even the Incas had. Throughout Europe, they were quite specific. A decree in France in 1283 forbade anyone of the middle class to wear "belts of gold, previous stones or cornals of gold and silver." In 1363, England's Edward II outlawed craftsmen and yeomen from wearing "cynture, cotel, fermaille, anel, garter, nouches, rubaignes, chenes, bendes, sealx u autres chos nor dragetnt." The same decree gave knights a bit more latitude, but they were not allowed gold or jeweled rings or brooches. In Germany, the sumptuary laws applied to esquires with land or rent of 200 Marks a year and assets of 500 pounds silver. There were separate and specific provisions for their wives and daughters. Spain kept it simple. A 1238 law said simply that only queens and princesses could wear gold or silk cloth, gold jewelry or precious stones.

The issue in all of these, of course, was not commercial; just the opposite. The laws arose from the fact the burghers were gaining the commercial power that allowed them to buy gold. The sumptuary laws were designed to prevent them from gaining that status separate from commercial success. It was an outgrowth of the religious idea that put gold and kings atop towers. Mark this idea and hold it, for along with the idea that gold is a hedge against chaos, it will come heavily into play in the 1980s and in the threat to the Blackfoot River.

THROUGH THE HISTORY of empire, through Roman to Spanish to British to American imperialism, there is an interesting pattern of former colony rising as new empire. A corollary of this seems to flow sometimes so neatly as to be not so much cart as horse. This notion can be followed in what the moderns call natural resources, trees for instance. Deforestation of the Mediterranean was carried out by seats of power. Lebanese cedars and North African forests were shipped off to build Hebrew temples. Greeks clear-cut Italy. Romans clear-cut Spain, England and even Scandinavia. Britain logged America's Atlantic seaboard to raise its navy. In the historical cases, the forays into the colonies presaged the fall of the empire, the rise of the new imperial centers in the former colonies and another run of the cycle.

Rome stripped Spain of its gold, but at the same time created a Spanish political landscape used to dealing in gold, a lust that would eventually create a Spanish monarchy tied to gold the way a junkie is tied to crack cocaine. This is the spirit that found and explored the New World, and the Spanish made absolutely no bones about it; they came for gold. It was a raid different only in scale from a heroin addict's carting off all the stereo equipment in a suburban house. This was explicit rather than implicit, stated in a proclamation the conquistadors would read to natives. They claimed all the gold, lands and people in the neighborhood as vassals to king and pope. Then the melted-down gold sailed to Spain, some of it up the mine-scarred Guadalquivir.

The 500,000 pounds of the stuff they would cart back to Spain was sufficient to tip all balances of power. It put Spain in charge of the oceans and everything else, but it was only a transfer of wealth, not its creation. It had its limitations, and once those were reached, Spain, like the golden Romans before, slipped into bankruptcy. Meanwhile, real change was coming, as it had with Rome's invention of hydraulic mining that suddenly made a lot more gold available.

THE GOLD FEVER of the Spanish left the early Americans largely uninfected, although there were exceptions: gold mines in Georgia in 1829, for instance. Largely, Americans dealt in trade in goods, such as "soft gold" (the fur trade), and with what to our modern ears is the misleading euphemism "black gold." Then the term referred not to oil but to slaves.

On January 29, 1848, James Marshall, a millworker, was going about the simple tasks of keeping a water wheel running at the confluence of the Sacramento and American rivers in California. He found a gold nugget the size of a grain of wheat, a nugget that would ruin the life of the mill owner, James Sutter. Word of the discovery leaked and his quiet piece of land at the edge of the Sierra Nevada was soon aswarm. Sutter didn't want gold; he wanted the mob gone, and he prosecuted the trespassers, a total of 17,221 squatters, demanding $25 million in compensation. A judge ruled in his favor; so a mob of 10,000 burned the court and prepared to lynch the offending judge. Gold will not be ignored.

Sutter never got his compensation and died poor, broke and broken, unable to avail himself of the cleansing powers of his own personal Pactolus, which was then being pressed into service to produce gold.

The setup on the edge of the Sierra, with abundant water and relief for hydraulic head, was ideal for a reprise of Rome's hydraulic vandalism of Spain. On one front it worked well. Between 1851 and 1855, California produced about 175,000 pounds of gold a year, peaking at around 200,000 in 1853. During the period, the Sierra Nevada's gold fields accounted for half of the world's gold production. At the gold rush's height, 120,000 people worked the hills. They built 5,000 miles of channels to move the river water that would chew away the banks of rivers to fill the banks of investors and miners. All of those fields, however, still bear the erosional scars of hydraulic mining that also filled San Francisco Bay with silt from which it and the entire Sacramento River basin have not recovered.

An enduring mental image of the nineteenth century is of the '49ers, the pick and shovel eccentrics of the California gold rush, just as our image of agriculture then is of cowboys and homesteaders. That event—which, incidentally, provoked one of the largest mass migrations in world history—was but one of a series of rushes worldwide. The century's fever began in an ancient mining region in the Urals, but there were subsequent strikes in South Africa, Australia, New Zealand, Nevada, Colorado, Idaho, South Dakota and finally the Klondike.

Gold fever pushed America's westward expansion. The most famous battle of the Indian wars, the defeat of Custer's Seventh Cavalry at the Little Bighorn in 1876, was the end of a chain of events that began with the discovery of gold in 1872 in the Black Hills. These lands had been given to the Sioux by treaty only four years before, but the treaty was gutted when gold fever pushed in prospectors, just as they had stormed Sutter's land. Not that there was much attempt to enforce it. Custer himself led the expedition that was an initial breach of the treaty lands.

Under the battles and headlines of this history, however, there was spinning a fundamental shift in the human relationship with its gold—oddly, a sort of democratization. Much of this gold was coming from lands taken from "primitive" peoples—in the United States, Africa,

New Zealand, Australia—with no history of working gold. Compared to the old world's exhausted sources, it was new gold and easy to obtain, available to every man with a mule, pick and shovel. This democratization was quickly reversed. In the period between 1850 and 1875, 89 percent of gold mined was alluvial, the surface deposits in rivers that were available to the independent prospector. As that period ended, however, the alluvial deposits had been picked over back to their sources, the rivers' headwaters. There was more gold to be had, but it would become increasingly harder to get, and mining became capital intensive. Control of the industry passed from the hands of colorful sourdoughs. These characters would survive in stories, thanks to Mark Twain's stay in Calaveras County and to Jack London's in the Yukon. The business, however, would quickly pass to oligarchs.

By 1890, the share of gold from the surface deposits had been cut in half to 45 percent. Forty-seven percent came from quartz veins, while another 8 percent came from conglomerate beds, which besides being deeply buried were low grade. Gold was becoming ever more hard to mine. South Africa, with its large holdings of conglomerate beds, now became the next hinge of development, just as Spain had been for the Romans.

If the alchemists made a mistake, it was in believing that gold could be pulled from nothing. The truth is, there was far more gold to be made by making it from next to nothing. South Africa miners, by the last quarter of the nineteenth century, must have been a terribly frustrated lot. They had lots of gold and knew it, but the deposits were so poor that they couldn't mine it profitably. By poor, they meant it took three tons of rock to produce an ounce of gold. Remember that dividing line. It will gain in significance through a modern perspective.

In 1887, alchemy occurred. Three Scottish scientists in Glasgow—John S. MacArthur and Robert and William Forest—discovered cyanide's affinity for gold and used it in combination with sodium to cheaply extract gold from low-grade deposits. South Africa was rich. In the period since that discovery until the 1980s, South Africa alone accounted for 49 percent of the world's gold. In 1971, it produced 78.2 percent of the gold mined worldwide and by the end of the period had produced 40 percent of all the gold mined in all the world back to the times the Egyptians sacrificed slaves for gold-tipped towers.

Meanwhile, the democracy of alluvial gold ended. By 1929, only 8 percent of all gold was alluvial, with 39 percent coming from gold veins and the rest, 53 percent, from conglomerate rock beds. Gold was building new towers of capital. The massively capitalized efforts relied on alchemy and economies of scale to squeeze a profit out of three tons of ore that made an ounce of gold. In extreme cases, such as in Nevada by the end of the period, mines could make a go of it on an ounce in seven tons.

Nevada's ores remained marginal as recently as the 1970s, but a set of developments since has placed it at the center of gold's new world. Even before, though, Nevada's low-grade ore could be worked because long-standing American policy meant for marginal economies to show a profit at public expense. Like Caesar, America has long been denationalizing its mines with a law subsidizing sale of public lands.

LARRY TUTTLE, a former commercial banker from Portland, Oregon, has formed a second career out of a crusade. An affable middle-aged man, he took his crusade to the highway instead of the streets, because he needs 1,872 miles of space to cover a place that has been punished by that very number. The law governing exploitation of hard-rock minerals, including gold, from all federal lands in the West is the 1872 General Mining Law. In public appearances, Tuttle has a unique way of underscoring the absurdity of the obsolete legislation; he carries a facsimile of a set of rules governing teachers' conduct, also drafted in 1872. They include requirements that teachers fill lamps and clean chimneys, carve pen nibs carefully and "after ten hours in school, the teachers may spend the remaining time reading the Bible or other good books."

The federal mining law is archaic, a bad idea now, and probably a bad idea even when it was adopted—but then it had a different goal, facing as it did a West depopulate of white faces and commerce. In some states, such as Idaho and Nevada, the public lands total nearly two-thirds of the total land area, a reserve belonging to 240 million Americans. Not all of them, however, have equal access. Mining has a unique status, above recreation, above wildlife and even above grazing and logging.

The 1872 law allows miners to explore for minerals on public lands not withdrawn for special cases such as military bases and formally designated wilderness. If they find them, they have a right to mine. They pay no royalty to the federal treasury. The law, however, goes a step further with a provision called "patenting." Once a miner strikes and works a claim for a certain time, he may buy or patent the land for five dollars an acre. The public land then becomes private and the miner may sell it as he pleases.

To a degree, this explains why Nevada could produce a profit from an ounce of gold pulled from seven tons of ore while South Africa had to work ore bodies twice that rich. But this is not the end of the story. When Nevada was doing this in the mid-1970s, the nation was producing a total of about a million troy ounces of gold a year, more than four times the annual average of the California gold rush. In a period of about a decade, U.S. production would jump by an order of magnitude to an annual total of more than forty times the gold rush years. The California gold rush was a mere blip compared to the modern rush, the one you've never heard of.

THE ROOT of the new rush was again the chemical cyanide. In 1969, the U.S. Bureau of Mines, like the Scottish chemists whose alchemy provoked a gold rush a century earlier, proposed using this reagent in a new way. Up until then, the ore had been ground to a fine powder and milled in an expensive process that required high concentrations of gold. The new idea was heap leaching, a process that had been used in copper mining since the eighteenth century, but never with gold. Low-grade ores are piled and sprinkled with a solution of cyanide. When the liquid trickles out of the pile, it carries the gold. The process is cheap and allows production from ore bodies earlier considered too poor to mine or even bother finding. This new idea played into a chain of events.

First, geologists reread the earth with eyes now attuned to low-grade deposits. They found plenty, mostly spread along the Rockies. Meanwhile, engineers perfected gargantuan trucks and shovels, a quantum leap in the efficiency of earthmoving tools. From that point on, gold would come mostly from strip mines, not adits and shafts. Technology alone, however, simply would have produced surplus and cheaper gold. There was another factor.

The pull coupled to the earthmovers' push was a bump in the price of gold that sustained itself through the 1980s, largely brought about by the Nixon administration's decision to decontrol gold and a subsequent surge in demand. The rush was on, and this becomes a story of numbers, of multiplication upon multiplication that escalated gold mining off the scale of precedent. Market and geological forces worldwide sustain the phenomenon, but its epicenter lies in the United States, particularly in Nevada.

The tenfold leap in production came in the decade that began with 1980. By 1990, 60 percent of American-mined gold came from Nevada, half of Nevada's total from a single slot in the Tuscarora and Independence mountains that was virtually untapped until 1987.

By 1990 that slot held Newmont Gold Company's South Operations, American Barrick's Goldstrike Mine and Independence Mining Company's Jerritt Canyon Mine, by then the nation's largest, fifth-largest and sixth-largest producers respectively. Barrick's operation will become the largest gold mine in the Western Hemisphere. If the county-sized area that holds the three projects were an independent nation, it would be the world's fourth-largest gold producer.

Yet the full weight of this does not become apparent until one examines another side of the equation: the low-grade ore. At some new-age mines, the invisible gold weighs in at the rate of an ounce for each sixty tons of ore, also an order of magnitude change in the profitable concentration. The miners move the weight of fifty or so automobiles to extract an amount of gold that fits neatly in a clenched fist.

To miners, that slot in Nevada is the Carlin Trend, the equivalent of the oilman's Prudhoe and the logger's Cascades. It slices through the town of Carlin, a spray of house trailers, machine shops and bars huddled on I80 in the rolling plain of sagebrush that is northern Nevada's high desert. The nearest town of any consequence is Elko, twenty interstate miles east. This highway gives the first view of the big mines; a mile north along Maggie Creek lie Newmont's digs.

Here 2,000 workers will spend $863 million to move, leach and mill 151 million tons of ore. When completed in about thirty years, just one of Newmont's three holes will measure a mile and a half long, a mile and a quarter wide and 1,755 feet deep, according to the mine's operating plan. It will not be the biggest mine of the trend, simply the beginning. The other mines roll out for twenty-five miles on the backs of the mountains that step north, the Carlin, Bullion-Monarch, Genesis, Post,

Goldstrike, Bootstrap, Dee, Rossi and Hollister. Farther north out of this main clot lies Jerritt Canyon, north as the sagebrush hills break to snowcapped peaks shouldered in larkspur, balsamroot, phlox and aspen.

Nevada's spaces being open, there is a single ridgetop in this place that offers a view of most of it. Even on a sunny spring afternoon, one has a sense here of begin transported to a planet surrendered altogether to industry. Sirens wail. Ore trucks roar. Most of the landscape—most once or still public lands—is either hole or pile, or lakes of cyanide wash. The adjacent unmined hills are woven with roads and cratered with the pads of exploration drills. Trucks with dump boxes wider than a street are barely discernible specks building new mountains on the new horizon.

The environmental activists and the regulators have at least come to agree with the miners on one issue: Almost no one thinks cyanide is the biggest problem. Not that the handling of one of nature's more lethal compounds is without potential and proven difficulties. "State-of-the art" leach pads almost always leak. Cyanide-contaminated waste ponds look like lakes to wildfowl, which have been poisoned by the thousands. But ponds can be covered by nets and spilled cyanide is relatively easy to neutralize. By focusing on the toxicity of cyanide, environmentalists have been distracted from the scale that cyanide allows, a scale that by its size also produces a laundry list of troubles.

There are problems simply social. During the five years beginning in 1987, Elko roughly doubled. It has more brothels (legal) than book-stores. It needed a new jail, and county officials now can predict when it will periodically overflow, based on which contractor is working in the mines. The Humboldt River that bisects the town also is demarcation for a swelling sea of mobile homes on one side of the river and a corre-sponding swell of upscale tract housing on the other. There is a standing citizens' committee on domestic violence where there was none before. The surrounding desert is netted with the new trails of dirt bikes and dune buggies.

There are 43 million ounces of gold reserves among the three largest mines, at present worth about $15 billion. Mining in Elko's immediate area produces 4,000 jobs directly and another 10,000 indirectly—this in a town of 30,000 people. Mine wages are the highest in the state. All this makes for a political gorilla that sleeps where it wishes.

In this context of political power, people in Elko usually mention the flap about the northern goshawk. Some of the bird's best aspen-grove habitat stood in the path of a mine's plan just when the federal government considered listing it as a sensitive species. All hell broke loose, with hell orchestrated by the Elko County Commissioners. The commissioners formally and publicly lobbied for firing any state official who agreed with protecting the bird. The local paper called for a "depredation hunt" on the state board whose sin it was to a hire a director who agreed with the federal government as to the bird's status.

"This is the most confrontational place I have ever been," says Steve Anderson, a wildlife biologist with the Humboldt National Forest. He also has stood service in the spotted owl country of the Pacific Northwest.

"It's an ugly bunch of people with ugly motives and not a lot of intelligence," says Robert McGinty, a schoolteacher, describing a county land-use board on which he serves. McGinty also is a member of the grassroots environmental group known informally as the "Elko County Subversives." Their meetings convene at a local casino and draw crowds that would comfortably fit around a blackjack table downstairs. Most of the members are either current or retired agency biologists sharing notes.

Merlin McColm, a retired state wildlife biologist, now chief subversive, says this group, maybe twenty at best, is the sum total of the environmental movement in northeastern Nevada. The group is simply too overwhelmed by the mines to do much about them. The mines have all the power, almost literally so. At full roar, the Carlin Trend mines will use about 250 megawatts of generating capacity, the size of a middling coal-fired plant and about 75 percent of all power used in the northeast corner of the state.

Yet when one speaks to the regulators and activists of these issues, they acknowledge them as problems but move quickly to what they hold as the real damage: disturbance of rock and water.

CAROL EVANS, a BLM wildlife biologist in Elko, bounces a four-wheel-drive pickup across a sagebrush desert miles from the mines visiting streams she knows well, fingers of streams insignificant by anything but desert standards, but here oases. Toro, Beaver, Coyote, Jacks and Little Jacks creeks hold a good chunk of the world's remaining habitat for

Lahontan cutthroat trout, a threatened species and desert resident by quirk of hydrology. Once creatures of the ancient Lake Lahontan, they inhabit what is left of it, streams and seeps that break the desert's surface.

Until now, Evans's war has been with backward ranchers who poisoned the protecting willows of these streams and grazed them to sterile ditches. Inching her way politically and bureaucratically, she has revived some streams. Grazing has been fenced to the uplands. Miners have given money, equipment and time. Mining executives and workers have ridden buses down desert two-tracks to spend weekends spudding in cottonwood and willow seedlings. Schoolkids have helped, and in this corner of the desert there are signs of resurrection. The work goes on, even though Evans knows many of the best stretches of these streams and the springs that feed them soon will be pumped dry, reversing her efforts.

Carlin holds the largest dewatering project in the world. To dig their holes the miners must pump the groundwater not only from their holes, but from the surrounding area, simply because water seeks its own level. The pool of groundwater will not be neatly sluiced by the walls of the pit, so to pump the pit dry, they must pump the aquifer dry. The pumped-out area is called, without a hint of irony, the "cone of depression." Around Carlin, this area will eventually cover some 400 square miles, a potential drying of streams and seeps in an area roughly the equivalent of that enclosed by the Washington, D.C., beltway. The pumping will discharge enough water into the Humboldt River to feed a large city, already about 100,000 gallons per minute. The power bill for pumping at one mine is $1 million a month.

When pumping stops in perhaps fifteen years, the water table will return to "near normal" within a century, according to a computer model. The problem is, the model is wrong. The model predicted that in 1993, two years into actual pumping, the average rate would be 10,330 gallons per minute from Barrick's Goldstrike, yet actual practice produced 60,000 gallons per minute.

This six-fold discrepancy, however, did not stop the BLM from pressing full speed ahead on approval of yet another adjacent project, also for Barrick, a mine where dewatering was based on the same leaky model. Further, an environmental assessment for the new mine said its dewatering issues would be covered by the existing pit, despite the fact the new mine was more than 500 feet deeper into ground and ground-water than the existing pit.

Officially, the BLM's response to this hole in its reasoning was a pledge to reexamine dewatering later, meanwhile proceeding with the new mine. Unofficially, a BLM staffer said in a memo to a third party, which he eventually gave to me, that the procedure "is incorrect at best and at worst an active distortion of the truth," largely because the mines' potential to desiccate Lahontan cutthroat habitat remains unassessed in the official environmental assessment.

The general lesson in this is not so much the BLM's malleability in the face of multibillion-dollar gold mines, although there is that factor. There is a larger problem. Who can blame public officials for not examining every environmental consequence when they are ultimately of no legal consequence? The 1872 law leaves a legacy in which the setting of public policy is not a weighing of the environmental costs against the social value of the gold. The decision to mine belongs to the miners and is based simply on geology and profit. Even if dewatering would be ten times that predicted, the mine would go on.

"As an agency we are in a somewhat difficult position," says Gary Back, a BLM biologist. "We've got the mining law to live with until or if it is changed. That gives the mines the legal right to be out there and extract minerals. My job as a biologist . . . is helping them get the minerals out with the least amount of disturbance."

LIKE BUTTIANS, we are all coming to realize that mining, the simple act of digging a hole in the ground, comes with a cost. Heap-leach mining has done much to spread that realization, in that it is a realization of Midas's wish. Because it works such fabulously low concentrations of ore, the process brings gold from most anything. The invisible gold is everywhere, to the point that whatever we touch turns gold. Now, the locations of mines are determined not so much by the presence of gold, but by the presence of cheap power and malleable environmental regulators. Yet we are reminded there is a demand for this gold, just as there was with the copper, and we are told "demand" is a synonym for "need."

The uses of gold in the manufacture of electronics is slight and could easily be satisfied with the gold hoarded in vaults and central banks. Fort Knox once stored thirty years' worth of U.S. gold production. Unlike any other commodity, gold is eternal. All that has been mined in all history is still with us. As late as 1960, 70 percent of the world's total stock of gold rested in vaults in the United States. During the buildup to World War II, France sold some of its hoarded gold to the United States. It arrived still in the wrappers the United States had put on when it shipped the gold to France to pay for the Louisiana Purchase. Says Robert Triffin of Yale: "Nobody could ever have conceived of a more absurd waste of human resources than to dig gold in the distant corners of the earth for the sole purpose of transporting it and reburying it in other deep holes, especially excavated to receive it and heavily guarded to protect it."

To a degree, this dominance of hoarded gold has shifted, and no one should be comforted by this shift. In 1992, 2,300 metric tons of gold, slightly more than was mined worldwide during that same year, went to jewelry, continuing the trend of brisk demand for jewelry that built through the past decade. In every year since 1989, annual consumption of jewelry has outstripped annual worldwide mine production.

"Nineteen ninety-two was an outstanding year for gold jewelry in the U.S. In a year beset by the lingering effects of a protracted recession, sales of gold jewelry rose 5 percent, reaching 9 billion dollars," said an annual report of the World Gold Council. It is an echo of the reports through those years of gold rush, the same years when the nation spread the gap between the rich and the poor.

"The market for 18 karat watches flourished in the 1980s, spurred by their image as symbols of achievement," enthused one jewelry industry publication.

"Jewelry fabrication has grown by more than sixty percent over the past five years," said Newmont's chief, Gordon K. Parker, in a 1992 speech. "We see gold demand improving steadily as long as increasing world prosperity is translated into growing demand for jewelry."

What really dug the holes in Nevada and in Colorado, Washington, Oregon, Idaho, California, Montana and soon on Montana's Blackfoot was a shift in ideas. During the Reagan years, greed again became legitimate, even fashionable. Greed, cloaked in the gilt of supply-side economics, allowed us to mark status with gold. In the film *Glengarry Glen Ross* there is a scene where the actor Alec Baldwin is spurring on a group of high-pressure salesmen in his charge. One of the salesmen questions his authority and Baldwin responds by ripping a gold watch off his wrist.

"You see this watch. This watch cost more than your car. That's who I am. You're nothing," he says.

The lines could just as well have been delivered from atop a ziggurat.

THE UNITED STATES WAS the leading consumer of gold jewelry until the early 1990s when that title slipped quietly to the Chinese. The shift was the measure of the expansion of a Chinese middle class, still relatively small as a percentage of the population, but given the enormous population, large enough to yield a supply of cash with enough clout to chase gold. To be sure, this trend is rippling though world commodity markets—not just jewelry stores. That same middle class, for instance, has begun eating more meat, mirroring the wasteful eating habits of Americans. (It takes about ten times as much grain to produce a calorie of meat as it does to eat the grain directly.) That shift in preference has sent world food experts back to their calculators to redraw the forecast of the world food supply, and it is becoming clear that supplying the grain to feed Chinese (and American) meat will deplete reserves for feeding people elsewhere.

The relationship between starving millions and the hoarded gold bars of a few is more than irony. The Chinese, and Asians in general, have their own long history with gold. China has its own sources and has worked them as long as the West has, although the modern gold rush has placed new strains on those deposits similar to those in the United States. Despite the Chinese government's best efforts, the nation's poor have flocked to the upper reaches of the Yellow River to illegally mine gold, spawning a marked increase in erosion and associated problems with working placer deposits.

Gold mining has taken on a new urgency in Asia, particularly in China, Hong Kong and Taiwan. The Chinese are indeed buying jewelry, but not primarily for aesthetics. Much of what they buy is uniform beads and chains, not highly worked craft, but simply a convenient medium for storing and transporting gold. They are buying gold to hide, not display wealth, and we have known since Gyges that gold has this power. When governments and currency collapse, gold will be there, portable and solid enough to be liquid.

JIM KUIPERS, the miner turned environmentalist, has steered our conversation off in another direction, working a vein that has always seemed odd to people not in the business. The gargantuan heap-leach operations such as the one planned at Lincoln have always seemed to be marginal investments. Consider for a second that a requirement that the strip miners fill in the hole behind them would pull all the profit out of the job. Cost constraints show on an even finer scale. A BLM engineer once told me that miners lay out their projects so the trucks hauling ore travel downhill while loaded, uphill empty. Any requirement by regulators, for whatever reason, that they reverse that order would mean the trucks would use enough extra fuel to push the project into the red.

This, says Kuipers, is why some operations are so notoriously filthy. They are ducking the costs of environmental regulation, or attempting to pass those costs to the future. He believes there are heap-leach operations that have never shown a profit, or only shown a paper profit, a defrauding of stockholders by management, as well as a defrauding of the land.

All of the heap-leach mines are enormously sensitive to the price of gold, and many have sets of contingency plans based on the price fluctuations during the decades-long life of the mine. If it stays below $400 an ounce, the hole will be only so big, but above $480 and the hole will expand to include another somewhat more meager ore body. Every operation cuts as closely as possible to the margin; the new mines work deposits that have been known for a long time and have been allowed to sit until a price rise makes them possible. This is why the personal decision to buy gold becomes crucial. That demand pushes the price up, and a few dollars' increase in the price of gold brings planned mines on line. A boycott seems in order, but then the miners aren't necessarily betting on your consumption.

Kuipers believes many mines are being developed today betting on what is to come. As they stand and as the price of gold stands, they are not profitable. But if the price rises, the development work is done, the hole is in and the mine is ready to make money. If the price rises.

"They are betting," says Kuipers, "on chaos."

I CAUGHT UP with Phil Hocker at a mall in St. Louis. Not that he's a mall rat with an affinity for the heartland. It's just that is where the convention of environmental journalists happened to be, a juxtaposition of facts that proves the supply of irony is unlimited.

As malls go, it is at least an interesting one, the city's old and cavernous Union Station, ornate vaulted ceilings, train rooms and all now converted to hold Body Shops, Nature Companys and a Hooters. It sits a few blocks from the Mississippi River in this town where Lewis and Clark began laying the groundwork for Manifest Destiny, but the railroad motif reminds one quickly that the heavy lifting of the work they started was done by steel rails, much of it from this station.

Hocker and I sit under the vaulted ceiling in a quiet lounge that overlooks the fields of retail consumption below. He is quick and ebullient as usual, with the on-task string of patter, the suit and the satchel of studies and pamphlets that mark the inside-the-beltway man-with-a-mission. Hocker still bristles at being pegged as a Washington operator. He snatches his wallet and from it a Wyoming driver's license, long since expired, but he doesn't have the heart to renew it in D.C. His heart's in the West but the federal law that so pisses him off must be rewritten, and that is Washington work.

Hocker trained as an architect at Princeton and Harvard then did some work designing oilfields in Alaska in the 1970s. Shortly thereafter he surfaced as a fly in the oilmen's ointment. He was a plaintiff in a lawsuit against offshore oil and gas leasing and eventually lobbied in the campaign for new federal legislation on that front. Then he switched his focus to mining.

In 1987, Hocker left Jackson Hole, Wyoming, for the District to found the Mineral Policy Center, an organization that has allied with a series of environmental groups to run point on reform of the nation's mining laws, particularly the 1872 Mining Law. His first ally in this was former Secretary of Interior Stewart Udall, who is still in the fight, still on the organization's board. Udall's involvement tells much about the long, twisted struggle for repeal of 1872, an action that most people initially think ought to be a no-brainer. Most people have thought that for at least twenty-five years, but the law is still with us. The net result of the battle, other than stalemate on repeal itself, is that we are actually worse off than before.

The drive for reform began during the Nixon administration, and in fact, then Secretary of Interior Rogers Morton testified in favor of repeal. Even the industry then accepted more stringent provisions than the miners will accept now. All of this evolved in an atmosphere of bipartisanship, when environmentalism had not yet become a wedge issue.

Not that the industry was leaning into reform. It in fact picked out a pressure point in Congress, a man who happened to be running for president, chairman of the Interior Committee and an Arizona politician, a westerner with ties to Arizona's copper heritage in general and in particular, a longstanding tie to the copper giant Phelps Dodge. That corporation is to Arizona what Anaconda is to Montana. The uneasy fact of all this is that Morris Udall caved in. He said simply and bluntly there would be no mining reform as long as he sat in the chairman's seat, and it died.

Then Morris Udall faded, and his brother Stewart believes there is unfinished family business.

Morris Udall's replacement upon his retirement was George Miller, a feisty Calfornian and friend of the environment. Miller put reform back on the agenda, and it heated up in 1986 when the Reagan administration allowed patenting 86,000 acres of public lands as oil shale leases for $2.50 an acre. You remember oil shale, the supposed answer to the nation's energy needs? The technology has generally gone the way of cold fusion and perpetual motion machines, but it turns out there was money to be made in oil shale. Those lands patented for $2.50 an acre were sold at $2,000 an acre. The general mining law allowed that and still does.

Meanwhile, Nick Rayhall from West Virginia weighed in to the battle. Hocker took Rayhall on a flyover of Golden Sunlight, an open-pit gold mine in Montana, and the representative from the coal strip-mine state said that if his miners did such a thing "they would be thrown in jail." He sponsored a bill, and the industry mounted a silent campaign to defeat it. Industry representatives often say that reformers are trying to kill hard-rock mining on all federal lands, an accusation born not of fact, but of a poll. The American Mining Congress found in its polling that when asked whether the law should be changed to require royalties and reclamation, the public sided with reformers eight to one. When the question was recooked with the assertion that reformers want "to stop mining on federal lands," the balance tipped slightly toward the miners.

The industry has given itself to publicly asserting that reform will kill all mining—which is a lie—and to privately leaning on selected targets.

"They are going to companies like DuPont and Caterpillar that sell stuff to the mining industry, and they are saying if you want to keep on selling stuff to us you need to join us in fighting this," Hocker says. So Caterpillar and DuPont go to their home-state delegations and political levers reach nationwide, spreading clout beyond western delegations.

Reform passed the House in 1993 and got beat in the Senate in 1994. The western senators came through, with Larry Craig—a rock-ribbed Republican from the mining state of Idaho—carrying the day for the industry, water he would continue to carry. Congress did, meanwhile, pass a temporary moratorium on the patenting of lands, pending reform legislation. The gambit then became one of sham reform; that is, Craig would introduce bills with grandiose titles like "The Mining Law Reform Act of 1995," which in headlines set royalties, but in the fine print set amounts at next to nothing and continued all of the more egregious provisions of 1872. That 1995 bill failed, but the industry had Craig push it as a rider to an appropriations bill in 1996 that died in the budget fight with the Clinton administration. At this writing, the stalemate remains. Save the moratorium, we are legally where we were in 1872.

A recent case can underscore the hopelessness of that position. It is especially appropriate because this one was a victory, albeit Pyrrhic, for the reformers. Yellowstone National Park was threatened with a mine, Crown Butte. The sensitive location quickly put the issue in the national spotlight, even leading to a series of Pulitzer Prize–winning editorials in the *New York Times* against the mine.

During the 1996 campaign, President Clinton traveled to Yellowstone to formally announce a deal to stop the mine, and some of those (but not all) doing the cheering quickly overlooked the fact it was an election year deal, on which some of the finer points were to be negotiated after the election. Because they had a legitimate mining claim under 1872, the miners, a Canadian corporation, couldn't simply be told "no." They had to be bought off, and Clinton agreed to do so with a trade of $65 million in U.S. assets. The government began casting about for lands to satisfy that deal, meaning Crown Butte will either get cash outright, or new land to press its extortionist's threat to mine.

Meanwhile, Plum Creek Timber, at the request of Montana's governor, has prepared a list of $20 million worth of Forest Service timbered lands, and says it would be glad to pony up the cash in trade for the land. How many such victories can we stand?

The legacy of that law can be measured—in dollars, acres, miles, pH, parts per million or per thousand—in arsenic, asbestos, cadmium, copper, cyanide, iron, lead, mercury, sulfur and zinc. There is not a firm count, but there are an estimated 557,650 abandoned mines scattered over 32 states, together accounting for 50 billion tons of untreated waste rocks. Mine wastes have polluted 180,000 acres of lakes and reservoirs and 12,000 miles of streams. In many cases, the pollution is not over, but will continue virtually forever. There is no money for cleanup, money that mining law reform was supposed to provide.

Obviously, some sites are worse than others, but the worst sites are the best known. Hocker says there are fifty of those, ranked "worst" simply because they are federal Superfund sites. Cleanup of those alone would cost between $12 and $17.5 billion.

There is, however, a cultural side to this legacy that is unmeasurable, the hardest issue to get at, but perhaps the most sobering from our point of view. There is an attitude of "rape and run" buried in these numbers, an attitude legitimized by antiquated laws.

Unlike many activists, Hocker does not vent his bile against the people who have done this. He will speak harshly of some miners, but is just as likely to turn around and speak well of other individuals in the industry.

"I speed too when there are no cops around," he says. And there are no cops around mines. The mines and the Superfund sites are not all on federal public lands, so not all our problems would be solved with repeal of the law. In my selfish case, for instance—the mine on the Blackfoot—1872 does not apply at all. The mine is wholly on state and private lands, but Hocker argues that the law is indeed relevant to all mining. It is the overarching attitude, the law relevant to most of the mines and the codification of the national disease that evolved from Manifest Destiny. It has created in turn a diseased culture of mining.

HOCKER AND I finish our talk. I walk out of the lounge into the maw of the train-station mall. It is packed on a Friday afternoon, and the crowds rush in, flush with the promise of practicing the national religion. I notice a group of kids being somewhat restrained by a dad. They are bouncing off the walls, the sort of excitement I remember when I was finally turned out of doors at their age. If, as Hocker suggests, culture counts, then what is all around me is really the story.

The crowds weave through the shops, and I walk with them. Finally I notice a shop called Union Gold specializing in ten- and fourteen-karat jewelry.

I am a long way from my river. It heads from the Great Divide west and I have headed from the Great Divide east, down the Missouri to where it joins the Mississippi a few blocks away. My river does not end here, but as crowds weave around me, I have the distinct sense it does.

HOLE IN THE HEART

WINTER HAS FALLEN since I was last here. The mountain that was then wrapped in bunchgrasses and deer is shrouded now in thick snow. Cold has persuaded a force as restless as the water cycle to sit still for a few months. Water that was and will be rivers pauses, suspended on hillsides. It is the season of rivers' resting. Down the slope of this hill lie two threads of river, to the south the Blackfoot and to the west the Landers Fork about to join the Blackfoot. Just creeks year round, they are mere trickles through the snow now, a slack-season crew of waters mustered from groundwater, seeps and secret springs. On the surface, everything waits as snow, gathering power from mass that gravity and warmth will launch as whitewater worthy of rafts, but later, come spring.

Winter of 1996 has begun. On this November hill, all animate beings seem to have taken their model from water, as surely they must. The life of

this place is gone or asleep or simply lulled to quiet by the tyrannical demands to conserve calories. Even my boot steps that only a couple of
months ago rang out on rock and snapped on summer's brush, fall now
as whispers among winter's stealth. I feel like a trespasser, a noisy human
unfit for silence.

Legally and technically, I am a trespasser. This is the place where the
mine will be. Technically it is state land. Because I am a Montanan, it is
my land. Phelps Dodge, the old mining corporation constituted here as
Seven Up Pete Joint Venture, does not yet have the state's permission to
mine this land; the company has only asked permission. That is enough.
The company controls the place, a temporary lease granted to allow exploration. I have no right to walk here. In the real world of mining, finding gold grants rights. Gold grants. All other legal formalities that follow
are just that.

It turns out I have a small part to play as a writer in this business of
formalities. It is my job, according to the established ritual of my craft,
to inform the public. That is, I am to look up the opponents of the mine
and write down their criticisms, and I am to look up the miners and
record their views, or rather, what they and their public relations consultants will represent as their views, all seamlessly passed on to you, so
that you can render an informed judgment. Only it turns out that Phelps
Dodge does not wish to play. That's why I'm in trespass. It turns out that
I don't want to play either.

I have made the requisite telephone calls to the miners' local mouth-
pieces requesting interviews and tours. Requesting to sit down over a
cup of coffee to press my request for a tour. Faxes requesting permission
to accompany other groups scheduled to tour the site. "We'll get back to
you." They never did. I did get one answer. I called a state regulator asking to be allowed to accompany a group of Salish and Kootenai tribal officials touring the site. I got a return telephone call not from the state
regulator, but from the company, denying the request. In all this, I was
not being singled out. In the summer of 1996, a group of journalists
from throughout the nation visiting the area under the auspices of the
University of Montana had been scheduled to tour the site. Phelps
Dodge had agreed. And then canceled at the last minute when it found
out the journalists would also hear from opponents of the mine.

None of this surprises or even disappoints me. Like the miners, I am tired of this game too. I haven't the slightest interest in providing balance to this story. Their plans for this place are on the record, filed with the state in maps, charts and drawings. They intend to dig a big hole here. Beyond that, there's not a great deal more that needs to be said, or permission from them that needs to be obtained. I don't want to talk to them, because they are evil. I prefer trespass. This is still Montana, and I'll walk the hills as I please.

THE SNOW IS FRESH AND EARLY, the result of a collision between an early Arctic cold snap blown down out of Alberta and a nation-sized wall of water-laden Pacific air. The storm blew in on a wind that I listened to all the night before because it demanded attention, moaning and roaring a promise that it carried weather no one had ever seen before. It must have carried out the promise elsewhere, because the result here was familiar. Two feet of powder fell overnight. Highway crews have cut a path, but still have not dug out pullouts and turnouts, and I get my little car stuck trying to find a place to pull off the road. Logging trucks and wheat trucks roar by, pressing toward port and mill. I abandon the car and begin walking though snow on what was last summer a blacktop road. Nearby, maybe under the snow and blacktop, lies the trail Meriwether Lewis took across the Divide.

A quarter-mile up the road, there is a set of deer tracks cutting across the road and into the ditch then a belly-flop mark where the deer hit bottom. I can't resist cutting off on the deer's trail to flop and hit bottom myself, drawn for a second by the childish illusion that flopping in snow is fun and must have been fun for the deer. Snow is work. Water is power, and it takes all I have to counter it, now bushwhacking, postholing my way up the ridge recorded in Lewis's journal. My gaitered, wooled legs poke through the powder with satisfying whumps (maybe just a little fun) and I unzip vents in my parka, meeting the power of the place with calories, as the deer did.

The writer now, I am using the snow here to cover this hill in the illusion of quiet and peace. The peace is ephemeral. Since we were last here I have taken you far away in time and place, down other rivers. While we were gone, time has passed, and during that time the people who think about this place have not been idle. They have been laying plans. Downslope toward the highway, a power line stilts on across the ridge, heading to cities, to seats of real power. The snow is ephemeral. The power line persists.

I remember now that my original plan was to counter problems of trespass by carrying a rifle. It is hunting season, and a man walking up a mountainside carrying a rifle would not be given a second thought, while one carrying a notebook might be. That was the face on my reasoning. Behind it lay the comfort of power. I am not at all immune to the gun-equals-power equation factored so deeply into our culture. I like the explosive burst of violence from the clean firing of a 30.06, 2,900 foot-pounds of energy at its muzzle, delivered within a two-inch circle at 300 yards. Here, though, even such definite and sure force is an illusion, so I left the rifle home.

I POSTHOLE ON UP the ridge to a vantage, turn and fall backward, confident the snow will catch me like the arms of a father. Water holds me up and I sit, easy-chair style. I am sitting somewhere over what will become the pit, the hole, which means I am sitting directly on $1.6 billion worth of gold. There is no evidence of gold. This seat only feels like snow. Snow on top of a mountain. Humans have always drawn comfort and a sense of security from sitting atop mountains. Our proverbs are full of the fact that mountains do not move, but sitting here, I need no proverbs to remind me of this. The substance of the perch seems to anchor at the earth's core, in turn anchoring me centered in this slice of world.

From here, I command a view of a small valley. Behind me, the ridge climbs away toward the Great Divide, a gentle roll set now mostly in snow. Tips of sagebrush, sprays of dried bunchgrass (mostly rough fescue) and last summer's browned yarrow poke from the blanket. There are lodgepole, fir, a few histrionic ponderosa pine and clumps of quaking aspen. To my right, the west, runs the terraced floodplain of the Landers Fork. Straight ahead, a few hundred yards below my perch, the ridge peters out on the broad, flat valley of the Blackfoot. I can see the river, maybe a mile away, a thin line demarking the opposite edge of a broad sagebrush plain. At the toe of the ridge, a two-lane highway marks the plain's other border, parallel to the river. The two lines and the plain itself run on east as far as I can see, maybe five miles. To the south again, just beyond the Blackfoot, mountains begin again, defining the south edge of the valley, so the whole scene is a bowl big enough to hold a small city, but holding now only a highway, a power line, a deserted campground, a few jack fences, and everything else pretty much as Lewis and Clark found it. It seems primeval in winter under a fresh, clean cover of snow.

It only seems so. If my eyes could see heavy metals pollution, then the river slit in the snow a mile off would glow with alarm. Just upstream on the Blackfoot, still within sight, a tributary of the creek enters— Mike Horse Creek. If the name rings a bell, it is because the Mike Horse gold mine serves as a sort of poster child for the hard-rock mine cleanup nationwide. The Mike Horse, about ten miles from the site as the crow flies, was the largest of a series of gold, silver, copper, zinc and lead mines that cover a small valley now called the Upper Blackfoot Mining Complex. It earned such an ominous name through a certain fame among water quality regulators, simply because it is such a mess. The Mike Horse is the worst mine of the bunch. It was started in 1898 as a silver, lead and zinc mine. Anaconda Company pressed it into full-scale production, especially in the buildup to World War II, producing primarily copper and lead, but gold and silver in the bargain. It was not a strip mine, but an old-fashioned array of adits and shafts.

In 1975, spring runoff swamped a tailings dam. The dam was repaired, but that deluge and the accumulation of heavy metals and acid drainage still give the site the photogenic quality that has brought it national attention. Its most famous photo shows a trickle of water downstream of the mine that is an impressive and otherworldly array of colors—yellows and browns, gurgling over rocks.

In 1991, a group of biologists completed a study of the Blackfoot that found evidence of heavy metals pollution—especially in the upstream reaches from the Mike Horse on down to the town of Lincoln— but also evidence of heavy metals like cadmium, copper, lead and zinc as well as sulfates along the entire length of the Blackfoot. Don Peters, a state fisheries biologist and one of the authors of the study printed in the *Canadian Journal of Fisheries and Aquatic Sciences*, said despite its relatively brief history and the small portion of the watershed's land base used, mining is still the biggest problem for the life of the Blackfoot. That's resulting from the old mines, which are the little mines.

The Mike Horse is a piddling hole in the ground compared to Phelps Dodge's plans for the McDonald site. Understanding this idea of relative size—of scale—is crucial to this place where I am sitting. We can begin to comprehend this by thinking about energy, the simple energy that pulled me up the hill. Nothing complex, not the informed, elegant organized energy, the sophistication that runs sun energy through evolution and chlorophyll to make the lodgepole pine poking from the snow over there. Just brute force. The trick here now is to grasp the concept of the energy of gravity and water then try to expand that understanding across the space of the hill. Maybe even throw a third axis into our calculation. Walk up the hill. Now run. The difference is speed, or time. Mass, distance, time. It's all very simple really, and we can wrap our brain around it easily. To a point. Yet this place takes us past the point. Like the deep time of evolution, the infinity of stars and the infinitesimality of quarks, the scale loses us. That's what this snowbound trip is all about, about scale.

It is not an unusual problem for those of us who write about the West. All the years I have lived and walked in it, written about it, tried to communicate the feel of the place, the scale defeats me. Always I find myself like the tourist getting the film back from his first western vacation, trying to understand how the camera made the mountains small. Yet always this puny feeling came from the place's natural physiognomy. Open-pit gold mining is the only enterprise I know of that matches the scale of nature here.

I HAVE COME to this hill to try to force my mind to envision this plan for a mine. In front of me in my snow chair, pinned from the wind between my fanny pack and my binoculars, is a straightforward drawing of the proposal. My car is parked at the point in the lower left corner of the map marked "power sub-station." It has taken me a half hour to walk from there across "Rock Pile Site D" to what I think is the edge of the "McDonald Open Pit." Were you in a light airplane flying over at such a height to give you the same field of view the map has, you probably couldn't see me, even though I am wearing a fire-engine-red parka. You would have some difficulty making out my car. Refer to the scale. The mine site is 5,400 acres, nearly eight square miles, more than half the area of Manhattan.

Think of a gravel pile half the size of Manhattan, and you begin to get the idea of an open-pit, heap-leach mine. I have just spent maybe half an hour huffing and puffing up a mountain that would no longer be a mountain. It would be a hole. Gold mining is about taking mountains apart, one of the most difficult ideas for me to imagine on this perch that seems irrevocably rooted to the Earth's center. All of my huffing and puffing barely brings me to the edge of the hole, just at its lip. Were I to walk across it to the hole's opposite edge, postholing in this snow, it would take easily another half hour.

Repeating this walk in the future, however, would not be a flat stroll from my car to the hole. On its east edge, the pit would be flanked by piles of rock labeled E and D on the map. That is to say, the mountain would not disappear, but simply move. These two piles are what is known as waste rock, rock that contains no gold and must be stripped off to get to the gold-bearing rock below. In this mine's case, most of the rock is waste. The potential hole beneath me contains 980 million tons of rock, a number that is itself hard to get ahold of. Imagine a freight train 100 cars long, each car fully loaded with rock. It would take 13,000 such trains to empty this hole.

About 575 million tons, or two-thirds of the total, contains no gold and would be simply piled up as rock piles E and D, from which one would look straight down onto the Landers Fork. These new mountains would be as high as thirty-story buildings of heavily mineralized soil. No gold, but therein are the sulfides and metals that have created acid mine wastes and pollution in all of the mined streams of the West.

I SURVEY a peaceful scene, or have described it as such. By urban standards it is. But every now and again the peace is broken by a truck pulling the straightaway through the valley below, gearing down for the climb through the Great Divide at Rogers Pass. The roar is the single greatest disturbance of this fine winter morning. That last truck used maybe two-tenths of a gallon of diesel fuel crossing our view, and that number gives us a handle on the future of this place. The busted-up buttes that stand over the pit will be covered with monstrous front-end loaders that snatch 23 cubic yards at a time. The rock and ore will be hauled away in a fleet of 25 190-ton trucks. The mine's fleet of trucks will use 7.6 million gallons of fuel a year, 20,896 gallons each day.

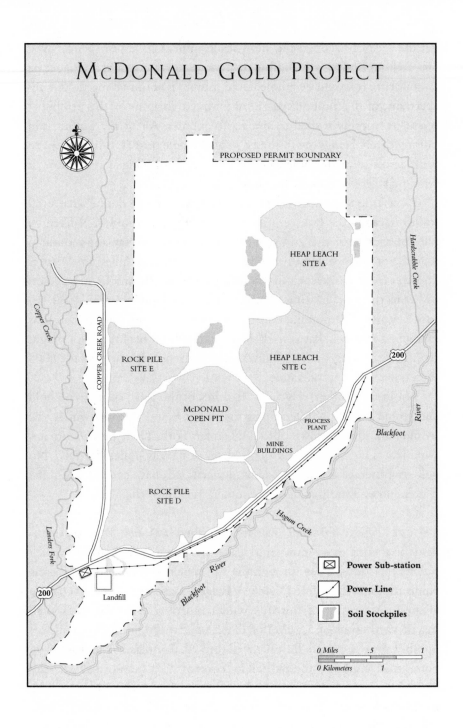

McDonald Gold Project

PROPOSED PERMIT BOUNDARY

HEAP LEACH
SITE A

Hardscrabble Creek

Copper Creek

COPPER CREEK ROAD

ROCK PILE
SITE E

HEAP LEACH
SITE C

200

River

McDONALD
OPEN PIT

PROCESS
PLANT

Blackfoot

MINE
BUILDINGS

Landers Fork

ROCK PILE
SITE D

Hogum Creek

River

Blackfoot

200

Landfill

Power Sub-station

Power Line

Soil Stockpiles

| 0 Miles | | .5 | | 1 |
| 0 Kilometers | | | 1 | |

Consider: Each day, the mine's trucks will use more than 50,000 times as much fuel as the truck that just punched the peace out of this mountain morning.

And it will be each day. The operating plan says the ore will roll seven days a week, twenty-four hours a day for fifteen years. This is just the ore trucks; back on the highway, there will be a string of trucks hauling in the fuel, blasting chemicals, soda, grease, transmission fluid, crankcase oil, diatomaceous earth, hydrochloric acid and, of course, cyanide, about 2,500 truck trips a year. Two out of three days for fifteen years, a truck loaded with cyanide will make the run up the twisting mountain highways, winding around sometimes icy curves with the river.

That the river may be asked to freight away spilled cyanide is only speculation, but it is almost certain the digging of the hole will saddle it with another burden. The rock will not go into those mammoth shovels willingly, but must be blasted from the layers of the buttes with a mixture of ammonium nitrate and diesel fuel, another 220,000 gallons used annually in addition to that burned in the trucks and shovels. This is the same stuff used to level the Alfred Murrah building in Oklahoma City, an effect achieved with only two tons of the mixture. The mine will use thirty-seven tons of this explosive each day for fifteen years, a total of 13,500 tons per year.

Heretofore, the numbers I have used in discussing this mine are all the company's estimates, listed in its operating statement, but I venture now into a calculation that comes from an outside source, an environmental consultant who reviewed the plan. Blasting typically has an efficiency rate of about 95 percent, which is to say that almost all of the diesel fuel and ammonium nitrate crosses to chemical oblivion. It also means 5 percent remains, so 675 tons of ammonium nitrate will accumulate in the waste rock each year. Ammonium nitrate is fertilizer, and during the duration of the mine, operation will lace the Blackfoot's banks with more than 10,000 tons of fertilizer.

Fertilizer is the death of mountain rivers. That's why we treat sewage and regulate runoff from farm fields. The nutrients cause plant life, especially algae, to flourish then die. The decaying vegetable matter saps the river of oxygen, slows it, warms it—in general, causes it to age and decay. Nutrients do occur naturally in streams, accumulating from the runoff from forested hillsides, but the Blackfoot now handles between one and two tons of such nutrients in a year, nothing on the order of the 675 tons the mine would produce.

THE REAL EXERTION in climbing this golden butte came from the snow, the problem of postholing through a knee-deep blanket. It takes unusual amounts of energy to push water, as any kid who has tried to run knee-deep in an ocean understands. As with most open-pit mines, the McDonald Project will need to move water, which is where much of its energy will go. There are two issues here, beyond energy use. As with the ammonium nitrate, there is concern about water quality but there is also the matter of water quantity.

Even the process of testing the water flowing below the mine (part of the process to obtain a permit) has already degraded the Blackfoot. This much is understood. They can't be seen in the snow now, but the whole area around this butte is studded with well shafts. The company has been pumping these to try to understand the big black box that is the underground network of fresh water. The area is worked in the medium of glacial till, sand and gravels piled in the creases between mountains that conduct an underground network of streams and pools. When we look at the Landers Fork and Blackfoot as the water of the place, it is a bit like looking at a person's eyes to see his brain. The streams are simply the surface expression of the water system. They give and take from the unseen world at various points through their course. Most of it is mysterious and deep.

Well pipes probe the mystery, but they probe deeply. The surface aquifer at the site is fresh as mountain snow, but the mine goes into deeper, mineralized strata and the water there in deeper aquifers reflects its origins. Specifically, it is heavy with arsenic, zinc, cadmium, lead and silver. Arsenic and zinc are the biggest problem; water from the wells tested more than double the state standards for arsenic and more than triple the standards for zinc. During testing, the miners pumped this water into the drainage at the rate of about 800,000 gallons a day.

It takes power to move water, especially polluted water. During the session of the state legislature just prior to the beginning of these tests the mining industry got a brand-new law governing such discharges. It became legal to pump any test water from the ground to the river, no matter how badly it is polluted. Then to cover problems beyond testing, the state loosened regulations of something called a "mixing zone," something we shall hear much about later, but for present amusement, we'll broach the concept here. If discharge water does not meet standards, a polluter simply claims a mixing zone. Standards are based on concentration, parts per million. To meet standards, then, one can take pollutants out or one can put more pure water in. Mixing zones apply this latter idea *in situ*. The zone is a stretch of unpolluted stream or aquifer. The substandard water is dumped upstream but its quality is not measured there. It is measured downstream, after it has been diluted by the stream.

Even in testing, the McDonald mine is using a section of the aquifer to cover its chemical tracks. And even in testing, there have been screwups. Twice, according to newspaper accounts, during a single month, the company shut down testing operations after the pumps blew apart pipes carrying away the arsenic- and zinc-laden water. In one case, a ten-inch hole sent the water who knows where. In and of itself, these were minor events, but they reflect mightily on the company's contention that it can handle an operation of this scale. The system that failed was not much more complicated than a farmer's irrigation pipes. There are two levels of concern here. The known, which is the amount of damage to the Blackfoot that will occur even if everything goes according to plan, and the unknown, the catastrophes that will occur when the big pipes break.

Mostly an aquifer is an unknown, best understood if this discussion switches from questions of water quality to quantity. First, a number that is hard to grasp: The miners will need to pump 15.8 million gallons of water each day to keep the hole dry. This is sufficient water to supply a small city of about 100,000 people, but there is a hard fact that is far more relevant than analogy.

Simply, this is more water than is flowing through the Landers Fork Valley and Blackfoot Valley at low flow. The mine will divert all of the valley's water. That is not to say the two forks will dry up, at least not for their entire length. Most of this water will be simply diverted, pumped from the hole, then dumped back in the river downstream. Some, however, will be used. The mine has applied for a "consumptive" use permit, the right to take water and use it for such processes as diluting, pumping and spraying cyanide on the mountains of ore. That permit asks for 1,800 gallons per minute, which is about 25 percent of the Landers Fork at low water and about 32 percent of the Upper Blackfoot.

The issue, however, is not limited to consumption. That larger volume of water diverted simply to keep the pit dry is the issue—as you will recall, the primary issue on the minds of federal mine regulators who have dealt with the bloom of gold mines around Elko, Nevada. Again, consider the mine view looking in from the side, as in this drawing submitted by McDonald in its operating plan. Notice the cone of the pit, then notice the dotted line that is the water level in the aquifer once the pit has been pumped dry, what the miners in Nevada refer to as the "cone of depression." This is simply the area in which all the surface water will be removed, and the issue is how far that water wall is removed from the pit wall. That depends very much on underground characteristics such as the porosity of the gravels in the alluvium and how much resistance they offer to water, which in turn determines how steeply the water can be banked.

This is the calculation the miners in Nevada and all miners erred on so badly, and with cause. Hydrologists of any persuasion will explain that their field of study is inside a black box. It is buried and unseen. However, in the case of the McDonald mine, the miners haven't recorded

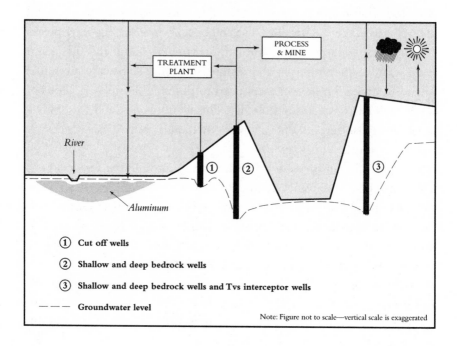

① Cut off wells

② Shallow and deep bedrock wells

③ Shallow and deep bedrock wells and Tvs interceptor wells

– – – Groundwater level

Note: Figure not to scale—vertical scale is exaggerated

this calculation. There is no accounting for a cone of depression. That's why the drawing they have submitted and reproduced here admits to being not to scale. The exact layout of this crucial scheme is not known.

Given the proximity especially to the Landers Fork, though, it is easy to imagine how far this cone will extend. Remember now that a river is a surface expression of the alluvial flows. If those subsurface waters beneath the Landers Fork dry up, then so will stretches of the Landers Fork. This is not pollution of the river; this is taking a river. No more river for stretches of its run, and likely highly critical stretches. Recall too that the Landers Fork is one of the key spawning sites for bull trout. This fact alone is prima facie evidence that the river is in intimate communication with its aquifer. Young bull trout live in spaces between streambed gravels, but can only do so in sections where subsurface water is boiling up through those gravels, keeping the nurseries constantly refreshed. The touchy nature of this process is one of the biggest reasons the bull trout is a threatened species. Touchy in a normal stream, and impossible in one that no longer has water.

Of course, most of the water the mine takes, it will return, probably with a bonus of some added chemicals. Much of the volume will still be there, potentially altering downstream flows. Depending on the timing of discharges, the extra water could raise levels in the main Blackfoot, creating wetlands where there were none, flooding meadows and changing the course of the stream.

All of this, of course, is temporary, or at least most is, unless the addition of a mile-wide hole in the aquifer might permanently alter a small valley's hydrology. But for the sake of argument, we'll assume they are temporary. The permanent plan, the long-term contribution of the mine—even if all goes well and there is no catastrophic spill of cyanide to the river and the resulting load of metals and acids settle to a level the river can choke down in perpetuity—is, of course, the mile-wide lake and sculpted landscape given as a gift to the state of Montana. Or maybe not.

The miners say there will be a lake, but one hydrologist who evaluated the plan says maybe not. The miners included no allowance in their calculations for evaporation. The summers here are hot and dry, and this valley holds its water by keeping it underground. The pit/lake surface will expose 304 acres of water to the lift of the summer sun, and the pit will *lose* more water than precipitation will replenish. That is, to keep the lake full, about 16 percent of what is now the flow of the Landers Fork will be diverted to the hole to be diverted to the sky. Forever.

THEN THERE IS CYANIDE. Once the overburden is made into those two mountains just west of where I sit, between the pit and Landers Fork, then the line of trucks will begin the haul east. They will head directly to what were marked on our map as the leach pads, or to a crusher, where ore lumps will be smashed to dust, then borne in trucks to the same leach pads. From the sky, it will look like an anthill in progress, the work of so many boxy, single-minded yellow ants. From the outset, though, it will be admitted that this new mountain is unearthly and can no longer be hydrologically linked to the planet that made it and now supports it. This severing of the hydrological link is, of course, impossible, the chief fallacy of heap-leach mining; but they always try.

The attempt is plastic. Before building the new mountains, the miners will lay down a massive sheet of plastic, actually a series of sheets welded with a special process. The sheet is about as thick as a nickel. You might think it folly to try to make seams in plastic that will stand the forces at a base of a mountain, and you would be right. The seams always leak in this liner meant to serve like a newspaper under a giant bad dog.

Truck by truck a mountain rises in layers, each layer maybe as tall as a house. As it rises, the miners build temporary rivers in pipes that spray the layers with a solution of cyanide and water. This is the heart of the process, the heap leach, the exercise of the simple chemical fact that gold adheres to cyanide. This affinity is at once the miners' method of operation and their defense; the industry argues it takes every precaution against cyanide spills simply because it is in their selfish interests to do so, a sort of Adam Smith of environmental regulation. They catch all the cyanide because it has their gold, just as the Exxon *Valdez* had Exxon's oil.

There are invisible hands in capitalism, and then there are invisible fingers. At a certain point, the extra steps necessary to ensure 100 percent recovery of the cyanide cost more than the gold it carries. A liner the thickness of a nickel may always leak—every one has so far—but installing one twice as thick may cost a few hundred thousand more, maybe a few thousand more than the gold is worth. Cyanide will spill from these mountains, if the past is an indication.

And they will be mountains, two of them covering about 900 acres, a footprint of more than one and a half square miles. From where I sit now at the site that will be the pit, I can see the truck that made all that racket earlier now fading from sight, a kid's toy truck down on a pencil line of highway off toward the horizon. That point is near the opposite side of the heap-leach pad. It will stretch from the edge of the pit to there. Except as far as the highway is concerned, there will be no there. If the state grants this mining permit, it will at the same time agree to move this highway, at the miners' expense. It must move to accommodate the leach pads and the mine's processing areas. Off at river's edge, a little Forest Service campground must also close. Too near the mine.

Like all mountains, these new leaching piles would have their own hydrology, boosted by pumps and cyanide spray. Like all mountains, there will be little fits and starts built into the flow, pockets that trap solution that may wash out later, maybe while the recovery system is still in operation. Maybe not.

The leach water will gather eventually into two ponds covering a total of 70 acres, a cyanide lake about 1,500 feet from the Blackfoot River. Perhaps this would not be so unsettling if this distance were not all downhill, the way water flows anyway, both on the surface and within the smear of alluvial gravels that is the floor of the valley. These ponds will be bermed to protect the Blackfoot, at least on the surface, insurance designed to withstand a 100-year flood, that is, a flood so severe it can be expected to occur only once every 100 years. We get those every now and again. It seems a safe standard until we look a bit farther up the valley to the gunsight pass and remember this site sits within shouting distance of the Continental Divide, where a winter's worth of snow to make the spring flood can begin piling up in October.

We remember that all of this—plastic, pumps, pipes and rubber pipe seals—must perform flawlessly ten minutes away from Rogers Pass, where the temperature was once the coldest ever recorded in the Continental United States, 70 below zero on January 20, 1954. And we remember all the mines now where the man-made mountains deserve to be called mountains because they and their attendant problems will exist "in perpetuity."

The miners' response to all of this is an invocation of the American article of faith, generally expressed in the phrase "state of the art." The assertion is that technology will deal with each of these problems. They further maintain that it is unfair to hold the McDonald Project accountable for mistakes at places like the Berkeley Pit or even Summitville, in that those mines used outdated technology. Generally the miners do not invite us to look behind the curtain for a better view of this wizard, but let's have a peek anyway.

To be sure, there has been a leap of technology in heap-leach gold mining. That's what has made this concept profitable. Aside from development of the concept itself, technical improvements have come largely in tools—computer-controlled trucks and shovels, and tools for exploration. The mining industry has been among the most aggressive in adopting satellite imagery and sensing to inventory the face of the Earth from space. Very little of this has anything at all to do with environmental problems.

Those environmental tools that do exist tend to be expensive, so miners avoid them if they can get away with it. Doubling the thickness of a plastic liner, for instance, is no great technological marvel; it is safer but is almost never done because of the expense. Cost, not availability, generally determines the level of technology employed in waste-water treatment.

There are indeed "state-of-the-art" systems. Mines in South Dakota, for instance, because of state regulation, use a reverse osmosis process, biological treatment and ion exchange systems that do (when they work right) remove metals and cyanide from waste water. Phelps Dodge, however, is not coming even close to these systems at the Blackfoot mine. That is, the claim to using the best available technology is simply false. The technology employed is the mixing zones, an old con covered with the canard: "The solution to pollution is dilution."

Outside sources who have reviewed the corporation's application for a permit are uniformly surprised at how primitive both the technology and assessment of the site have been. On the key issue of hydrology, for instance, one consultant who reviewed the documentation—the same one who noted the corporation had neglected to consider evaporation from the lake—said, "Standard, widely accepted public domain hydro-logic software has not been used to characterize the site."

In a larger sense, though, the insertion of technology into the issue is a red herring. The problems are not technological. The environmental problems are the direct result of scale. It requires knowledge not much beyond high-school chemistry to neutralize sulfuric acid or to stop the leaching of heavy metals. At least on the scale of a chemistry lab's table, under a chemistry lab's roof and inside a chemistry lab's walls that block out the real-world conditions of the northern Rockies Continental Divide. When the sulfuric acid and metals move from mountains, however, we all become students. This is the scale reserved for the Earth's own forces, not humans.

No amount of technology will cancel the simple fact of this hole in the ground. The presence of gold dictates its size and the demands of profit dictate its ultimate disposition. Technology has nothing to do with it. The pollutants, in fact, are difficult to consider as such. They are not the polysyllabic Frankensteins derived from chlorine, the man-made organics we have come to associate with such atrocities as the burning of the Cuyahoga River in Ohio. All are simple inorganics and—except the cyanide—naturally occurring on this very site or derivatives of naturally occurring processes on this site. These simple facts the miners will use to assert that their enterprise is benign.

The argument works, until one considers scale. The metal and acids occur, but not here on the surface, not in quantity. The earth stores them out of reach of oxygen and surface water. Except for volcanic eruptions, in human experience there is almost no precedent for exposing what the earth has safely stored on such a massive scale. When such natural events do occur, we have a name for them. We call them catastrophe.

ON THE HILL that day, I faced a more immediate dilemma: My car was stuck where I had left it. But this is Montana and it's not much of a problem. Back at the car I simply wait roadside, my predicament obvious. Long-haul trucks roar by, oblivious. The rush of their passing seems to lift me out of my footsteps a bit, and each throws a long rooster tail of snow dust across my bow. Then the first pickup crests the hill. It is, of course, enormous, a four-wheel drive, and the back seems full of such tools as one might need to pull an idiot writer's car out of the ditch. It stops, and guys in watch caps, wool pants and suspenders de-truck then wonder why a fellow would be out here in a little car instead of a proper pickup truck. Their logging chain hook is too big to fit the Japanese idea of a tow-hook on my Honda, so we jury-rig a hook out of a hunk of nylon rope I find under the dog and twelve-pack in the back of the truck.

"Just throw a bowline in her. That will hold her," comes a logger's advice. (Large and stubborn mechanical devices are feminine.) I'm already halfway through the bowline by the time he speaks. Work on power-line construction crews put me through college, so I once was fluent in knot.

The truck's tires barely spin and the Honda snaps out like a loose tooth.

"Let's move this shit outta here before a trooper comes along. They'll give you a ticket for not calling a tow truck."

This three-minute scene is Lincoln. Begin with that last somewhat enigmatic statement, which is, of course, bullshit. It is nonetheless the sort of folklore that flushes small-town life. It is assumed and believed that those in authority over the state exist to prevent one from solving problems and in general leading a meaningful life. Thus, the constable has nothing better to do than drive around the state issuing citations to good Samaritans in monster trucks.

This is the vein of folklore that is high-grade political ore. If highway patrolmen are anathema to the good deed, then it follows that the work of environmental regulators is so much silliness, geared to prevent a man from getting his job done. And that's what resonates most here: getting a job done.

Lincoln has been a refuge of on-the-edge, hand-to-mouth, pick-and-shovel types from the beginning. It is, of course, named for the president, deriving, as many of the names in the West did, from reverberations of the Civil War. His name came to mind when five early sourdough types struck gold in a gulch just outside of town in 1865, the year Lincoln died. The town has been more or less continually mined and logged ever since, but usually on a relatively small scale.

This legacy shows up now as four-wheel-drive pickup trucks with chains in the back and men inside who know what a bowline is and think solving the general problems of life is simply a matter of hooking up the right machine in the right fashion, and believe in extending the

benefits of their hard work to anyone who needs a hand, including id-
iots in Hondas from Missoula. Because my education came in equal parts
from universities and power-line crews, I have more than a little sympa-
thy for all of these views, especially when stuck in a ditch.

It is not clear whether the mining corporations sympathize with
these views, but that doesn't matter. What does matter is they are able to
exploit them.

All of the numbers in the above description of the mine are not the
ones grabbing the attention of many of the people of Lincoln, the men
in pickup trucks. The number that rings loudest is this: During the
course of the project, it will generate 390 "good paying" jobs (the company's term) and $550 million in purchases, some of that in the state and
in Lincoln. Included in this is an unveiled promise of a more general
prosperity worked through the magic of an ephemera of economics
called the "multiplier effect." That is, the paychecks of the few who win
jobs will get cashed in town and generally rattle around the various cash
registers to replace what has heretofore been an archetypal Rocky
Mountain village economy, a place that until now ensured prosperity by
everyone doing everyone else's laundry.

The numbers ring in Lincoln because, like many small towns, it is
full of people on the edges. That's what a frontier is all about, and it is
still an economic frontier of sorts. People move there and live there for
reasons other than economy; call it a mountain mystique, or lay it to the
fact that it is gorgeous, wild and peaceful. It is not, however, very prosperous, so unless one brings a trust fund or pension (many do) one winds
up perpetually underemployed. Further, it attracts many of the sort who
drive pickup trucks and the mine is offering them a better-than-average
wage driving trucks or loaders, welding, wrenching, drilling holes and
blasting. It's heavy construction work, and one does not live on the edge
long without learning something about doing construction work. All
this appears to mean the mine is an antidote for Lincoln's economic
problems. This would be a good argument were it not for the fact that
this experiment has been tried many, many times in the West. Most of
the places where it has been tried are ghost towns now.

First, mining is not, as the miners argue, a significant factor in the
general prosperity statewide. It's true that by any reasonable standard
Montana is a mining state. Hard rocks founded it, and it produces more

holes in the ground than most with far fewer people than most. Still, there are only 2,605 jobs in metal mining statewide, which is 0.61 percent of the labor force. The McDonald mine's contribution to that would be another 0.09 percent. Of the twelve western states including Alaska, mining accounts for 0.15 percent of all employment, still not significant. Further, its share of total employment was cut in half between 1980 and 1990. That's not all because there was a drop in mining jobs (although there was, despite the gold boom, thanks partly to automation). It is because most of the West during that period was in an economic boom, leading the rest of the nation in job creation, and that general prosperity was coming not from mining, but from more modern sectors of the economy, such as medical care, tourism and services.

That principle applies locally, even to the point of denying the contention of a link between general prosperity and mining on Lincoln's relatively small scale. Thomas Power, chairman of the economics department of the University of Montana, has studied this issue throughout the West and found almost uniformly that towns prospered independently of mining. Some saw their greatest periods of job growth when mines closed. Says Power:

> Those who argue that continued public subsidization of hard rock mining on federal lands is crucial for the economic prosperity of the West face an enormous historical factual problem: The mining towns of the West have been anything but prosperous. They have been run down, depressed communities for many decades. Butte, Montana; Kellogg and Wallace, Idaho; the copper towns of Arizona: Lead and Deadwood, South Dakota; the iron towns of Minnesota and the coal towns of Appalachia: None of these, despite the production of billions of dollars worth of valuable minerals over many decades have been visited by prosperity.

On the contrary, the towns experience a boom and then a bust and suffer on both slopes. During the run-up, a dinky village like Lincoln suddenly grows a ring of house trailers, more than doubling its population in months. No one builds homes because the mine is only expected to last maybe twenty years. The schools quickly crowd. The sewers strain and wells run dry. The town builds to accommodate and pays for the building—then comes the bust and with it a string of boarded-up store-fronts and falling-down trailers. None of this looks like prosperity. Nor does it look like wilderness, and strangely, wilderness turns out to be the biggest indicator of prosperity.

Power has done quite a bit of work tracing this phenomenon, as have others. During the 1980s, Montana did see an upturn in job creation and a number of other economic indicators, but Power found growth was localized. The jobs grew fastest in those counties adjacent to designated wilderness areas. The reason was quite simple. People wanted to live there and brought independent incomes or movable jobs. They spent money and the money did jingle on through town. Ironically, some of those places still had chronically high unemployment rates, but Power argues that will always be true, no matter how many jobs are created. People move there for reasons other than jobs, and there will always be a certain number of people willing to live marginally, trying to figure a way to attach roots.

Lincoln's promised ring of mobile homes and the roar of trucks building and wrecking mountains is not wilderness. That hole will un-dermine this community's prosperity.

Still, the miners would have the town believe otherwise, which is why the local paper runs cover photographs of mine officials presenting eight-foot-long checks to such as the Lincoln Emergency Services for rescue equipment. The miners paid to insulate a senior citizen clinic and bought an X-ray machine for a clinic and helped pay for a visit of a chil-dren's theater troupe. The money spent has some direct benefits for the miners. For instance, the school principal who asked for and got the do-nation for the theater troupe later testified at a public hearing in support of the mine.

Of course, all of this could be simply an act of charity from the good hearts of the miners, a contention that would be easy to swallow were it not for the fact that the mine took out newspaper ads in both the Black-foot Valley *Dispatch* and Helena *Independent Record* listing each donation: "The McDonald Gold Project is proud to support these organizations and to contribute financially to their important work."

Environmental activist Jim Jensen told the Great Falls *Tribune*: "They are spending this money to grease the skids of public opinion for their mine. . . . Back in the old days of the copper kings it was just called pay-ola. . . . I'm not sure who's most guilty, the john or the prostitute, but they are both at work here."

THE QUIET OF a winter's mountainside and the panorama of the valley below bestows a sense of well-being. It is the same sense sought by the people who have chosen to live here, on the edge, the hard edge. When the economist says people are willing to suffer some unemployment and underemployment to be here, that's what he means, a position on the hard edge bought with a real economic cost. Any economic argument that fails to account for this willingness to pay to be here is nothing more than abstraction. Prosperity ought to include the notion of well-being, which at least in part derives from wilderness. How then can the trucks digging this hole create prosperity when they destroy its peace?

The plan to blast away this mountain and cart off its gold raises questions of values. Beneath the momentary illusion of the peace here now, that is ultimately what is so unsettling about this scene. A social question is being asked on this hill, and society has no satisfactory means of answering it.

The mining lobby's public relations broadsides these days focus on the issue of use. We cover this with the idea of need, and yes there are costs, real environmental costs to mining, but what we dig from the ground goes far in dealing with human needs. This is what the miners mean by the hard edge, by paying the costs of our lives. The miners are right and do us a service in raising this issue. This is the notion that makes Butte a town of stoic acceptance. Butte digs copper from the ground. We have achieved what we have achieved as a people because much of our ingenuity was and is freighted on hard, straight lines of copper. In this we are all together. All are complicit. Economic demand is a measure of real need. People and the mountain paid the price.

The miners extend this argument to gold. If there are people to buy the gold, then this is evidence enough to justify the violence planned for this place. Careful. The pea of this logic has just slipped from shell to shell. From "need" to "want." Drawing the line between those two concepts is the most important task before us. It is the line that separates adolescent from adult. Failure to draw this line makes addicts.

No one needs a gold bracelet. It's that simple, and that is the biggest problem in all of this. We are simply no good at solving simple questions of ethics, especially when there is profit to be made in obscuring these questions.

Here's all it takes to push this argument off the Tower of Babel: I say no one needs a gold bracelet, and the miners at the back of the room leap to their feet to call me an elitist. Who am I to say? And if I say so, might someone else say I don't "need" peace? After all, I have just argued, in part, that wilderness is valuable because people pay a real economic cost of underemployment. Demand equals need; I said it myself.

Our society's need for peace—not imagined peace, but the real commodity as dealt out by quiet mountain valleys—has become and will become more self-evident as it becomes increasingly scarce. We will not be able to go on without it. We will crave it long after most of the world will have forgotten gold ever existed.

For a moment, however, grant an edge of the miners' argument, because it leads us to a very real problem. Peace does have an economic value just as gold does. Given that, the national religion tells us the market can weigh and decide this issue. If the peace of this valley is more valuable than gold, then price ought to reflect that. People ought to be willing to pay more for preventing the mine than for the mine.

So where do I pay? Where is the store that will sell a small bit of insurance of wilderness the way the corner jewelry store sells rings? The jewelry store pays people to dig holes. Where is the store that pays people not to dig holes? Even if there were such a store, how would the few of us who live in this place or even know about this place come up with enough dollars to offset the beam of heat focused here, the desires of 6 billion people concentrated on this tiny valley by the lens of international markets?

FIGHT

THIS IS NOT the beginning of this chapter. It is a
story, a scene that will not go away. It seems largely
irrelevant, but its persistence in my mind as I think of
the Blackfoot would suggest otherwise. It happened
several years before the gold mine on the Blackfoot
was proposed and years before I knew much about
gold mining, or the tortured history of rivers.

It was Montana cold that winter's day, maybe
January, maybe February, and I was a newspaper reporter on assignment. I was driving the Interstate
highway that winds east along the Clark Fork River
upstream of the mouth of the Blackfoot to Garrison Junction, where I would leave it and take the
two-lane on to the capitol at Helena to cover a
meeting of the state legislature. I was in a hurry. Icy
roads had trimmed my car's speed, and I had cut my
schedule fine. The prospect of being late plagued
my mind. I was a reporter then, carnivorous and un-
accustomed to being beaten on stories by being late.

K. Ross Toole, the historian of our place, said something important in contending that our legacy is all around us while we are ignorant of it. My car on the Interstate sped past Gold Creek, so named because some of the earliest fur trappers in the state, based at Fort Benton, took a break from the slaughter of beaver to prospect for and find gold right here. This pulled a subsequent string of prospectors through these draws and ridges to eventually find gold at Helena, and that became the state's capital. The quaint walking mall of the downtown threads Last Chance Gulch, where they dug the gold and where they set the boom-bust go-for-broke creed of this state. Much rides on a last chance.

The railroad that parallels the Interstate was the old Milwaukee, now the Burlington Northern. It came together, complete with a ceremonial driving of the golden spike, at Gold Creek on September 8, 1883, join-ing Atlantic to Pacific. As we have seen, the ties that built it logged the Blackfoot for the first time.

Yet what helped most in all this building was not beside or behind me, but straight ahead in Helena in a statehouse built on a capital itself located by, quite literally, corruption and bribes, bribes flagrant and unimaginable to a modern mindset. But then there was copper and gold to be dug.

That I was oblivious to all of this on that morning and still thought of myself as a reporter, despite being a reporter for a paper not so long ago owned by the Anaconda Copper Company, was less remarkable than the development that became the scene that keeps coming back. I had seen eagles soar that morning, and there is nothing unusual in that, but as I wound toward the turnoff from the Interstate at Garrison, I saw, re-vealed by its shadow, a smooth slit in the snow, a line, a trough like a child's snow saucer would make running straight down the bank into the river. Then, at the trough's base, I saw a soft whiskered head pop from the river and scan the surrounds, then another head. I stopped the car. My business could wait. The two river otters slid out the Clark Fork onto the bank, climbed the bank and used their slide. I watched as they did this again and again. The story could wait.

THE PRIMARY DECEIT of this book and many books is concealing chronology. It is also a primary service, what we mean when we say a story allows us to escape time. It is the way in which we remove ourselves from the roar of events long enough to think about those events. I have a story to tell, and to tell I must manipulate; especially I must manipulate time. Deceit, however, cannot last forever.

In the case of this book, the deceit has been particularly trying in that as I have written it, my time in this, my real time, has spanned a bit of a political storm, and so far I have told you nothing about it. It has not been an easy matter to keep from you, because my space, literally the space in which I have written most of this book, has almost daily been invaded with the details of this fight. I try to poke away at a paragraph and the fax machine a few feet away whirs to life. My wife snaps up the machine's issue, reads it and faxes back. This is how war is waged.

This takes us to the matter of yet another deceit, not as widespread in books as tweaking time, but one more worrisome in the contract between reader and writer. I am compromised in the telling of this story, a plain old conflict that can only be dealt with through disclosure. So I disclose. The gold mine proposal on the Blackfoot has provoked opposition, grassroots environmental opposition. That in itself is deeply relevant to this story, the politics, the fight. My own fax whirs in this fight because my wife, Tracy, bless her, is involved in the fight against the mine. So are most of my friends here in this little mountain town. For a couple of years now, friends here could not gather for dinner or drinks without talking about the mine, and often as not, when we did gather, it was after some hearing or such, or during some fund-raiser, twisting each other's arms for a few more bucks for leaflets, polls, consultants, TV time, mass mailings and faxes. Of course there are organizations carrying all of this out and of course I am still enough of a journalist to honor the pro forma code of taking no active role in these organizations. But my heart is with them; they are my friends and my wife and the truth is it's not their fight alone. It is mine.

IT IS A RULE of evolution that the adaptations and growing abilities of one creature will be matched with adaptations in those beings closest in the circle of its life. This holds for allies as it holds for enemies. As the wolf gets stronger, the antelope gets swifter. It is the dynamic of evolution that makes evolutionary biologists quote Lewis Carroll's Red Queen, that survival of a species requires constant running just to hold its place. Politics evolve under the same rules.

This notion was my comfort when I first heard of the mine. I knew the people who would fight it; I knew their abilities. From all the wars I have described in this book and from many more that were not, Montana and the Rocky Mountain West in general have created a cadre of environmental warriors that are nothing if not battle-tested. Consider, for instance, a recent case involving activist Dan Funsch. He was arrested and charged in a tree sit protest in northern Idaho attempting to block the clear-cutting of yet another stretch of old growth. A tree sit, you will recall, is that form of aerial sit-in wherein protesters take up a position of passive resistance at treetop. Think Gandhi with climbing ropes. Funsch adds his highly personal twist in that he lashes himself in like everybody else, but he plays the accordion. This led to his undoing, in that when the police who came to break up the whole affair ordered him down, he was unable to comply immediately, the logistics of accordion playing and rope rigging and the relationship between them being somewhat complex. Accordingly, he was charged with resisting arrest.

Everybody hears about the tree-sitters and the noisier string of protesters, but they are on their own in a small corner of the movement. I am glad they are there, but I take more comfort in knowing who else is in this fight.

The troops are organized under names like the Clark Fork Coalition, Montana Environmental Information Center, Trout Unlimited, the National Wildlife Federation and Women's Voices for the Earth, but I think in a different set of names: Meg Nelson, Karen Knudsen, Geoff Smith, Bruce Farling, Tom France, Jim Jensen, Bryony Schwan, the ones I know, but the circle spreads wider. A case history of a few of these tells something of their weight in the fight.

Meg Nelson runs the Clark Fork Coalition, which is an independent river watchdog group that takes its charge as protecting the entire Clark Fork drainage, including both the Blackfoot and the Superfund site at Butte, not to mention some active and proposed mines downstream. Meg is a sober-minded and serious woman who got her start with another Montana group, the Northern Plains Resources Council. That's a coalition of ranchers and environmentalists who successfully fought strip mining of coal in eastern Montana, and that background is key.

Missoula is the hotbed of the state's environmental movement because Missoula is a college town, and that is exactly what is wrong with our politics. The movement, especially the headline-grabbing wing of it, is flushed with idealistic but transient college students willing to march and protest and sign petitions. Nothing wrong with that. It's the beginning, but it tends to evaporate without a trace with the change of each season, especially summer, when activists become kayakers or followers of bands, once the Grateful Dead, now Phish. To work, a movement must mature, and by maturing I mean account for the political realities and the history of the place. It must account for the lives of ranchers and even loggers, and people like Meg Nelson learn to do that.

A mature movement also incorporates science, which is where Geoff Smith, the science director of the Clark Fork Coalition, comes in. The group has always had somebody poring over the studies and impact statements, finding the weaknesses and deceptions and feeding their findings into the hearings and the courtrooms. Bruce Farling used to hold that same position before he moved on to direct the state's chapter of Trout Unlimited, an organization of fly fishers. Bruce is as sharp on the science as any environmentalist I know, but he is trained as a journalist, so he tells the story well. He is politically astute and likes and deals well with ranchers. He can walk their land and know every range plant, which impresses them. He's honest.

Tom France is a lawyer, and nails down much of that front for the movement. He works for the National Wildlife Federation, an organization I think rightly accused of being bloated and bureaucratic to the point of existing for its own perpetuation, rather than the perpetuation of species. The Federation is a creature of Beltway politics, but France is not. He too started with the Northern Plains Resources Council, then went to law school and took his environmental commitment to the courtroom. He grew up in Minnesota, but now middle-aged, he has worked for and lived, hunted and fished in Montana most of his adult life. Some of the key national battles on high-profile issues such as grizzly bears, wolves and clear-cutting bear his fingerprints.

Jim Jensen is hard driven and feisty, a sort of one-man environmental organization that grew beyond that but still bears his indelible stamp. He is a hardball politician, the sort that reporters call when they need a quote that drives a point like a spike. His base of operations is in Helena, because he's a lobbyist.

These names make up only a sampling of the troops, but I give them by way of setting up a battle.

THERE IS A PROBLEM in a long-running war, in that finally all the battles begin to look the same. And finally there comes the urge to go for broke, a maneuver that will win not just the fight at hand, but the adjacent battles as well. In 1995, an idea began percolating through the group of people listed above and their wider circle of friends and allies. It was in some sense a direct reaction to the Seven Up Pete mine proposal, but it drew a wider inspiration and was in an even more immediate sense a direct reaction to the 1995 session of the Montana legislature. That in turn also grew from the mine proposal. During 1995, events mirrored, perhaps even surpassed, the changes occurring in Washington, D.C., when industry lobbyists suddenly felt free to overtly and openly attempt to rip apart the fabric of environmental legislation. In Montana, mining money had built the corridors of power, and it was no real trick for it to walk the halls again. Industry lobbyists sought and got a relaxation in the state's water quality laws.

It was not a make-or-break issue for the mines, or for mining in general. As we have seen, clean water is a matter of money, how much the mine is willing to shave from the profit margin to spend on cleanup equipment. So in that sense, environmental regulation is a make-or-break issue for some individual mines. That is, relaxation of the standards pushed some from the red to the black. It made possible the marginally possible mines. The betting was and is that the McDonald Project mine is one of those marginal operations, which is why the miners lobbied so heavily for the new law. Certainly, the changes the legislature allowed made the mine more profitable, but probably they made it possible. Specifically, the changes relaxed standards for arsenic alone, and the McDonald mine, unlike most others, has a specific arsenic problem. The new law had McDonald's fingerprints on it.

After a lot of head scratching and some fairly sophisticated polling to fine-tune the strategy, the state's environmentalists made their move. They mounted a petition drive pushing a citizen initiative that would place a straightforward and remarkably simple amendment to the state's water quality laws on the ballot. It said that miners had to either meet state water quality standards at the point of discharge or remove 80 percent of the pollutants. The practical bite of the proposal came in the former provision in that it would ban mixing zones, the practice of dumping dirty water in a specified reach of a clean stream and declaring the resulting mix clean enough.

If this proposal would not outright stop the McDonald mine, it would at least make it cleaner and give regulators a tighter handle on it, but the target was more than McDonald. The state's waters and people were at the time facing problems from expansion of the Zortman and Golden Sunlight mines plus proposals for new gold mines in the Sweetgrass Hills in the north as well as Crown Butte near Yellowstone National Park. These were just the gold mines.

Even if passage did not stop a single one of these mines, it would still send a loud and clear message. By overriding the legislature, it would tell the state's politicians the residents did not want mining operating under political conditions that allowed the industry to simply walk into Helena and buy the legislature. In that losing the ballot initiative would send just the opposite message, mounting this campaign was an enormous gamble.

I watched from the sidelines as the move took shape, which is when the argument of political coevolution occurred to me. The state's history had at least given us enough political sophistication to summon a cavalry to ride to the rescue, and ride they did. This is the battle that roared all of the time I have been writing this, the chronology I have deliberately ignored. Now we pick up that story.

Behind the scenes, the environmentalists first moved to broaden their base. The movement's best moves historically resulted from coalitions, and those old and well-worked lines of communication began again to buzz. Particularly, they began crossing that relatively recent barrier that says environmentalism is a partisan issue. Gary Buchanan, a longtime Republican, friend of the state's Republican governor, former manager in Republican administrations and a stockbroker, signed on as one of the chairmen of the drives. Land Lindbergh, the soft-spoken, low-profile rancher, became its treasurer.

The move was to cost Buchanan in particular. During the campaign, his house in Billings was heavily vandalized, and miners quite openly approached a school district that used Buchanan's stock brokerage firm as bond consultants, a conservative town where the miners' pleas were likely to be heard. They lobbied to have the firm fired, simply because of Buchanan's stand. He was not swayed.

The first flush of hope came early, in May of 1996. Even before the petition drive gathered enough signatures to qualify for the ballot, independent polling began. Responding to the question "Would you favor or oppose toughening Montana's treatment standards for water discharged by metal mining operations, even if mining companies said it is aimed at shutting them down?" 59 percent of the respondents said "yes." Another 22 percent said "no," while only 19 percent were undecided. There were not enough undecided votes, even before the campaign had begun, to sway the results to the miners' column. Further, this was the tough version of the question, loaded with the assumption that stricter standards would shut down mines. The poll also asked the more straightforward question of whether respondents favored the ballot initiative. Sixty-seven percent did. In May.

Then the campaign began. The miners organized under the banner of "Montanans for Common Sense Water Laws," a name straight out of the Wise Use textbook. Wise Use is a political movement widespread in the West and backed heavily by various extractive industries like mining and logging, as well as the American Farm Bureau, the National Association of Realtors and groups such as associations of snowmobile manufacturers. Organized in the late 1980s during the height of the timber wars, it was an attempt by industry to outmaneuver the grassroots organizing by the environmentalists. Industry did not have a grassroots, so it bought one, a tactic that has worked.

The Wise Use influence on the miners' campaign is apparent. First, Montanans for Common Sense Water Laws were not Montanans. When the first campaign finance disclosure forms were filed it showed that 92 percent of the drive's money came from mining companies already digging or planning to dig holes in the state. The list included prominently Pegasus and Golden Sunlight, both with existing mines, and of course Seven Up Pete Joint Venture, which was to become the largest donor, eventually kicking in at least half a million dollars.

The term "common sense," however, is even more consistent with

Wise Use modus operandi, and really set the tone for the campaign. It is a way the movement at once fights specifics and claims the touch of the common folks. It lays the course of discourse and boils the matter to sentiments that will fit on a bumper sticker, which is too often how we conduct our politics. Anything other than "common sense" is "radical." Trust us on this, they say, and ask no further questions. We wouldn't want you to be confused with all that talk about parts per billion and point discharges.

The Wise Use movement—which, by the way, is changing its own name to the even more Orwellian "New Environmentalism"—has been (with the help of industry-hired consultants) conducting campaigns like this throughout the nation with all the care and attention to detail normally given to selling cars and soap. It is smart, and it is effective, appealing all at once to anti-intellectualism, antiscientism, suspicion of outsiders and a native, bedrock belief in "common sense."

So what's in a name? The state commissioner of political practices eventually ruled there was enough in that particular name to constitute a violation of the law. Specifically, the group was found not to be simply a bunch of Montanans. It was a mining industry front. Fines for such violations are based on spending, so the group's campaign qualified it for a fine of $1.6 million, at least in theory. The fine remained theoretical. The commissioner of political practices turned the case over to the Lewis and Clark County Attorney for prosecution, the county in which most of the development from the McDonald mine would be located. There was no prosecution.

The money-raising did not stop. The issue qualified for the ballot and would become during that political season—a presidential election year when Montana would reelect a governor and replace a popular Democratic congressman of six terms—the hottest political issue in the state. About this, there was no question. It's where we spent our money. It's what we talked about. The resulting superlatives, however, extended even beyond this election year. The miners eventually spent more than $2 million in this state of 800,000 people. It was the most ever spent on a ballot issue in the state's history.

Said the *Washington Post*: "It is not much of an exaggeration to say that the mining industry once owned Montana. . . . The days of the copper kings are now a distant memory, but in this election season Montana's mining industry is once again flexing its political muscle, like an aging giant roused for one final battle."

Nice copy, but the story can be told with two numbers. You have one of them: $2 million that the industry used to buy newspaper and television advertisements, many that were, like the name of their fronting organization, false. For instance, one showed a former state regulator drinking water from a creek that was purportedly a mine's discharge. It wasn't. The creek in question was downstream of a mine, but that particular mine pumped its wastes into an aquifer.

You need one more number. The backers of the ballot initiative raised—through auctions of donated goods, backyard barbecue fundraisers and door-to-door knuckling plus a few major contributions from organizations such as Trout Unlimited—a total of $321,700, one-sixth the miners' total.

After the election, Bruce Farling analyzed the results like this: "We could have come up with an initiative that said 'Don't rape grandmothers.' If those guys opposed it with $2 million, it would have lost."

Toward November the polls narrowed. We began to count the days to the election, wondering whether the rate of erosion from the stream of cash was greater than the number of days remaining. By election day, the same polls that had shown the issue a cakewalk now showed it too close to call. But it wasn't. The measure lost in a landslide, 56 to 43 percent. Beyond that, it must be reported that on the same ballot there was another question that would curtail corporate spending on ballot initiatives. The reasoning was we Montanans were sick and tired or corporate money ruling our politics and with that measure we would assert our independence. That one passed.

IT'S NOT OVER. The next fight for the Blackfoot will be waged on a much narrower battlefield, arguably, deep in enemy territory. Where the initiative fight was broad, general and indirect, this phase must be specific and direct. The biggest responsibility for permitting the mine rests with the state, which must review and approve an environmental impact statement. That process is already under way as I write this in December of 1996. The impact statement is scheduled to be completed about a year from now.

The fate of the river depends on the administration of a popular young Republican governor, Marc Racicot, who was reelected with 80 percent of the vote in 1996 after taking an active stand against the clean water initiative. (The fact that his opponent died two weeks before the election may have played into that number.) Technically, approving the McDonald mine is not strictly his call. The lease must come from a state land board made up of elected officials such as the commissioner of education and the attorney general. They are not political appointees or even Racicot's allies.

The lease, however, is but one leg of the process. The second is approval of the environmental impact statement, which is the responsibility of the Racicot administration's Department of Environmental Quality. It is unclear if either of the two legs predominates over the other, but some analysts believe that if the administration approves the impact statement, the land board will have little legal ground to deny the lease. This is the sort of issue that will occupy lawyers' time on all sides before the hole is dug, but to all it is clear the governor has considerable sway over this mine.

Racicot is popular because he is the feel-good, made-for-television face on a vicious administration. Ronald Reagan inspired a rash of cloning, but Racicot offers some advanced features over the original model. He is young and occasionally lapses into the touchy-feely, a new-age Republican. He is, however, like Reagan, a front man, the face for the billboard and the sound bites for the bumper stickers. The infrastructure of his administration often looks like an extension of industry's machines. Mines in Montana dig holes with trucks, shovels and the Racicot administration.

The governor, for instance, "streamlined" environmental regulation by creating the Department of Environmental Quality, which took an old mining regulation agency, the Hard Rock Mining Bureau, and combined it with the Water Quality Bureau. The former was an unrepentant advocate of mining, the latter, at least in theory, a watchdog. The effect of this combination was to infuse the whole with mining advocates. Racicot appointed to head the new agency a former timber industry executive and then aide to Republican Senator Conrad Burns, who was and is a point man for Wise Use.

During the campaign for the clean water initiative, a former officer of the Water Quality Bureau who had ended a twenty-five-year career in environmental regulation went public with a remarkable op-ed piece that ran in many Montana papers. Kevin D. Keenan wrote:

> With astonishment, I watched the evolution of corporate conduct relative to environmental legislation and regulation. As I reflect on this period, it is not the polluters' foot-dragging in the 1970s or the overt corruption of the Ann Gorsuch Environmental Protection Agency era that most offends me. It is the corporate and political activity of the past five years, during which polluters have mounted a frontal attack on the legislation, regulation, enforcement policies and budgets of state and federal environmental agencies. . . .
>
> Enormous amounts of money, unlimited legal and lobbying resources and constant political access characterize this attack on environmental and public health policies and on the agencies that administer them. . . .
>
> The mining industry and its well-financed lobby have been the champions of these kinds of influences.
>
> Even before the 1995 Legislature weakened Montana's environmental laws, the ability of regulatory agencies to require compliance with the existing legislation was severely compromised. Any agency employee who tried to hold his or her ground on a regulatory issue would simply be ignored, and a higher level supervisor would be sought. The employee would be branded an obstructionist, and the issue resolved politically in favor of the industry.

Phelps Dodge, through its front, Seven Up Pete Joint Venture, has invested heavily in this new machine for approval of the McDonald mine. Here's how it looks to the weary eyes of someone who has watched Montana's raw politics for more than a decade: The corporation feeds its application into the machine, punches a few buttons and the whole thing can be expected to perform as routinely as an ATM.

IN APRIL OF 1996 FBI agents from around the nation converged on Lincoln to arrest Ted Kaczynski, the hermit eccentric accused of being the Unabomber. His cabin is maybe ten miles from the McDonald mine as the crow flies, but for at least six years he was a part of a tiny town that for the last couple of years of his residence talked mostly about the McDonald mine. He has never said what effect the threat to his home had on his views, which, if the charges are true, were in more than a remote sense related to destruction of the environment. He is charged with mailing the bomb that killed a timber industry lobbyist in California; Lincoln is surrounded by clear-cuts. Probably we will never know what connection exists in his mind, given that the glare of television lights has melted any discrete issues to an unrecognizable glob. Besides, it's dangerous to try to impute any motives or rationale whatever to someone who may be either innocent of the charges or an off-center, twisted crank.

That's not to say we ought to ignore Ted Kaczynski. I think now of a friend of mine who, on being told of Kaczynski's arrest, said, "Another promising career cut short."

Does this surprise you, that there might be environmentalists who sympathize with mad bombers?

Thomas Hobbes, among the most conservative of political philosophers in democratic political tradition, so favored order that he favored a sovereign, and he granted that ruler immense powers. Yet even Hobbes left an out for revolt, a time when it was appropriate to defend oneself against the sovereign. It is from Hobbes that we get the body metaphor of politics, as in "the body politic." He permitted violent revolt when the politics of the body went beyond metaphor, when the sovereign posed a threat to the body. He allowed self-defense against the sovereign.

My body is water.

MONTHS BEFORE KACZYNSKI'S ARREST, I drove early one morning through Lincoln past the McDonald mine site and on over Rogers Pass, then down the front range to eventually visit another mine. I was walking the slipperiest of slopes, especially in the details of the visit that would stack up during that day, but occasionally there are good stories on slippery slopes. Besides, Ric Valois's demand did make sense. His sole condition for my being allowed to accompany him on an armed mission into enemy territory was that I wear camouflage. I told him I had no such clothing, and he said that was okay, he had plenty, so I drove that sunny June morning three hours east across the Great Divide to Ric's hand-built log cabin on the high plains of Montana.

The camouflage he offered was standard Army issue, Vietnam era, much like Ric. Seeing it sent me back, as I imagine it does him, and I imagine that's why he keeps it. Only I am different from Ric. He was an Army Ranger whose combat came deep in Laos. He fought where there officially were no Rangers and where there would be no help in case of troubles. I was antiwar and the uniforms I saw in those days stood on the other side of the barricades with billies and German shepherds. When I shucked my jeans and pulled on the fatigue pants, my skin crawled with old but indelible passions. Ric handed me a beret, as in green, as in "fighting soldiers from the sky," as in "love it or leave it," as in John Wayne, Nixon and napalm. I took it, and he left the room. I tried it on then forgot about it, pacing around the cabin, checking gear, questioning Ric about the mission, about the building of his cabin, small talk, getting ready. Then I happened to walk by a mirror and recognized someone else. My reflection formed a real character who looked back at me, and I said to myself, "Geez, I look like some sort of Latin American revolutionary," what with my beard and beret and the half-year since my last haircut. Then Ric walked in the room and said, "What the hell. You look just like Che Guevara."

I liked this and played with the idea at least for a minute of taking a nom de guerre, Commander Zero or something stylish like that, but the fantasy evaporated when Ric handed me his assault rifle, a CAR-15, loaded and real. Hanging on the wall nearby was a Chinese-made AK-47, just as real. Neither was going with us that day, but as we climbed into his Ford pickup for the long drive east, he dropped a loaded and holstered .45 automatic pistol, a Thompson model of the famous Army Colt, straight on the seat. It would go the whole way up the mountain with us to the peak, where we likely would break the law in the battle against the razing of the environment of the West.

I had left my own pistol at home. Officially I was an observer, and the camouflage was slippery enough. Its overt purpose was simply to make me unseen, and I could live with that.

RIC VALOIS, a compact and wiry man of forty-one, is founder and the most visible member of a group called the Environmental Rangers. His eyes are dark, deep and lively, pushing their punch with a mustache that droops a tad below Army regulation. Otherwise, he probably could still pass military muster. He is fit, stomach flat, erect and muscled, just as a homemade weightlifter's bench on the living room floor of his cabin would suggest.

When I rode with him that day in June of 1994, the rangers already were a couple of years old, and still there is no telling how many members exist. Maybe the group is just Ric, although he says that's not so. He says he has recruited members in every region of the country except the Northeast. Many of them are people much like him, Vietnam vets or just vets, many with special forces training like Green Berets and Navy SEALs. The members, says Ric, pay their own way so the group has no outside support. He said he did apply for a grant one time but the granting foundation insisted he have nonprofit tax-free status from the Internal Revenue Service. It wasn't altogether clear how he would fill out the federal paperwork, given that one of the most urgent needs for cash is for assault weapons.

The group has some goals that are less than bellicose, at least as stated on its pamphlets. Rangers do work such as shooting videos and distributing educational material to classrooms. Still it's easy to see how certain public officials might overlook these services, given that the rangers' most in-your-face tactic is to show force, especially firearms, at every opportunity. Ric makes a habit of attending official public hearings in full uniform, including the .45, which has more than once caused him to be called a terrorist. "It's okay if they call me that as long as they spell it 't-e-r-r-a-ist,'" he told me. The rangers exist to defend nature and defend those defending nature.

In the West, the environmental confrontation has escalated beyond cherubic schoolkids dropping empty soda cans in recycle bins. There have been violent confrontations, and people have been hurt. In particular, Ric cites the rise of Wise Use. This has contributed to mean-spirited and vituperative politics throughout the West, but behind the scenes, it has produced thuggery. Environmentalists have been beaten and threatened with violence. Houses have been burned, much of which must be reported in the passive voice because it happens in the night, in remote places. No one claims credit. Little evidence accrues. There are, though, certain cases on videotape, on the public record, especially in the events surrounding a long-term protest of a planned Forest Service timber sale in northern Idaho called Cove Mallard. One man was convicted and fined for beating a protester. One protester was dragged by a car. Ric's response to this was to show up and threaten violence against anyone who harms protesters. "They beat the shit out of a good friend of mine over there. He is the gentlest guy you would ever want to meet."

The main body of the radical environmental movement, especially at Cove Mallard, has formed under the wing of Earth First. In recent years, Earth First has become especially conscious of its image, expelling elements—never mainstream, but there were elements—who advocated vandalism, advocated a technique called "monkeywrenching." Now the organization is dominated by pacifists. They go limp when facing violence; Ric does not.

Valois claims that the rangers are in no way connected to Earth First and will not do the group's bidding. He is acting on his own, but does so by providing an armed presence in the woods.

"Civil disobedience and nonviolence have their place. I've got a lot of respect for those guys [the protesters]," he says. "But those [harassing the protesters] are a bunch of bullies and thugs, and they've got to be dealt with.

"My mom says I'm full of a lot of anger and I guess I am. I try to keep it under control. . . . I really don't enjoy the role of being confrontational, but I am. What the hell. I figure if I'm going to be a son of a bitch, I may as well be a son of a bitch for a good cause."

RIC PULLS HIS FORD into a Mini Mart to gas up just about the time I notice that the camouflage shirt I am wearing, the sort just about any archer or duck hunter might wear around here, bears an arm patch that says "Environmental Ranger." The slope just got slipperier, and I scrunch down a bit in the seat, hoping that the wheat farmers and truck drivers pulling up to the pumps—we are in Great Falls, a place where even Rush Limbaugh is suspected of liberal leanings—will have heard by now that Che Guevara is dead and no longer a threat to civilization as they know it, which is to say wheat, church, ball caps and large pickup trucks. I realize suddenly that clothing designed to make me unseen seems to be having the opposite effect.

We clear the Mini Mart and I steer the conversation in the direction these usually take. If a fellow in his forties forswears mufti, carries a pistol and says his life is ruled by anger, then the obvious question is: What did you do in 'Nam? Ric says he was in combat in Laos as a border Ranger for only four months, six months in the Army altogether. Why so short?

"I was wounded a couple of times, and there was that other stuff."

That last clause sounds to me like a slamming door, and I understand by his set of face that the word "stuff" covers some darkness. There needs to be another question, but I'll save it. We go on. Growing up in Toledo, Ohio, Ric was one of those kids who spent all his time on the outskirts of town, out where a few trees and vacant land could front the illusion of wild.

"That was before the malls came in, and ten years later that woods was destroyed."

Back from Vietnam, he wandered farther afield, cowboying, just him and a horse riding around the West in the old way. He worked at maybe fifty ranches in almost every western state and a couple of Canadian provinces, then along the way stumbled on a copy of Edward Abbey's *Desert Solitaire*. Ric did not finish high school and still has a hard time reading a book all the way through, but Abbey's hymn to the solitude of Utah's slickrock canyons grabbed him.

"This guy puts into words exactly the way I feel, and I said to myself that I got to go meet this guy," and he did, riding his horse to Arizona where Abbey was then tending a wildlife preserve.

He said he got along well enough with the writer, working with him on that preserve for a time, then things went bad, and Ric left. Still Abbey's influence stuck, especially through reading (at Abbey's suggestion) his early novel, *Brave Cowboy*, in which the solitary cowboy hero fights encroachment on the wild by shooting down a helicopter with a carbine.

After Arizona, Ric returned to Toledo for tree-trimming jobs until he saved enough money for his land and cabin in Montana. All of this— his time in Vietnam, his time of wandering, his thinking—finally led him to the founding of the rangers.

"All I was seeing is Vietnam all over again. Big government telling us what we've got to do, and it's all based on lies. It is total destruction for no purpose. I'll be goddamned if I'm going to let this happen in my own backyard."

Then he's blunt about a threat to finally draw the line at the Cove Mallard timber sale. When we talked that June day, the controversy had been raging in northern Idaho for years, but still was unresolved, still in court and fought to a standstill with protests. The main logging had not begun, but it might at any time. Ric told me something he has also stated for the record to Forest Service officials: "I tell them if they start logging then there's going to be a war over there. Not a metaphorical war, but a shooting war."

This raises the dilemma of whether he means to carry out this threat, an uncertainty he himself cultivates. The uniform, for instance, and the fact he goes armed to innocuous events such as public hearings—these are, by Ric's own admission, a part of the bluff. A person who encounters a belligerent grizzly bear in the back country is supposed to puff up his shoulders, even raise a jacket on spread arms, in order to look bigger. Bears do something similar to each other, and so the bluff lies encoded in genetic memory of combat.

Ric does not call this a bluff, but rather "psy-ops." That's why he won't tell me how many rangers exist, and for all I know, he's alone. He says he went to Cove Mallard one time to show a presence but for some reason or another, his compatriots couldn't make it. Some presence. So he went straight to the Forest Service law enforcement officers and said, "Look, if you see a bunch of guys out there carrying pistols, don't worry, they're all right. They're with me."

He said the Forest Service guys replied, "Yeah, we've seen them already, and they're all right."

"A person sees one ranger, and he tells everybody there are four. The next guy reports it as forty, and pretty soon there is a whole army out there." But then psy-ops is merely a tactic aimed at the end, and when it plays out, I believe Ric would escalate.

"Nobody in his right mind who has ever been in combat would want to be in combat again. We can settle this thing without violence. The point is, each man has to stand up and say 'no.'" But then he adds, "I see myself as playing the same part as the early abolitionists played in ending slavery. I see myself as the John Brown of the environmental movement. When only money buys justice and freedom then we have lost the battle, and it's time for a harder line."

MAYBE TWO HOURS EAST of Ric's cabin we pull into the high plains town of Havre, its pronunciation hayseeded to "have 'er." Jim Hill the railroad baron named it, just as he named Glasgow and Malta in Montana for places in Europe he liked. Havre is another wheat and railroad town set on the high end of the Missouri Plateau. Ric has recruited a couple of locals who will assist in the day's mission, and we are to meet them at a pawnshop one of them owns toward the edge of town.

The sign—MERT'S II HAND, BUYSELL$TRADE$—is threatened with being upstaged by the riot of bumper stickers Mert has plastered all around the place. The sum of these indicates Mert is a partisan of the NRA: "You'll get my gun when you pry it from my cold, dead fingers," and that sort of thing. The taxonomists of American politics tend to sort environmentalists to the left and gun nuts to the right, and that's mostly true, but out here on the high plains, or south in the backwoods or northwest in the mountains—any place where isolation skews the stream of arguments, information and propaganda—affiliations can go weird.

Ric says he and Mert have had some heated discussions about the NRA. Ric is not a member, nor is he a believer. It's not that he doesn't subscribe to the right to bear arms.

"If you carry a bazooka over your shoulder when you go to the supermarket, well then more power to you," he says.

It's just that he believes that the right to defend oneself is not so much a constitutional question or even a right that government can grant or deny. Allowing groups such as the NRA to carry that battle to government amounts to surrendering one's control to bureaucracy, both government's and the NRA's, he says.

"You've got a right to defend yourself. That's a law of nature. I've got a right to live."

Hobbes's idea lives, just as it lived in the minds of some of his successor theorists, who wrote: "When in the Course of human Events, it becomes necessary for one People to dissolve the Political Bands . . ."

I SHAKE HANDS with Mert behind the counter, a big man, maybe fifty, gray hair, deep scooping sideburns and a surly set of face. He is wearing camouflage pants and a T-shirt, and his gear is at ready. Ric asks where Dave is, and it is revealed that Dave has been whining about the day's mission. His assigned task is, in Ric's words, "to sentry the vehicles." Dave is balking because it's going to be 90 degrees that day, so hanging around the rigs promises to be sweltering as well as boring. Besides, there is more glory in heading up the mountains with the real guys. Then Dave arrives and pitches a snit, resolved when it is at last decided that a couple of parked pickup trucks in remote rural Montana may not need armed sentries after all.

Dave is twenty-seven, empty eyed, slack jawed and terribly over-weight. I decide maybe he's the one needing the anonymity of a nom de guerre, something like Commander Whole Number Less Than Zero. We mount the pickup trucks (Ric has begun to call them LVs) and drive the remaining two hours to the LZ.

Our target is a gold mine, a giant strip-mining operation that has re-moved the top off a mountain in the Little Rockies in north-central Montana. Isolated and gargantuan, it has pretty much had its way with the land, to the point that its operators reacted to controversy by closing it to visits from opponents. Those fighting the proliferation of strip mines throughout the Rockies can't see and use the experience of one of the largest and most egregious as ammunition against the others.

That's where the rangers came in for an assignment. At the request of some people fighting one of the same company's mines elsewhere, Ric had agreed to hike across some adjacent land that is part of the Fort Belknap Indian Reservation, cross on to company land at the top of a mountain and videotape the mining operation below. The tape, when compared with maps and a formal mining plan that is part of the public record, would help environmentalists confirm their suspicions that the mine had expanded beyond the limits of its permit. Not that the gov-ernment would do anything about such a violation, but proving it might serve the case against the other mine.

The risk in this operation was a charge of trespass. I was not wild about breaking the law, particularly not now that I was wearing the same camouflage as the rest of this odd crew, but figured I'd cross (or not cross) that bridge when it presented itself.

A couple hours past Havre we drove onto the reservation and found a young man, who in the soft lilt of an Assiniboine Sioux or Gros Ven-tre gave us the detailed directions of how to attain the hilltop. We bounced in the pickups up ruts and dry washes, through a needle's eye of a steep-rocked canyon, past a pow-wow grounds where the tribal members were gathering for a weekend of traditional celebrations, past a Sun Dance Lodge and on to the end of the road, a dry wash set in a steep draw blanketed with scraggly lodgepole pine.

Mert slipped on a camouflage shirt to cover his T-shirt—Kmart camouflage he called it, the same stuff he wears bow hunting for elk. Ric walked straight up to him.

"Are you armed?" he says.

Mert stares straight at him and says nothing.

"Are you armed?"

Mert raises the right tail of his Kmart camo to reveal a prodigious beer gut and the butt of a revolver. Ric is pleased. Dave, on the other hand, is not armed, and for this I am pleased.

Ric says the guns are not for show. We are in a remote section of a remote state. Ric has trusted Mert, Dave and the man who gave us directions. Any one of these people could betray us. We are inviting targets to any locals or miners who decide nosy environmentalists threaten their livelihoods.

The way to our target is up, a fact that soon splits us into two groups. Ric and I forge out ahead, crashing through the thick lodgepole and underbrush; the other two drag back a bit, stopping ever more frequently to puff and wheeze while their faces return to something paler than rich red. A couple of golden eagles soar over the gap between hills. Ric stops every now and then to apologize for his troops. He tells me he's got to work with what he's got and besides, who is he to judge the sincerity of a person's contribution. He assures me that there are other rangers besides Dave and Mert. We wait for the other two to catch up, then Dave tells us he has been swimming twice a week at doctor's orders to lose weight. Mert says little except to speculate as to the best route to the top and eventually it turns out he is right. He has spent years in these hills.

Now and again we get a glimpse of the mine through the saddle notches and draws, but it takes more than an hour and maybe two or so winding miles of uphill slog to give us a vantage of the whole place. Ric unpacks his video camera and sets to work.

Below us, what had been a ridge of the Little Rockies has been blasted apart and hauled a couple of miles away. The mine played out as a panoramic scar that looked to be three miles long. Where once stood a mountain, gaped a hole. Off to one end, giant-tired loaders scratched away at the headwall. Two mountain-sized mounds of terraced ore stood at center. At the top of one, there was a reservoir of cyanide water the size of a couple of football fields. Sprinkler pipes squirted cyanide across the top of the other pile.

As with all mines, this one was built with the usual "state-of-the-art" assurances. We were promised it would not leak. After the first spill, the miners promised it would not leak again. The second was detected when downstream homeowners caught the sickly burnt-almond whiff of cyanide in their tap water. There were at least nine serious cyanide spills in one fourteen-month period. One spill alone sent 52,000 gallons of cyanide solution downstream. In the summer of 1993, the creek draining the mine was as acidic as vinegar.

That day on the ridge, all of the couple of miles of clear-air distance between us and the mine was filled with the heaves, scrapes and roars of industry. From the hill where we stood one of us could have fired a .45 pistol. We could have emptied a whole clip trying to turn all this back. Still the pistol shots would be unheard by the trucks below, as silent to them as the eagles soaring above us.

"ALL I AM SEEING is Vietnam over and over again," says Ric and in this context he mentions government, greed and lies. In the context of the gold mine, I am seeing the same. We are sitting by a fallen tree halfway back down the mountain, and both of us have replaced the berets with sweat bands made of camouflage handkerchiefs, the '60s warrior and the '60s antiwarrior looking the same.

"I ain't no goddamn hero," he says. And then for some reason this launches him back to telling me what happened to him in Vietnam. I had it in my head to steer him there, but he went on his own. The physical wounds he suffered there were not that big a deal, not enough to earn him an early trip home. He took a rifle round in the leg and later a piece of shrapnel from a mine opened the same leg almost on top of the bullet scar.

"I didn't tell you what happened back there. I've never told anybody but my old man and a buddy."

He drops his gaze, as if just admitting to a felony.

"I assaulted a superior officer. The son of a bitch had got this kitten, this little kitten and he had this pot of boiling water. He had been drinking. Sure. But that was no excuse. He was going to put the kitten in the boiling water, and I couldn't take that so I put his own goddamn head in the boiling water, and he ended up with some scars."

We wound our way back down the mountain without incident and found the little creek that flowed to where we had parked the trucks. The headwaters of that creek arose near the cyanide-washed ore heap. We were thirsty, having long before drained our drinking water, but no one was thirsty enough to drink from the creek. Still Ric bent over and stuck his face in it.

"It's okay," he says. "At least it won't take your hide off, at least not right away."

I AM USING RIC now to suck you into our political dilemma. He's different, but by no means unique, nor does his militancy cover the spectrum of possible radical behavior. Did Ric seem reasonable to you? He did to me. Does he seem more reasonable now that you have followed the course of this mine and the politics it engenders? You see the dilemma. By raising this, do I advocate violence? Am I suggesting armed resistance as a legitimate means of protecting the Blackfoot and all of the rivers it becomes? Were this only an ethical question, I could answer it in a second. The sovereign *does* threaten the larger body and I am capable of acting in self-defense. I would kill someone in a heartbeat if I thought it could stop that mine. It won't.

But it's not just an ethical question, and we know it and have known it since our state developed coercive powers sufficient to make rebellion impossible. This is so obviously true as to make our dilemma no longer interesting. I raise it here for another purpose. The question is no longer interesting to me for the same reason it is no longer interesting to most who have followed and been a part of the environmental wars through the generations, and it has now been generations. The issue of violence illuminates nothing about where we might go. It does, however, illuminate something about the nature of the opposition.

I set this up with the question about Ric Valois's apparent grasp on reason. Now another setup: Does Land Lindbergh appear reasonable? And of course he does. His quiet neighborliness, his patience and his grasp of the tool of conservation easements have gone very far in protecting our river. He can refer to acres protected, a finite and real number, and not many among us can cite such tangible evidence of success. He is what we wish we all could be, and would be, if all of our opponents were rooted in nature. It is the *nature* of his opposition that makes reason possible.

The ranchers and loggers of the Blackfoot have done damage, but like the rest of us, they speak in terms of generations. There is pride in their longevity as families, which is a measure of the attachment to the place that supports them. In this attachment to generations is contained an attention to regeneration. They live within cycles. The grass and trees must regrow if they are to claim a legacy for themselves and their ways of life. They work in life cycles.

They have done damage, but what has been done is against their self-interest. The worst damage, of logging for instance, is instructive to this argument, in that it has been carried out by corporate loggers such as Champion International. In this, we need to remember that the Latin root of corporation is "corpus," the "body," an artificial body to stand in the business world, but an artificial body has no place. Champion demonstrated this by clear-cutting all of its lands using practices that undermined the ability of the forest to regenerate, because such practices were cheaper. Then Champion simply disappeared from the place. It had no interest in future generations.

Real loggers and real ranchers do look to the future, to the point that ensuring the health of the system is in their self-interests. Yes, they do damage, but out of ignorance, from lack of information. It is the sort of ignorance that can be corrected in quiet show-me sessions held over the tailgate of a pickup truck or in a serious conversation at Trixi's Bar. It is in this same way that environmentalists correct an ignorance of their own, when they learn where their real enemies and allies are and when they too learn that they have an interest in the political health of succeeding generations. The strategy of winning the next battle, future take care of itself, is as destructive to the political ecosystem as are clear-cuts to the natural. Environmental activists need to learn an attentiveness to longevity as well. In this way, communities coevolve to relationships that can survive.

All of this evolution is no longer possible when the nature of the enemy changes. Walt Kelly's often-quoted aphorism, concerning the meeting of the enemy that is us, ignores a part of the problem. We are life, and when we meet an enemy also rooted in life, then he indeed is us and something can be done. We may grow.

Mining is not rooted in life. Gold is not one of those gifts of nature that flows from and back to the life cycle. It is eternal, the deadest form of dead in that it never lived and cannot die. It does not grow or regenerate, so miners, by definition, have not the slightest interest in generations. This enemy is not us. Reason does not apply against this enemy, resistance does.

CHRONOLOGY: It is late fall, just before the clean water initiative would be defeated in the ballot box. The membership of the Clark Fork Coalition is gathered for its annual meeting, plotting out fund-raising and spending against the McDonald mine. The featured speaker for the annual pep talk is the writer David James Duncan, my neighbor, probably most remembered by the audience for his early work *The River Why* and his *River Teeth* rather than for his more famous *Brothers K.* Duncan reads a parable about the Big Blackfoot and Norman Maclean. It's funny and angry, but mostly he speaks of anger. He apologizes, says the threat to the river has made him too angry to write well.

Art is supposed to be nuanced and layered. Art is possible when the Blackfoot is well, but impossible when the threat we face is clear-cut, ominous and thoroughly evil. We are consumed by the real, and our art is consumed in the process.

He ends the speech that day wishing folks well: "Strength to your sword arm."

MORE CHRONOLOGY: December 10, 1996. Eleven days before Solstice. People who live at the 48th parallel keep track of Winter Solstice, when the light begins to return to bite the edges from the long, black nights, this year in particular, because winter set in hard and early. There's a feeling of hibernation about, and in the quiet, we let the events of November's election sink in, and wonder what comes next. The night and quiet are deceptive. There will be a rising again. There's always a next fight.

The morning edition of Missoula's newspaper that particular day carries a banner headline on page one: The story's lead reads:

HELENA—A Canadian-based mining company wants to explore gold reserves three miles west of Lincoln, only a short distance from the site of what could be Montana's largest open-pit gold mine.

Big Blackfoot Mining Inc., based in Calgary, Alberta, is seeking federal and state approval to core drill on mining claims containing an estimated 200,000 ounces of recoverable gold. The site of those claims, off Highway 200 50 miles northwest of Helena, is a mere 10–15 miles west of Seven Up Pete Joint Venture's proposed McDonald Gold project.

AFTER

THIS BOOK will end in Astoria, Oregon, 1,800
twisted river miles from the headwaters of the Big
Blackfoot. It does so for the same cause that propels
most of life's events: coincidence. I live in Astoria
now, at the very mouth of the Columbia River.
That is the coincidence, that a chance offering of a
job to my wife brought our life here for some years,
out of the Rockies and as far west as one can go on
the Blackfoot's web. In a sense, the Blackfoot ends
here, so it is appropriate on several levels that I have
come here. My story ends in Astoria because it does
not have an end, which is often true of stories, and
certainly true of rivers.

It is said the settlers on the Oregon Trail were
advised to travel west until their hats floated. Astoria is that place. It sits on the edge of America. From
this city one sees the coastal range, the river's last
barrier of mountains before the sea. These are end-
lessly pocked with clear-cuts. The big trees—the

Douglas fir, western cedar and hemlock—are mostly gone. Just west of the hills, the Columbia ends in ocean. My house overlooks the breakers out at the jetties, those long arms of artifice engineered to settle one of the world's most violent meetings of river and sea. All the sand brought down the basin made a bar. All the river's force driven by a half continent's gradient collides atop this bar with some of the world's most histrionic tides. Together, these primal forces made the violence that wrecked at least 2,000 vessels, 200 of them major ships.

The soft roll of hills swathed almost in mists and gray, the pastels that water spreads on even sunny days, make this place seem peaceful, but it's a place of catastrophe. The seaward edge of Willapa Bay, the estuary just north of the Columbia, one of the nation's best surviving estuaries, is formed by Long Beach Peninsula, a twenty-mile-long spit of sand washed down the Columbia and smeared north along the coast by the Pacific's currents. It was not all built gradually, but is the result—as is most of the Columbia Basin's topography—of the breaching 4,000 years ago of the ice dam that made glacial Lake Missoula. Montana's waters made this place what it is. It was carved in catastrophe, and catastrophe surely is in our future. Astoria faces water and water's power, so it seems the place to end this, which is to say, the place to point this story off to where it goes from here.

It is coincidence I am here four miles or so from Fort Clatsop, where Lewis and Clark wintered in 1805–06 before marching back up the Columbia, over Lolo Pass, past the yard of my old house two states away in Montana, up the big Blackfoot, past the McDonald mine and the rock cairns that guided them then down the Missouri to St. Louis to begin the history of the American West in the sense we understand history and beginnings. Coincidence too that I once began the story of the American grasslands, only to find myself on the trail of a wandering elk that left Montana and followed the rivers for 1,800 miles east, winding up in Independence, Missouri, a few miles from Lewis and Clark's trail.

One cannot consider the West without crossing and recrossing Lewis and Clark's trail, which was drawn by rivers. The life of the place and the death of the place can be read in its rivers, especially at river's end. The trail ended here where hats float. The place where rivers meet the sea is a place where our own ceaseless motion, our westering, meets the unmovable permanence of ocean, our limit, our end. This is crossroads,

crossroads in the sense that a man of another river, the bluesman Robert Johnson, meant when he said, "I went to the crossroads, and I fell down on my knees."

THIS HAS BEEN the story of a single small river, especially as it is threatened by an open-pit gold mine. This is where the end ought to come, where I resolve the conflict and tell you whether the mine will be built or whether my friends were successful in stopping it. You recall that the decision rested with the state along a couple of paths.

The short answer is, as I write this, the question is open. This is the winter of 1997, and the first round of decisions won't be out until this fall at the earliest. Any ruling then will not settle much. In the first place, this will be a running battle and the environmentalists will throw up breastworks at every opportunity for a quick skirmish. Each event will delay the impact statement, and the process could go on for a couple of years. But everyone in the process, even the most optimistic, when drilled and pressed, predicts the state will approve the mine.

That's not to say the matter is settled. There are other possibilities— the Salish, for instance. That tribe lost the Blackfoot Valley in the Hellgate Treaty of 1855, but the treaty reserved for them the right to hunt and fish the place forever, which in turn gives them some rights over developments that would harm the hunting and fishing, developments like the mine. They intend to assert those rights to oppose the mine.

Further, there are some federal obstacles that may emerge. The Army Corps of Engineers is weighing in to the case, which hardly sounds like the bugles of the cavalry riding to the rescue to the people of the West. The Army Corps is the agency responsible for much of the reengineering of western rivers, the sum total of which is the clear evidence of hubris on the planet. The agency is the sworn enemy of running water. Nonetheless, we have learned some things about rivers in the past few years, especially in the Mississippi Basin where reengineered rivers have flooded—dikes and levees be damned. We've learned that wetlands are worth more than dikes, and the agency has been placed in charge of protecting wetlands. The McDonald mine would do particular violence to wetlands, so there may be a lever there.

There is also the matter of the Endangered Species Act, the best legal tool environmentalists have had through the most intense of our battles. The species in question here is the bull trout, that magnificent resident of the Blackfoot imperiled by logging and ranching. Its habitat has been squeezed now to a couple of small tributaries, one of which is the Landers Fork. Everybody admits the mine would damage that animal, and there is a prima facie case under the law to stop the mine. There is also a Congress of a mind to gut the act, largely because it has been effective, so here is a battle that will be played on a much larger field. But here, nonetheless, is a possibility for a battle.

So do you see a possibility for a happy end in any of these courses of events? Think again. Say one issue raised here leads to someone somewhere saying "no." That means the gold will go nowhere, and that's the sticking point. It's a known deposit, and can't become unknown. When have men forgone the gathering of gold, given time?

That second mine proposal that surfaced at the close of the last chapter is actually a recurring nightmare. In the 1980s, another company proposed working the same ore, but for one reason or another folded its tent and went away. The gold remained. Conditions, especially political conditions, change. Expressions of environmental will are temporary. Legislatures become more compliant. Internationally, population pressures undermine stability. Chaos increases, and always the price of gold rises. Meantime, it's there in the ground, and it will keep.

There can be no victory in the fight to prevent the Seven Up Pete Joint Venture mine, just as there are seldom victories in environmental battles. The last generation won the Endangered Species Act and the Clean Air Act, only to see a new generation emerge. These people have forgotten the grizzly was nearly extinct and the Cuyahoga River once burst into flames. We'll fight it again. The last generation cleaned cities by forcing cleaner cars, only to see the Reagan generation of affluence flee to the suburbs, begin driving many more miles per capita and begin buying Suburbans and Blazers that get half the mileage, and smog lays on cities once more. We'll fight that again.

If you are looking for an end of this story, you may stop now. There isn't one.

ALDO LEOPOLD invoked Paul Bunyan when he wrote of the Round River. A mythical creation, it was designed (by Leopold, not Bunyan) to make us think differently of rivers. That this place Astoria is a crossroads testifies to our notion that rivers were lines that went away. They led to the frontier, especially the western frontier. They were the escape hatch, the line to someplace else when we used up the place we were in, the underlying notion of Manifest Destiny.

Because they were veins and because the landscape is arid and because rivers are by definition the center of valleys in mountains, cities everywhere, but especially in the West, were built alongside rivers. Only recently have those cities started to face their rivers. Before, the strip along the riverfront was reserved for warehouses, depots, slaughterhouses and whorehouses. Storefronts and good people looked the other way. With cause. Rivers were lines that led to that mythical place "away." Our trash and our sewage and the effluvia of our enterprise was the burden, the curse of these rivers, and they reeked of this curse. We could not face them.

What Leopold knew, and what we are only beginning to know, is that there is no such place as "away," so rivers can't go there, and if rivers can't go there, they must be round. Paul Bunyan's round river was a river where the mouth joined the source. How might we treat our places differently if we saw all rivers as round?

That idea comes easier here in Astoria, first impressions notwithstanding. Of course the Columbia first appears for all the world to end here. There is undeniably an end, a river's end. There is an unbroken line of oceangoing ships parading by. I watch them every day from my living room. Wheat from the Palouse and lumber from Montana headed out; Toyotas and Sonys headed in. It's not round; it's a line.

Or so it would appear until one spends a few months in the gray sodden wrap of the place. It rains and it rains, sheets of water breaking on the hills like ethereal extensions of the sea's breakers, which they are. The ancients were mystified by the source of rivers. They believed they must bubble up from underground, through springs connected to oceans, so underground must purify oceans of salt. They believed hell was a salty place, until French scientists bothered to measure rainfall in a drainage, and from then on we understood rivers come from rains and snow. The Columbia flows west past Astoria, but the Columbia also flows east over Astoria in those clouds. It's round, if we could see it.

The biologist Paul Ehrlich believes our inability to foresee and admit our species' long-term depletion of the globe is a function of our

inability to see, or more accurately, to see long-term change has occurred. We are undeniably a visual species; our most finely tuned sense
is sight, the way other species are attuned to a sense of smell or sound. A
bat finds its way in the dark world through fine hearing; a cat by feel.
We, with our discriminating eyes.

Throughout the millennia of our evolution threats presented themselves fast and furiously in the foreground. The threats were such as
predators and avalanches. The objects of our attention were agile moving prey and predators and plants that needed identification on sight as
food, poison threat or poison ally. Our sense of beauty rests on sight, as
does our racism, as does our addiction to television. In all of this, sight
deals with the immediate, the foreground and the fleeting. Because we
evolved in a world where our survival depended on perception of the
immediate, it also depended on our blurring or ignoring the background. We are not tuned to see gradual change.

Leopold himself put this same problem in another way, he who saw
rivers as round. He said, "One of the penalties of an ecological education is that one lives alone in a world of wounds."

Our perceptions of the state of the world are based on our varying
abilities to perceive. Part of that comes from variation in education and
abilities, but part lies in the fact that we are struggling to see an unsee-
able threat. Consider all of this in light of the salmon. Humans have
lived at the site of Astoria for probably 10,000 to 12,000 years. In all of
this time, their culture was based on salmon, even to this day, even when
there are few salmon left. We still learn from salmon, although now the
promise is of a hard negative lesson.

Astoria itself grew as a result of one such hard lesson. In its early
years, it was never much more than an outpost of explorers and fur trappers, never much of a town. True enough, it is the oldest American settlement west of the Mississippi, but by 1844, thirty-three years after
John Jacob Astor established it as a fur trading fort, it had dwindled to a
permanent white population of four. Then in the 1850s it boomed. It
became a salmon-fishing town after hydraulic mining from the California Gold Rush wiped out the salmon of the Sacramento River. Salmon
fishers moved here. The miners got their gold, but the miners still
needed to be fed, which required unspoiled rivers. My move here is not
without precedent.

IT WOULD BE EASY to follow me through this book and think it has always been about gold and rivers, but if rivers have no end then they enclose all things, including that which we care about the most: human survival and human well-being. Rivers enclose gold and salmon. Gold is "want." Salmon is "need." Gold is greed, a greed so set in our culture that our mythology preserves Midas and Crassus. It is simply an evil, a failing of bad people. This then is not so much a matter of rooting out gold as it is of defeating or eliminating or reforming bad people. It is excess, and if there is a lesson in our present, it is in the harm of excess. In a sense, as a first cut, as a bumper-sticker argument, I buy all of this. Much of the drive to grab gold is nothing but greed. I am hardest on myself for my own moments of greed, so why should I not be hardest on others exercising a greed so undiluted and bald as grabbing gold?

The bumper-sticker argument, however, misses something. If we know anything from our study of evolution, it is that enduring traits figure in the endurance of a species; the traits of humanity are as relevant in this as are those of any other species. The love of gold is an enduring trait, which is the same as saying greed is a part of the human condition. It crosses time and culture.

Gold is the mark of a species whose cleverness negotiated adversity. We learned to hoard. We learned to accumulate wealth. It accumulated as piles of food and piles of wisdom we call culture, then it accumulated as gold that could substitute for that food, make it abstract and portable and everlasting. Like a vestigial tail, though, gold now stands alone with no relation to its function. It is a symbol of well-being, but it is not well-being. We negotiated a difficult world, which gave us a love of security, a craving for well-being. People with an insatiable drive for wealth survive, and survival activates evolution. In a harsh world that has prevailed through all of human history this hunger for wealth was an asset, but it no longer is, because the world has become more harsh because of our own success.

Gold was the instrument of hierarchy and wealth. By this we are reminded that the well-being and security of those able to hoard it were achieved through the exploitation of others. Some of us find this distasteful, as I do, but we need to remember that our egalitarianism is a very new idea, and across species, a unique idea. Survival is based on a certain amount of exploitation. Equanimity is a luxury. Survival is necessity. A salmon lays thousands of eggs, but only a very small percentage, less than 10 percent, survive to adulthood. Young salmon survive by eating other eggs and each other. A species sends out its numbers to gather wealth, but that wealth must be concentrated in the few to carry a generation to the future.

Human reproductive success and cleverness in hoarding, however, has run the world to its limits. The Pactolus could give up its gold and its life because somewhere there was a Guadalquivir, and somewhere beyond that a Yukon and a Sacramento and beyond that a Columbia. The number of rivers is finite, though. This scarcity limits the productivity of exploitation as a survival strategy. We could take freely from others in our species because there was always a supply of unexploited people somewhere, but reaching this limit has had a curious effect. Those of us who live well can no longer live off the wealth of others; there is too much poverty for that. There is little wealth for the poor to gather so that we may exploit them, certainly not enough to satisfy the rich world's insatiable demands. We now live off the natural wealth of coming generations. We do not exploit others; we exploit our children. When there are no more rivers to kill, then we take the next generation's rivers. Other species exploit their kind, but to ensure, not undermine, the survival of the next generation.

We need gold now as a symbol, just as kings need it for a crown, but it is the symbol of excess and excess is what we need to learn to see. By this, I mean there is gold in all things. I cannot draw a clean line between "need" and "want." I know that gold is all want, that much I can tell, but as I consider the things I use to sustain my life, it is always true I can get by on less. And should. That part of a house that is too big is gold; those extra shoes, gold. And a part of gold is, as it has always been, beauty. I own guitars made of fine wood made of trees the rainforest needed. In the strictest sense, I do not need these guitars, but they give my life beauty, so it turns out I don't draw the line nearly as well as some of my posturing would have you believe. But I draw it. That's the business of a life, and I am aided in this by seeing.

I have seen the beauty of an unbeaten river, and I use that perception to guide me. Because I have seen what gold can do to these rivers, I cannot call it beautiful. This is about seeing.

Now I sit here at the mouth of the Columbia and try to see the Blackfoot in its waters. How would that work, how would we behave differently toward the planet if we were trained to see the essence of beautiful rivers, ones we know and love, flowing through each of our places?

A SALMON IS NOT a visual species, but it deals in wealth. It hoards. It is born in a river somewere upstream; once, before the dams stepped up the Columbia, the fish were born by the billions ranging across thousands of miles of streams, nearly into Montana, well through northern Idaho. They headed downstream when they were still the size of a cigar and migrated to the ocean to feed in rich pastures, then, three years or five or six years later, returned to the very spot where they were born to spawn, coming back twenty pounds, thirty, sixty. Then they would die and that mass they had taken from the ocean would feed a bear, or more likely, the carcasses would winnow along creekbanks in waves we would call carrion and stench, but the forest and river would call wealth. Calories. Bear and coyotes ate them, but so did deer and elk. So did trees. Biologists have learned to spot isotopes of ocean-derived nitrogen and have traced them, finding out that on the order of 20 and 30 percent of the living mass of streamside and rainforest trees comes from ocean-derived nutrients, wealth gathered and brought home by salmon. Then the trees shed nutrients to the streams and free-flowing rivers trap them to feed insects to feed fish. Rivers and salmon hoard and exchange wealth. The forest raises salmon, but the salmon raise the forest, and a healthy river mediates the bargain.

All of this depends on a salmon's ability to return to a natal stream, or more precisely, a natal site. This is the only way that evolution can pass on the information the next generation will need to negotiate the specifics of that very stream. The demands of migration are as varied as rivers, and each local population must evolve to match those demands. The whole system is based on a specific knowledge of place that is wisdom, and the wisdom is passed in genes.

Consider: There is a species of salmon that is born in streams but almost immediately migrates to lakes on the stream to spend its first year. Depending on where it is born, it would have to migrate either upstream or down to find the nearest lake, and given the range of streams, any possible direction on the compass. Biologists gathered eggs of this species, the sockeye, from a variety of sites, then hatched them in a laboratory. In each case, the fingerlings emerged and faced a given direction, according to where the eggs came from. In each case, it was the compass direction those fish would need to travel to find a lake had they been born where their eggs were taken from. The power of survival is the power to ensure the next generation's information.

A salmon in the mouth of the Columbia could distinguish the Blackfoot's water from all other threads the Columbia gathers. A salmon can detect as little a quantity as one molecule of certain organic chemicals added to its pool. Forget parts per billion. One molecule. This is how it finds home and fulfills its responsibility to survival, or how it found home before the chemical tracing of its natal streams became confused with polychlorinated biphenyls, chloro-organics, phosphates, nitrates, sodium cyanide, sewage, silt and dams.

Still, a salmon sitting off Astoria knows something of the Blackfoot 1,800 river miles above. It can detect headwaters. It can detect Silver Bow Creek, the Landers Fork, Copper Creek, the Clark Fork, the Snake, Henry's Fork, Bruneau, Salmon, Clearwater, Lochsa, Palouse, Owyhee, Malheur, the Kicking Horse, the Illiciliwaet, the Kootenai, the Flathead, Pend Oreille, the Spokane, the Okanogan, the Wenatchee, the Yakima, Walla Walla, Umatilla, John Day, Deschutes, Willamette. Each is a strand discernible here at the mouth of the Columbia. It is as if the record of human behavior in the Northwest is gathered to a single line and fed to an animal that can detect a single molecule of pollution in a single whiff. How do you think we fare? How would we behave differently if we could see what a salmon perceives, if we shared its profound sense of reality?

In all of this, the salmon must sense Pactolus, as should we. Remember that Midas sapped the life from his daughter by turning her to gold before he passed the curse to a river. Our piles of gold are as eternal as our pile of mine tailings, and this will be the legacy, a generation turned to gold.

I cannot draw the line I need to draw, but I can draw this much of it. Gold is not life and I do not need it. Salmon, which is to say a river, is life, and I do.

ASTORIA WRAPS AROUND a round knob of a hill, like a mini San Francisco, complete with the roller-coaster streets winding among Victorian houses. I am running on the streets, headed up in the rain, more a mist. There is sun off in the distance. I take my daily run on this route because it earns me vantage, a point where I can see. I stare at the river, trying to wring information from it the way a salmon does. It carries news of our health and well-being, if I could learn to see it. This is my daily exercise of the human illusion that sight grants insight. Behind me is the river, the line of ships. Around me is this old town, its sad, streaming face that has survived so much as to earn a place on this hillside. Unlike many western towns, Astoria appears to belong where it is. To my right I see Youngs Bay at the base of the hill and behind that a few miles the thread of the Lewis and Clark River and upstream the site of Fort Clatsop, duly marked and preserved as monument to the expedition of the two explorers.

My run winds uphill, and I follow a route marked by white-painted castles stenciled on the pavement, the route to "the column." The run's pitch is a thigh-burner, but worth it. On top, the whole emerald world of the coastal range unwraps like a giant relief map rolling down to the sea. I see ten or fifteen miles off in any direction. The view is picturesque in the sense that it is beautiful, but also in that it frames a picture. Much can be read therein.

The column that is my destination at hilltop is also a monument to exploration, to Lewis and Clark and to Robert Gray, the Yankee sailor whose ship *Columbia Rediviva* discovered this river and gave it its name on May 11, 1792. Only "column" is not quite the right word. It is a round, phallic tower, an obelisk, a sort of ziggurat, painted mostly in yellows, but in gold at its top. I wonder if those who built it knew the lineage of its form. Through time, we have used these towers to elevate us as gods, to grant status, but wrapped with this yearning is another more deeply religious, the need to see and to understand.

As the road breaks to the clearing around the tower I notice a sign advising of a side trail, leading away from the column. It tells me if I follow, it will lead to something called the cathedral spruce, a giant old-growth spruce among a patch of trees that somehow escaped logging. The sign says the spruce is "taller than the column."

I go, and it is.

ACKNOWLEDGMENTS
AND SOURCES

THIS PROJECT and anything else I do is first indebted to my wife, Tracy Stone-Manning. She keeps me going. Always. In this case, however, the debt runs deeper. Following her work and her activism led me into much of the detail that makes up this book. She is my hero and inspiration.

The rest of the book is just journalism, which is a simple business, only one step removed from writing washing machine manuals. It is just a matter of finding people, talking to them and writing down what they say. Therefore, any quality in a book belongs to the people who lend it their stories, and this one is no exception. My name gets to be on the cover, but the book belongs to all those people named herein.

This was not a cloak-and-dagger operation. There were no Deep Throats, nor clandestine meetings with unnamed sources. By and large, Montana does not work that way. People are willing to say what they have to say straight out in the open air. That is to say, most of those to whom I owe mention in this section are named in the main of the book. Note those names; many of them are heroes, so the debt is not mine alone but accrues to everyone who believes in wild rivers and the integrity of wild places. Understand also that the ones named are not in this fight alone. If everyone fighting this particular battle were listed herein, this book would read like a telephone directory. A good river has a way of producing a long list of good people.

Aside from these individuals in the fight, this project got some special help along the way. There was first an assignment for *Audubon* magazine from my editor there, Roger Cohn. That work underwrote much of the research that produced the chapter on the history of gold and modern gold mining in Nevada's Carlin Trend.

The idea was shaped especially with research I was able to do while on a John S. Knight fellowship in journalism at Stanford University, and I thank that program, particularly its directors Jim Risser and Jim Bettinger, for protecting a bit of intellectual sanctuary in what is mainly an unthinking world.

More than most book ideas, this one was shaped by the first editor on the project, Bryan Oettel. He spotted the idea hidden in my original idea, and that's what this book has become. His effort was ably continued by David Sobel, and I thank them both. The link to them came from my agents, Anne Dubuisson and Elizabeth Kaplan, and as much as characters, agents make books happen.

Help in the heavy lifting of research came from a number of sources. The folks at the Clark Fork Coalition, besides waging a hell of a fight for a river, also keep a thorough research library. I am particularly indebted to the organization's staff scientist Geoff Smith for providing access to his voluminous research, pointing me to other information as well as for reading the manuscript. Meg Nelson, the coalition's director, likewise provided considerable assistance and guidance.

Bruce Farling, in addition to putting up with my crankiness on antelope hunting expeditions, opened his files at Trout Unlimited. Farling also wrote a summary of the mine proposal called "A Bad Place to Mine," which served this project. Tom France of the National Wildlife Federation provided access to research material. Likewise the Mineral Policy Center in Washington, D.C., provided much of the information.

Statistics on gold mining and consumption came from the World Gold Council, based in New York.

I also relied on the University of Montana's Mansfield Library as well as the capable work in several local newspapers, particularly the Great Falls *Tribune's* excellent series on the mine by Mark Downey and the *Missoulian's* coverage, especially the reporting by Sherry Devlin.

Most of the information on the mine itself came directly from Phelps Dodge's own records filed with various regulatory agencies. All are public record. Included is a particularly helpful historical inventory called the "Final Cultural Resource History," prepared by Timothy Light, Daniel Hall and David Schwab.

Books that formed this work are generally cited in the text. Some that deserve particular mention as general sources are:

Deitrich, William. *Northwest Passage: The Great Columbia River*. Seattle: The University of Washington Press, 1995.

Green, Timothy. *The World of Gold*. New York: Walker and Company, 1968.

Marx, Jenifer. *The Magic of Gold*. Garden City, New York: Doubleday & Company, Inc., 1978.

Mosley, Leonard. *Lindbergh: A Biography*. New York: Doubleday & Company, Inc., 1976.

Schwantes, Carlos Arnaldo. *The Pacific Northwest*. Lincoln, Nebraska: The University of Nebraska Press, 1989.

Sutherland, C. H. V. *Gold: Its Beauty, Power and Allure*. New York: McGraw-Hill Book Company, Inc., 1959.

Toole, K. Ross. *Montana: An Uncommon Land*. Norman, Oklahoma: The University of Oklahoma Press, 1959.

Toole, K. Ross. *Twentieth Century Montana: A State of Extremes*. Norman, Oklahoma: The University of Oklahoma Press, 1972.

Turney-High, Harry Holbert. "The Flathead Indians of Montana." *Memoirs of the American Anthropological Association* 39, 4, part 2 (48 1937).

INDEX